Evidence-Based Psychotherapy
With Adolescents

Evidence-Based Psychotherapy With Adolescents

A Primer for New Clinicians

JOANNA ELLEN BETTMANN

OXFORD
UNIVERSITY PRESS

OXFORD
UNIVERSITY PRESS

Oxford University Press is a department of the University of Oxford. It furthers
the University's objective of excellence in research, scholarship, and education
by publishing worldwide. Oxford is a registered trade mark of Oxford University
Press in the UK and certain other countries.

Published in the United States of America by Oxford University Press
198 Madison Avenue, New York, NY 10016, United States of America.

Library of Congress Control Number: 2019950999
ISBN 978-0-19-088006-4

Contents

SECTION III: SPECIAL POPULATIONS
AND APPROACHES

Acknowledgments

I would like to acknowledge with gratitude the support of my parents and family during the process of developing and writing this book. In particular, Pete, Ellie, and Henry, I couldn't do any of this without all of you. All my love—

Contributors

Gretchen Anstadt, research assistant, University of Utah College of Social Work.

Joanna Ellen Bettmann, PhD, LCSW, Professor, University of Utah College of Social Work.

Taylor Berhow, MSW, research assistant, University of Utah College of Social Work.

Anthony D. Bram, PhD, ABAP, private practice in Lexington, MA, part-time lecturer at Cambridge Health Alliance/Harvard Medical School, faculty at Boston Psychoanalytic Society and Institute.

Jerry Buie, assistant professor/lecturer, University of Utah College of Social Work.

Bryan Casselman, research assistant, University of Utah College of Social Work.

Jake L. Checketts, research assistant, University of Utah College of Social Work.

Katherine V. Ovrom, MSW, research assistant, University of Utah College of Social Work.

Tracie Peñúñuri, LCSW, adjunct faculty, University of Utah College of Social Work.

Michael Riquino, MSW, doctoral candidate, University of Utah College of Social Work.

Mindy J. Vanderloo, senior research analyst, University of Utah College of Social Work.

Contributors

SECTION I
BACKGROUND AND THEORY

1

Introduction

Joanna Ellen Bettmann

I had only been a therapist for a few years when I encountered a client who refused to speak with me. She was a new client in a wilderness therapy program at which I was working. When I arrived to see my adolescent client in the wilderness that day, the staff said, "She arrived two days ago. She hasn't talked to anyone yet." I thought to myself, "Well, she'll talk to me. I'm the therapist." Usually adolescent clients in that program were anxious to speak to me as I was the program staff who communicated with their parents, bringing word from home. I walked over to the client and introduced myself. I asked her if she would like to speak with me and we walked about 200 feet away from the staff to give us some privacy to speak. Once we sat down on the grass, I explained who I was, what my role was, and what we would be focused on that day. I invited her to speak and to ask questions. She stared at me silently with a hostile expression on her face. I said, "I'd really be interested in hearing what you have to say. Anything you want to share with me, I'd love to hear it." She continued to be silent and looked away. I issued a few more invitations to speak, letting her know that I was interested in getting to know her. She continued to be silent. A deep anger welled up in me. "How dare she not even speak to me?" I thought. "Why won't she even say what she is thinking?" I felt powerless, upset, enraged. I sat with her silently, internally raging, for about 10 minutes. I then explained to her that I would go speak to the staff, but that I would be available to speak with her later if she changed her mind and wanted to talk.

I felt rejected by her, inadequate for the job of therapist, and impotent. Her refusal to engage with me brought up all of the inadequacies I felt as a new therapist. I thought she could see that I wasn't up to the job, that I wouldn't be able to help her, that I was a fraud. In fact, she was simply a deeply hurt adolescent whose strongest defense was withdrawal. Her refusal to speak with me had really nothing to do with me and everything to do with her involuntary admission to a wilderness therapy program, her sense of disconnect from her family, and her strong walls against adult relationships. During the seven weeks that I worked with this client, she eventually shared a lot of her pain with me and we built a strong relationship. I developed deep respect for her resistance to adult relationships, understanding how her defenses had been built to deal with her sense of rejection from family members and others.

Adolescent clients present particular challenges for clinicians. They are often resistant to forming relationships with unknown adults, seeing adults as authority figures and not friendly or helpful ones. Unlike child clients, they often perceive themselves as quite capable of independence, wishing adults would give them space to do what they want. However, their brain capacities are not fully developed until early adulthood (Johnson, Blum, & Giedd, 2009). While they often perceive themselves as capable of full independence, they lack the cognitive capacity for successful and complete autonomy. They need strong attachment relationships with adults, but often act as if such relationships are a bother to them, and sometimes they display more hostility than affection. Parents of adolescent clients often report confusion about how best to support their adolescent children who used to be affectionate and interested in closeness, but now only want autonomy, financial support, and access to a car.

This is one of the central dilemmas for clinicians of adolescent clients: how to connect to and support clients who appear to flee adult relationships. How can clinicians support an adolescent client who seeks autonomy, but lacks full capacity for this? How can clinicians work with an adolescent client who needs support and guidance but resents this at the same time? How can clinicians work with an adolescent client whose interests or beliefs oppose those of their parents—parents who have custody as well as financial control of and health-care decision making over the client? These are some of the dilemmas which clinicians working with this population must face. This book provides new clinicians with tools to address these central concerns.

Evidence-Based Practice

This book proposes how to do evidence-based psychotherapy with adolescents. Strikingly, evidence-based approaches outperform typical psychotherapy both in direct comparisons and when contrasted to control conditions (Weisz, Jensen-Doss, & Hawley, 2006; Weisz et al., 2013). Evidence-based practice sets quality standards for the care provided by individual clinicians (Weisz et al., 2006). These standards protect clients against research-to-practice gaps that may expose them to iatrogenic or outdated modes of practice (Bloomquist et al., 2016). Despite the numerous evidence-based psychotherapeutic treatments available, many adolescents continue to receive poor care for psychiatric issues (Whiteside et al., 2018). Thus, clinicians must become informed about what constitutes evidence-based practice for adolescent clients, as such education increases the probability of clients' positive outcomes (Kazdin, 2013).

The integration of evidence-based practice into adolescent treatment is especially important because adolescent treatment is enormously complex, typically involving caregivers in the treatment process, and because co-morbid conditions, family dysfunction, and family stress are highly likely (Weisz, Jensen-Doss, & Hawley, 2006). Utilizing evidence-based practice in adolescent treatment also decreases the risk of clinician bias in the provided treatment (Burgess et al., 2017). If I am to be an effective clinician, I will need to scrutinize my treatment approaches regularly, updating them in accordance with the published literature (Kazdin, 2013). Thus, the focus of this book is how to provide treatment to adolescent in accordance with the best research available.

You will note that some of the case examples in this book derive from my experience working with adolescents in residential and wilderness therapy settings. Adolescent residential treatment shows efficacy as a modality (Bettmann & Jasperson, 2009). Wilderness therapy has also established an evidence base illustrating its efficacy (Bettmann, Gillis, Speelman, Parry, & Case, 2016; Bettmann & Tucker, 2011; Conlon, Wilson, Gaffney, & Stroker, 2018; Hill, 2007; Norton et al., 2014; Russell, 2003, 2005; Tucker, Bettmann, Norton, & Comart, 2015; Tucker et al., 2016). Wilderness therapy is a specific type of residential treatment—treatment in a wilderness environment, usually where group and individual therapy is provided in the context of back-country exploration, adventure, and wilderness skills (Tucker et al., 2016). Wilderness therapy and residential treatment are best utilized for adolescents who are struggling at home or display resistance to traditional and less intensive therapies (Bettmann & Jasperson, 2009; Bolt, 2016).

Structure of the Book

This book is divided into three broad sections:" Background and Theory," "Treating Mental Health Issues," and "Special Populations and Approaches." The first section, "Background and Theory," provides clinicians with key concepts and information for beginning treatment. Chapter 2, "Theory for Working with Adolescents," explains psychodynamic, intersubjective, and relational models in terms of their application to working with adolescent clients. While theory may seem strange to new clinicians, theory helps us to understand why clients do the things they do. Theory provides the basis for hypotheses that we form about our clients and underlies our conceptualizations of our clients and their problems. Chapter 3, "The Neurobiology of Adolescents and Its Implications for Treatment," explains how an understanding of neurobiological research can help clinicians to better understand adolescent clients and their cognitive capacities, limitations, and emotional regulation difficulties. Chapter 4, "Assessment in Adolescent Treatment," explains concretely what information clinicians should collect from adolescent clients and how to ask questions to obtain this information. Chapter 5, the final chapter in this section, "Building Therapeutic Alliance with Adolescents," focuses on strategies for connecting with adolescent clients. It provides clinicians with tools for bringing the gap between the adult clinician and their younger, often resistant client.

The second section of the book, "Treating Mental Health Issues," introduces evidence-based approaches for working with some of the most common presenting mental disorders in adolescent clients. Chapter 6 addresses evidence-based interventions for adolescent anxiety, while Chapter 7 addresses evidence-based interventions for adolescent depression. Chapter 8 addresses evidence-based interventions for adolescents with disruptive behavior disorders including ADHD, oppositional defiant disorder, and conduct disorder. Chapter 9 presents evidence-based interventions for traumatized adolescents and chapter 10 presents evidence-based interventions for substance-abusing adolescents. Whether you are seeing adolescent clients in a school setting, an outpatient community clinic, an inpatient psychiatric unit, a residential treatment center, or a wilderness therapy program, these are the mental disorders you are most likely to see: anxiety, depression, disruptive behavior disorders, PTSD, and substance use disorders. The five chapters in this section of the book will give clinicians evidence-based knowledge and tools for working with each of these presenting problems.

The third section of the book addresses "Special Populations and Approaches." Chapter 11 describes how clinicians can work successfully with issues of adolescent sexual orientation, sexual behavior, and gender identity. The chapter covers how adolescent development intersects with these topics, exploring the "coming out" process, stigma, suicidality, familial issues, and protective factors for LGBTQ adolescents. Chapter 12 presents strategies for successful psychotherapy with adopted adolescents, who are typically over-represented in many treatment settings. Using case studies to illustrate strategies for navigating attachment wounds and forming strong therapeutic alliances, the chapter also includes a discussion of how to work with foster families. The final chapter of the book explains "Family Therapy with Adolescents." Family work is a part of every adolescent case. Since adolescents' caregivers typically have custody and the legal responsibility to make medical decisions for the adolescent, working with adolescents involves coordinating with their families, making sure that treatment is cohesive with family values, and helping adolescents make their families a place where they feel valued. Conflicts between adolescents' wishes and those of their families are common and complex. This chapter provides tools to new clinicians on navigating these difficult waters.

Conclusion

My hope is that this book helps new clinicians to feel more prepared than I did when I entered clinical practice following graduate school. The countertransference that I describe at the beginning of this chapter—the sense of rejection, inadequacy, and rage—is relatively common to new clinicians. We often feel that we are not up to the job. Adolescent clients are likely to see our vulnerabilities and to respond to them. When we as clinicians are prepared with evidence-based approaches, knowledge of our own countertransference, and tools for working with difficult situations, we can inspire confidence in our clients. Our adolescent clients thus are more likely to trust us and to want to work with us. This book prepares clinicians to work with a challenging population and to be successful in doing so.

References

Bettmann, J. E., Gillis, H. L., Speelman, E. A., Parry, K. J., & Case, J. M. (2016). A meta-analysis of wilderness therapy outcomes for private pay clients. *Journal of Child and Family Studies, 25*, 2659–2673. doi:10.1007/s10826-016-0439-0

Bettmann, J. E., & Jasperson, R. A. (2009). Adolescents in residential and inpatient treatment: A review of the outcome literature. *Child & Youth Care Forum, 38*, 161–183.

Bettmann, J. E., & Tucker, A. R. (2011). Shifts in attachment relationships: A study of adolescents in wilderness treatment. *Child & Youth Care Forum, 40*, 499–519. doi:10.1007/s10566-011-9146-6

Bloomquist, M. L., Fiovanelli, A., Benton, A., Piehler, T. F., Quevedo, K., & Oberstar, J. (2016). Implementation and evaluation of evidence-based psychotherapeutic practices for youth in a mental health organization. *Journal of Child and Family Studies, 25*, 3278–3292. doi:10.1007/s10826-016-0479-5

Bolt, K. L. (2016). Descending from the summit: Aftercare planning for adolescents in wilderness therapy. *Contemporary Family Therapy, 38*, 62–74. doi:10.1007/s10591-016-9375-9

Burgess, A. M., Okamura, K. H., Izmirian, S. C., Higa-McMillan, C. K., Shimabukuro, S., & Nakamura, B. J. (2017). Therapist attitudes towards evidence-based practice: A joint factor analysis. *Journal of Behavioral Health Services & Research, 44*, 414–427. doi:10.1007/s11414-016-9517-8

Conlon, C. M., Wilson, C. E., Gaffney, P., & Stoker, M. (2018). Wilderness therapy intervention with adolescents: Exploring the process of change. *Journal of Adventure Education and Outdoor Learning, 18*, 353–366. doi:https://doi.org/10.1080/14729679.2018.1474118

Hill, N. (2007). Wilderness therapy as a treatment modality for at-risk youth: A primer for mental health counselors. *Journal of Mental Health Counseling, 29*, 338–349. doi:https://doi.org/10.17744/mehc.29.4.c6121j162j143178

Johnson, S. B., Blum, R. W., & Giedd, J. N. (2009). Adolescent maturity and the brain: The promise and pitfalls of neuroscience research in adolescent health policy. *Journal of Adolescent Health, 45*, 216–221. doi:10.1016/j.jadohealth.2009.05.016

Kazdin, A. E. (2013). Evidence-based treatment and usual care: Cautions and qualifications. *JAMA Psychiatry, 70*, 666–667. doi:10.1001/jamapsychiatry.2013.2112.

Norton, C. L., Tucker, A., Russell, K. C., Bettmann, J. E., Gass, M. A., Gillis, H. L., & Behrens, E. (2014). Adventure therapy with youth. *Journal of Experiential Education, 37*, 46–59. doi:10.1177/1053825913518895

Russell, K. (2003). An assessment of outcomes in outdoor behavioral healthcare treatment. *Child and Youth Care Forum, 32*, 355–381.

Russell, K. C. (2005). Two years later: A qualitative assessment of youth well-being and the role of aftercare in outdoor behavioral healthcare treatment. *Child and Youth Care Forum, 34*, 209–239. doi:10.1007/s10566-005-3470-7

Tucker, A. R., Bettmann, J. E., Norton, C. L., & Comart, C. (2015). The role of transport use in adolescent wilderness treatment: Its relationship to readiness to change and outcomes. *Child & Youth Care Forum, 44*, 671–686. doi:10.1007/s10566-015-9301-6

Tucker, A. R., Combs, K. M., Bettmann, J. E., Chang, T. H., Graham, S., Hoag, M., & Tatum, C. (2016). Longitudinal outcomes for youth transported to wilderness therapy programs. *Research on Social Work Practice, 28*, 438–451. doi:10.1177/1049731516647486

Weisz, J. R., Jensen-Doss, A., & Hawley, K. M. (2006). Evidence-based youth psychotherapies versus usual clinical care: A meta-analysis of direct comparisons. *American Psychologist, 61*, 671–689. doi:10.1037/0003-066X.61.7.671

Weisz, J. R., Kuppens, S., Eckshtain, D., Ugueto, A. M., Hawley, K. M., & Jensen-Doss, A. (2013). Performance of evidence-based youth psychotherapies compared with usual clinical care: A multilevel meta-analysis. *JAMA psychiatry, 70*, 750–761. doi:10.1001/jamapsychiatry.2013.1176

Whiteside, S. P. H., Leffler, J. M., Hord, M. K., Sim, L. A., Schmidt, M. M., & Geske, J. R. (2018). The compatibility of clinical child mental health treatment and evidence-based treatment protocols. *Psychological Services*, 1–8. doi:10.1037/ser0000267

2

Theory for Working With Adolescents

Joanna E. Bettmann and Katherine V. Ovrom

In this chapter, we present psychological theories that help clinicians understand and interpret adolescent behavior. Skilled psychotherapists use theory to understand the roots of client behavior. We do not cover all psychotherapeutic theories here, but rather focus on those that both inform adolescent treatment and underlie the interventions we present later in the book. We do not endorse any one theory as the best but believe that theoretical combined wisdom underlies the strongest treatment plan for each adolescent.

Sigmund Freud's Structural Theory

Sigmund Freud was the first to write substantively about adolescent psychology. Freud believed that human behavior is driven largely by conflict between three parts of the psyche: the id, ego, and superego (Freud, 1923/1960). In Freud's conceptualization, the id is comprised of instinctual material seeking pleasure and aggression. The superego is comprised of internalized social strictures. Considered the moral component of the psyche, the superego typically represses id drive material because it is generally not socially appropriate. The ego negotiates between the id and superego, marshaling resources which include defense mechanisms (Freud, 1923/1960).

In adolescents, one can often see imbalances and tensions between id, superego, and ego structures. For example, Angela (a pseudonym) was a 16-year-old girl who presented to community outpatient treatment with a possible eating disorder. She described that her parents were worried about her eating and exercise habits. She reported that she ate only a few pieces of vegetables for each meal, making sure to exercise at least an hour or two a day. Angela described intense conflict with her parents whose behavior she termed "controlling." Angela believed herself to be significantly overweight, despite being notably underweight. She daily evaluated her worth on the basis of her appearance and weight; if she thought she looked fat on a given day, she restricted her eating even more, exercised even longer, and berated herself for her weaknesses and inadequacies.

In the case of Angela, we can see heavy superego presence. Angela has internalized—from society, her family, her environment—that to be thin is to be good and worthy. This message, now embedded in her superego, drives her self-injurious behaviors. She is weighed down by a superego which tells her that she is bad and fat. Her id drives are largely suppressed under the overwhelming superego; she rarely expresses aggression to others (only against herself) and never seeks pleasure. Her ego is failing at its Herculean task: moderating between the id drive material and the superego strictures. If her ego were strong and well-developed, we would see greater capacity for healthy emotion regulation, more flexible responses to societal strictures, and better utilization of environmental resources. Her internal world is rigid and inflexible. Her cognitions are fixed, unhealthy, and maladaptive.

Treating Angela from a Freudian structural perspective would focus on enhancing ego functioning, unpacking superego messages, and releasing id material to be expressed in healthy ways. Angela would need to become de-pendent upon the therapist. This healthy dependence would model healthy relationships for Angela. During treatment, the therapist lends the client her ego strengths. Angela would see what healthy and adaptive responses to stressors look like. She would begin to re-examine her rigid cognitions through a treatment process which might take months or years.

Erikson's Theory of Psychosocial Development

Erik Erikson is best known for his theory of psychosocial development. He proposed that life consists of eight chronological stages, each of which contains its own particular demands or crises that the individual must nego-tiate in order to cope with the demands placed on them by society (Erikson, 1968, 1982). The ability of the ego to negotiate each of these crises determines whether an individual is able to progress to the next psychosocial stage (Erikson, 1982).

In adolescence, individuals must negotiate the crisis of identity versus role confusion (Erikson, 1982; Zastrow & Kirst-Ashman, 2015). According to Erikson, adolescents must work to define who they are by examining components of their identities in order to integrate all of these components into one cohesive identity. These components include identifiers such as race, gender, religion, as well as academic, athletic, and other identifiers. Those who are unable to effectively examine these components and integrate them into their roles or who struggle with conflicting roles become stuck in role confusion which causes them to feel uncomfortable with their own identity and sense of self. One example of a situation that could lead to role confusion is that of an individual who is attracted to persons of the same gender, but who is a member of a religion that rejects homosexuality. These conflicting roles and feelings can lead to confusion, uncertainty, and, in some cases, clinical issues such as self-harm and depression (Claes, Luyckx, & Bijttebier, 2014; Ghandi, Luyckx, Goossens, Maitra, & Claes, 2016).

Erikson's theory is useful when working with adolescents because it highlights the impact that social, extracurricular, and familial activities can have on the formation and negotiation of their identity. He also presented an explanation for the adolescent tendency to switch roles, identities, and social circles frequently as a process of free experimentation before their final identity is established (Erikson, 1959).

An adolescent who is struggling with Erikson's stage of identity versus role confusion might look like Anthony, a 15-year-old who is struggling in high school to fit in. He is not sure what peer group he most identifies with, what activities he most prefers, or whether or not he endorses his parents' religious beliefs. He has one or two friends, but doesn't feel that he is like others. He feels lonely a lot of the time and adrift. He spends time on his computer, searching for online communities where he could fit in. As an adult, Anthony will struggle to find peers he relates to or a job he feels passionate about. He feels uncomfortable about who he is and isn't sure where he belongs. While many adolescents experience this identity confusion, Anthony has become stuck in it. He is confused and ambivalent; he often feels depressed. Therapy will need to help Anthony identify his own passions and to develop skills to speak assertively to others about what he wants. Helping Anthony connect to his deepest beliefs and articulate them will be the therapeutic work.

Margaret Mahler

Another theorist who used psychosocial stages to explain human development was Margaret Mahler (Mahler, Pine, & Bergman, 1975). Mahler attempted to understand individual psychology by developing the notion of the psychological birth of the individual through a "separation-individuation process" (p. 3). This process is a lifelong cycle through which one establishes a sense of separateness from and relatedness to others. The separation-individuation process consists of a linear progression through three phases: autistic, symbiotic, and separation-individuation. The separation-individuation phase is further divided into the sub-phases of differentiation, practicing, and rapprochement. A key concept of Mahler's stage theory is that children move slowly away from their caregivers, both physically and emotionally, in a process of normative development (Mahler et al., 1975).

The final sub-phase of these stages, rapprochement, is particularly relevant to adolescents. According to Mahler et al., rapprochement is the phase in which a toddler seeks to explore and move further away from caregivers, while checking in regularly for emotional refueling. Mahler suggests that, during this stage, caregivers need to allow for the toddler's distance, while also remaining available for when the toddler wants to reconnect (Mahler et al., 1975). Some scholars link rapprochement dynamics to adolescents who both demand autonomy, yet still need parents and family for security and support (Esman, 1980). These apparent contradictory needs can cause anxiety and confusion both for the adolescent and for their caregivers (Esman, 1980). We can see Mahler's rapprochement in the example of Jane, a 16-year-old girl who wants independence from parents, demands freedom from their rules and strictures, but still wants to be taken care of, fed, and housed. We can see in this dialectic what Mahler termed *ambitendency*, the wish for two things simultaneously: the wish to both explore and to be close.

One important cultural factor to note with Mahler's theory, like that of several other theories discussed in this text, is that she implies that autonomy and individuating behaviors are the hallmark of psychological health. While these values are representative of predominately white Western cultures, other cultures do not share this perspective, embracing collectivism and interdependence of the family system and the community's collective health (Boucher & Maslach, 2009; Kwan, Bond, Boucher, Maslach, & Gan, 2002; Slote, 1992).

Another important critique of Mahler's theory comes from one of her former collaborators, Fred Pine (1992). In his later work, he explored the idea that human development is not linear but developmental, suggesting the humans achieve developmental moments rather than move linearly from stage to stage (Pine, 1992). He noted that humans are often too complex to progress steadily along a line and are more likely to move forward and back, hitting developmental moments across the lifespan (Pine, 1992). Pine's critique is helpful to those of us who work with adolescents, as such clients often appear older and then younger than they are. Their developmental flip-flopping is easier to understand using Pine's perspective: perhaps such adolescents are growing along a healthy developmental trajectory, but that process appears less like climbing stairs than moving one's piece forward and then back in a board game.

Pine's critique is made clearer through an example. Josh was a 17-year-old who lived with his family in a low-income neighborhood. His family lacked the resources to put him in physically active after-school activities, so Josh struggled to manage his high levels of energy in a restrained school environment. He often ended up in the principal's office or was suspended for mouthing off to teachers, failing to follow directions, or not staying in his seat as directed. Josh sometimes managed his sense of failure and disappointment by acting out, getting drunk, or being disorderly with peers in public. But many times, he handled his frustration maturely, venting his feelings to his girlfriend or talking with his best friend at length on the phone, a process which calmed him. In Josh's strategies for managing difficult emotional experiences, we can see his mature, adult-like moments and his child-like regressions to acting out. Such behavior exemplifies Pine's points: adolescents move both forward and back in a developmentally normative process.

Peter Blos: The Second Individuation

The work of Peter Blos (1962, 1967/1975, 1968, 1979) extended Margaret Mahler's stage model, focusing specifically on adolescence. Blos (1967/1975) described adolescents as going through a second process of individuation, the first occurring as Mahler et al. (1975) conceived it in infancy and toddlerhood. He credited adolescent turmoil to this second individuation, which requires one to decrease dependency on family and move away from familiar activities in preparation to enter the world as an independent adult (Blos, 1975).

One important component of Blos' theory for clinicians is his link between unsuccessful individuation and psychological disorders. He viewed behaviors such as self-harm, substance abuse, and illegal activity as an attempt to reject the family and society and to avoid the slow negotiation of the individuation process (Blos, 1967/1975). He presented such behaviors

as signs of understandable regression and avoidance because the individuation process requires a level of maturity, responsibility, and independence
that adolescents may find overwhelming (Blos, 1967/1975). Thus, regressive
behaviors serve to avoid the individuation process. Blos framed this period
of regressive behavior as an unavoidable and necessary part of adolescence
(1968). However, when an individual gets stuck in this regression/avoidance
and their behaviors become habitual and destructive, they have likely developed a pathological disorder that may necessitate significant intervention.

Two-Person Theories

During the mid-20th century, psychological theorists began to consider not
just individual psychology and the societal forces enacted upon people, but
the impact and meaning of interactions on human development across the
lifespan. Author Stephen Mitchell clarified this distinction:

> In this vision, the basic unit of study is not the individual as a separate en-
> tity whose desires clash with an external reality, but as an interactional field
> within which the individual arises and struggles to make contact and artic-
> ulate himself. . . . Mind is composed only of relational configurations. The
> person is comprehensible only within this tapestry of relationships, past
> and present. (1988, p. 3)

Mitchell's words speak for the theories covered below which posit that
relationships, be they with key people (relational model) or clinicians (intersubjectivity), are central to the treatment process. Delgado, Stawn, and
Pedapati (2014) use the term "two-person models" to describe these theories
in which relationships are created and utilized to cause therapeutic change.
These theories push clinicians to examine the relationships between adolescent clients and their caregivers and even with clinicians.

Relational Theory

In his book *Relational Concepts in Psychoanalysis: An Integration*, Stephen
Mitchell (1988) proposed the need to consider an individual in the context of all their relationships. Mitchell stated, "the most useful way to

view psychological reality is as operation within a relational matrix which encompasses both intrapsychic and interpersonal realms" (1988, p. 9). Thus, the clinician's unit of study shifts from the individual to the relational web within which the individual exists.

Applying his model to work with adolescents requires the clinician to inquire about all important relationships and to place primary focus on the individual's thoughts, feelings, and beliefs about these relationships. Given that adolescents are typically part of a family unit and that peer relationships are tremendously important to this age group, the relational model promotes the examination and integration of these familial and peer relationships into the therapeutic conversation.

We can find an example of Mitchell's model in the case of Adam, a 14-year-old who struggles with depression and suicidality. He feels isolated from his peers, citing that he used to be close to a few other boys, but that they are not interested in him anymore because "I don't play sports like they do." He feels distant from his family, explaining that he "used to be close to my mom when I was little, but I'm not a baby anymore." Caught between his strong desire for close peer relationships and his need to establish independence from his warm relationship with his mother, Adam is isolated and alone. He spends hours on his computer in his room, playing interactive games online. He wishes for more connection, but is not sure how to do this, how to establish important peer relationship like other kids do. We can understand Adam's symptoms evolving from the relational web in which he finds himself, not separate from those relationships but emerging from his relational isolation.

Intersubjectivity and the Two-Person Model

Intersubjectivity informs many of psychotherapy's relational models. To understand intersubjectivity, it is helpful to first understand the concept of subjectivity. Subjectivity is defined as the way that a person perceives and experiences herself and her world (Buirski & Haglund, 2001). Intersubjectivity, the interaction of subjective experiences, posits that interactions and relationships impact our individual subjective experiences and beliefs (Buirski & Haglund, 2001). In this framework, we see the interaction of client and clinician as the most important component of the therapeutic process. From the perspective of intersubjective practice, intentional interaction shapes and creates the client's subjective world, rendering that intentional interaction the most powerful tool available to the clinician (Buirski & Haglund, 2001; Stern, 2004). Buirski and Haglund (2001) explain that, in intersubjective practice, therapists view the client's current presentation as their best effort to cope with the world as they have subjectively experienced it.

Theorist Daniel Stern (2004) elaborates on the definition of intersubjectivity: "the capacity to share, know, understand, empathize with, feel, participate in, resonate with, enter into the lived subjective experience of another" (Stern as cited in Delgado et al., 2014, p. 95). Stern put particular emphasis on the importance of working with the client in the present moment, rather than focusing on past events or future outcomes (Stern, 2004). Intersubjectivity rejects the notion that the therapist has a clearer view than the client of who they are and why they are (Buirski & Haglund, 2001). From the intersubjective stance, the clinician's perspective is colored by her own subjective experiences and this is no more valid and valuable than that of the client (Buirski & Haglund, 2001).

In sum, intersubjectivity is the idea that both client and clinician influence each other's subjective realities in the present moment. Thus, the therapeutic process is an interactive experience between client and clinician. Through a series of present-moment-oriented interactions between client and clinician, clients can experience and learn a new model for relationships (Stern, 2004). The interaction between client and clinician becomes the primary focus of the treatment process (Delgado et al., 2014). The intersubjective stance expands the role of clinician from observer and reflector of relational patterns in the client's life to one who is actively entering and engaging in a meaningful relationship with the client.

In a two-person model that embraces intersubjectivity, the client and clinician engage in a treatment relationship in which both examine the feelings provoked in them by the other. We can see an example of this kind of treatment in the case of Aurora, a 15-year-old girl with a long history of criminal behavior. Aurora was a client in a residential treatment center, sent there by her parents who worried about her years-long membership in a gang. Aurora described the other gang members as her closest friends, explaining that she didn't connect with or feel close to her parents. But Aurora held a great deal of shame about the crimes that she had committed with her gang friends. She refused to speak about what exactly these crimes were, but stated that if the therapist knew about them, "you wouldn't want to talk to me anymore." The therapist spent weeks building a strong therapeutic relationship with Aurora, focusing on transparency, warmth, and establishing trust. The therapist encouraged Aurora to write down 10 crimes or behaviors of which she was most ashamed. Aurora took several weeks to do this, but eventually shared with the therapist that the task was complete. The therapist asked Aurora to share one of the items on her list. Aurora was deeply resistant to this, worried about the relational impact that might come from such a disclosure. The therapist assured Aurora that she wouldn't leave and would continue to feel warmly about Aurora no matter what she shared. After much hesitation, Aurora shared that she had shot both wrists of a young man who she believed had stolen her friend's drugs, while two of her friends held the young man up. The therapist was shocked and saddened by the disclosure, sharing with Aurora her authentic reaction as well as her commitment to working with Aurora long-term. Aurora became slightly tearful, explaining that she was sure that she was a bad person, not worthy of the therapist's attention or time. The therapist reassured Aurora that their therapeutic relationship was strengthened by Aurora's disclosure, by her willingness to share something of which she was ashamed. Both the therapist and Aurora expressed being moved by Aurora's disclosure and processed what impact this might have on the therapeutic relationship.

This example demonstrates several key principles of intersubjectivity and two-person models. First, the clinician allowed herself to recognize her own feelings and experience in relationship with her client. Next, she engaged in a meaningful conversation around these feelings. Both client and clinician acknowledged and recognized their subjective experiences of working together. Through this intersubjective experience, they built a relationship and utilized it to work through the treatment process as an interactive two-person unit. This example illuminates how an intersubjective approach might strength a therapeutic relationship in adolescent treatment, allowing the client to experience her therapist as an authentic human being with feelings and allowing the therapist to engage more deeply in the clinical exchange. Both intersubjectivity and two-person models can be utilized successfully in adolescent treatment. Beyond analyzing important relationships in the adolescent client's life, the clinician can engage in a meaningful working relationship with the client in which both acknowledge and interpret their feelings toward one another, as in the case of Aurora.

Psychological theory is useful to clinicians as it allows to more deeply understand our clients' behaviors, motives, and drives. Why do our clients do what they do? Why would an adolescent client who had been abused as a child choose to enter into an abusive relationship with a peer? Why do our adolescent clients seem to seek contradictory things: distance and closeness from adults at the same time? Why are our clients hard on themselves, blaming themselves for things entirely out of their control? Why would a client seek to hide important information from a therapist he admired? Theory illuminates answers to these questions, providing insight into why people do what they do. Theory allows clinicians to create informed hypotheses about clients, seeing beyond their bluster and behind their defenses.

References

Blos, P. (1962). *On Adolescence: A Psychoanalytic Interpretation*. Glencoe: Free Press.

Blos, P. (1967/1975). The second individuation process of adolescence. In A. H. Esman (Ed.), *The Psychology of Adolescence: Essential Readings* (pp. 156–176). New York, NY: International Universities Press.

Blos, P. (1968). Character formation in adolescence. *Psychoanalytic Study of the Child, 23*, 245–263.

Blos, P. (1979). Modifications in the classical psychoanalytical model of adolescence. In S. C. Feinstein & P. L. Giovacchini (Eds.), *Adolescent psychiatry, developmental and clinical studies* (Vol. 7, pp. 6–25). Chicago, IL: University of Chicago Press.

Boucher, H. C., & Maslach, C. (2009). Culture and individuation: The role of norms and self-construals. *The Journal of Social Psychology, 149*, 677–693.

Buirski, P., & Haglund, P. (2001). *Making sense together: The intersubjective approach to psychotherapy*. New York, NY: Jason Aronson.

Claes, L., Luyckx, K., & Bijttebier, P. (2014). Non-suicidal self-injury in adolescents: Prevalence and associations with identity formation above and beyond depression. *Personality and Individual Differences, 61-62*, 101–104. doi:http://dx.doi.org/10.1016/j.paid.2013.12.019

Delgado, S. V., Strawn, J. R., & Pedapati, E. V. (2014). *Contemporary psychodynamic psychotherapy for children and adolescents: Integrating intersubjectivity and neuroscience*. New York, NY: Springer.

Erikson, E. H. (1959). The problem of ego identity. *Psychological Issues, 1*, 101–164.

Erikson, E. H. (1968). *Identity: Youth and crisis*. New York, NY: Norton.

Erikson, E. H. (1982). *The life cycle completed*. New York, NY: Norton.

Esman, A. H. (1980). Adolescent psychopathology and the rapprochement phenomenon. In S. C. Feinstein & P. L. Giovacchini (Eds.), *Adolescent psychiatry, developmental and clinical studies* (Vol. 8, pp. 320–331). Chicago, IL: University of Chicago Press.

Freud, S. (1960). *The ego and the id*. New York, NY: Norton.

Gandhi, A., Luyckx, K., Goossens, L., Maitra, S., & Claes, L. (2016). Sociotropy, autonomy, and non-suicidal self-injury: The mediating role of identity confusion. *Personality and Individual Differences, 99*, 272–277. doi:http://dx.doi.org/10.1016/j.paid.2016.05.040

Kwan, V. S. Y., Bond, M. H., Boucher, H. C., Maslach, C., & Gan, Y. (2002). The construct of individuation: More complex in collectivist than in individualist cultures. *Personality and Social Psychology Bulletin, 28*, 300–310. doi:10.1177/0146167202286002

Mahler, M. S., Pine, F., & Bergman, A. (1975). *The psychological birth of the human infant: Symbiosis and individuation.* New York, NY: Basic Books.

Mitchell, S. A. (1988). *Relational concepts in psychoanalysis: An integration.* Cambridge, MA and London: Harvard University Press.

Pine, F. (1992). Some refinements of the separation-individuation concept in light of research on infants. *The Psychoanalytic Study of the Child, 47*, 103–116.

Slote, W. H. (1992). Oedipal ties and issues of separation-individuation in traditional Confucian societies. *Journal of the American Academy of Psychoanalysis, 20*, 435–453.

Stern, D. (2004). *The present moment: In psychotherapy and everyday life.* New York, NY: Norton.

Zastrow, C. H., & Kirst-Ashman, K. K. (2015). *Understanding human behavior and the social environment* (10th ed.). Boston, MA: Cengage Learning.

3

The Neurobiology of Adolescents and Its Implications for Treatment

Joanna E. Bettmann and Katherine V. Ovrom

This chapter presents recent findings in neuroscience that help explain adolescent risk- and reward-seeking behavior, as well as adolescents' increased cognitive capabilities and impulse regulation difficulties.

Neurobiological Development in Adolescence

The pace and scope of development which takes place within the brain during adolescence is second only to the neonatal period (Montgomery, 2013). The basic steps of neuromaturation are synaptic overproduction, pruning, and myelination. Synaptic overproduction refers to the proliferation of neural connections throughout the cortical area, which causes an increase in gray matter throughout the brain (Johnson et al., 2009). This process occurs in childhood and peaks around age 11 and 12, while pruning and myelination begin in adolescence (Johnson, Blum, & Giedd, 2009).

During adolescence, neural connections not frequently used are pruned in order to make the connections that remain more efficient in terms of communication and function (Johnson et al., 2009). The process of pruning is highly influenced by the environment: the demands of an individual's environment dictate which connections are utilized enough to warrant development and consequently which will be pruned (Johnson et al., 2009). Those neural connections that remain after pruning then undergo the process of myelination. Myelin is a substance that insulates and protects neural connections and which promotes faster movement of nerve impulses, allowing more parts of the brain to work together efficiently (Johnson et al., 2009). Myelinated nerve cells and their axons make up the white matter of the brain. Thus, while the process of pruning reduces gray matter, myelination leads to an increase in white matter. While white matter is sometimes referred to as a passive tissue when compared to gray matter, it is crucially important for the transmission of information and efficient communication between different parts of the brain.

Importantly for adolescent development, the processes of pruning and myelination, which lead to a reduction in gray matter and increase in white matter respectively, are not complete until young adulthood (Johnson et al., 2009). Both of these processes begin at the back of the brain in the hindbrain and progress forward, reaching the prefrontal cortex in early adulthood (Johnson et al., 2009). This means that even while adolescents are making gains in cognitive capabilities (Steinberg, 2007), the subcortical areas of the brain involved in emotional processes, risk, and reward seeking, including the ventral striatum and limbic system, undergo neuromaturation well before the regulatory centers of the frontal and prefrontal cortex (Casey et al., 2008). This helps to explain why adolescents sometimes choose to do very risky things, such as dangerous snowboarding tricks, when they do not have the skills or equipment to achieve such feats. These adolescents may be motivated by the good feelings they can achieve through such feats without thinking through the major physical consequences of a potential fall and injury.

Adolescent Risk Taking and Rewards

The adolescent brain is highly responsive to neurochemicals such as dopamine, oxytocin, epinephrine, and norepinephrine (Atkins, Bunting, Bolger, & Dougherty, 2012; Wahlstrom, Collins, White, & Luciana, 2010). Dopamine in particular is critical in understanding adolescent development and behavior. Research suggests that dopamine plays an important role in the adolescent propensity toward risk seeking and reward-driven behaviors (Wahlstrom et al., 2010).

Risk seeking and reward-driven behavior is not unique to human adolescents (Shulman et al., 2016). Studies of both humans and animals reveal adolescence to be a time of greater risk-seeking behavior than any other time of life (Telzer, 2016). Risk-seeking behaviors are those "with potential rewarding outcomes . . . but high potential negative consequences" (Padmanabhan & Luna, 2014, p. 28). Examples of risk-seeking behaviors include drug use, reckless driving, and unprotected sex (Padmanabhan &

Luna, 2014). However, increased risk seeking is not always detrimental. For many adolescents, risk seeking is a highly adaptive function (Telzer, 2016). The drive to seek out new experiences prepares adolescents to leave the childhood family home and enter adult life (Padmanabhan & Luna, 2014), an important developmental step for many Western adolescents. Risk-seeking experiences increase adolescents' social interactions which widen their social circle to include peers and potential sexual partners.

However, while the majority of adolescents survive and thrive, the potential for harm and death are alarmingly high for this population (Dahl & Gunnar, 2009). During adolescence, the likelihood of experiencing a traffic accident or experimenting with alcohol and tobacco, as well as rates of suicide, depression, anxiety, and other psychological disorders, all spike (Dahl & Gunnar, 2009; Van Leijenhorst et al., 2010). Adolescents are capable of critical thinking, and, by age 15, often possess logical-reasoning skills comparable to those of an adult (Padmanabhan & Luna, 2014). However, in the context of very emotional or high stakes situations, especially those involving peers, risk-seeking behaviors increase dramatically (Casey et al., 2008; Steinberg, 2007).

One explanation for this risk-seeking is adolescents' heightened sensitivity to the neurotransmitter dopamine (Wahlstrom et al., 2010). Research has found that those areas of the brain which produce and receive dopamine are more active in adolescence than other times of life (Wahlstrom et al., 2010). For example, the quantity of dopamine receptors in the prefrontal cortex peaks during adolescence, then decreases in adulthood (Padmanabhan & Luna, 2014). Adolescents' heightened sensitivity to dopamine, the neurochemical responsible for most human pleasure and reward-seeking behavior, may give some insight into why adolescence is a time of increased risk seeking.

One case example which illustrates this problematic risk taking is the case of John (a pseudonym), a 15-year-old with drug problem. John entered residential treatment following his parents' demands that he do so. He had responded poorly to one year of intermittent outpatient therapy, often refusing to attend sessions or attending them but replying monosyllabically to the therapist. John entered residential treatment with an angry pose, telling anyone who asked that his life would be fine if his parents would just stay out of his way. He demonstrated no interest in reflecting on the drug use which brought him to treatment, explaining that he "had everything under control." He told his therapist at the residential treatment setting that he had been using drugs since age 12, starting with readily available alcohol and marijuana. He explained that he loved the feeling that being high gave him, stating that he felt more confident and comfortable among his peers when high. He described that he and his buddies often took whatever pills were available, combined them with alcohol, and then cruised around town, finding bridges to climb underneath, buildings to scale, or cliff edges to walk along. John had begun dealing pills in order to ensure that he had a ready supply available to him. John evaluated his own behavior as reasonable, describing that life was "boring" and "stupid" without his friends and risky behaviors. He stated his belief that adults just didn't understand what having a good time was.

We can see the case of John as illustrative of adolescents' heightened sensitivity to dopamine, the neurochemical which is responsible for most human pleasure and reward-seeking. John's behavior is driven, in part, by pleasure seeking. What he is doing feels good to him. The case is also illustrative of adolescents' particular cognitive capabilities. The subcortical areas of the adolescent brain involved in emotional processes, risk, and reward seeking undergo neuromaturation well before the regulatory centers of the frontal and prefrontal cortex, which helps to explain why John evaluates his own dangerous behaviors (getting high and then putting himself in risky situations) as appropriate and reasonable. John is motivated by the good feelings such behaviors provide, as well as the peer support which is linked to these behaviors. He does not conceptualize his behavior as putting his life at risk; he believes his parents' worries are misplaced.

Other Neurobiological Models That Explain Adolescent Risk Seeking

Some research attempts to explain the paradox between adolescents' strong cognitive abilities and their likelihood to engage in high-risk behaviors by using one of two models, the dual systems model or the imbalance model (Casey et al., 2008; Steinberg, 2007). Neither the dual systems nor the imbalance models attribute risk-seeking behavior to cognitive deficiencies (Casey et al., 2008; Steinberg, 2007). Instead, both models attribute the spike in adolescent reckless behavior to the differences in timing between the development of the socioemotional/limbic/incentive-motivational systems of the brain and the regulatory/cognitive control systems. The socioemotional sectors of the limbic system and ventral striatum develop earlier in adolescence, while the prefrontal cortex and other structures that regulate impulses do not fully develop until the early twenties (Shulman et al., 2016).

The dual systems model proposes that the development of humans' socioemotional system follows an inverted U-shaped course, where risk and reward-seeking behavior increases during early adolescence and then declines in early adulthood (Shulman et al., 2016). There is some support for this model in fMRI research in which adolescents of different ages completed high-risk, high-reward tasks (Van Leijenhorst et al., 2010). In this research, younger adolescents exhibited increased sensitivity in the socioemotional sections of the brain associated with incentive-motivational behavior, while older adolescents and young adults displayed less activation of those same areas (Van Leijenhorst et al., 2010).

In contrast to the inverted U shape of the dual systems model, the imbalance model proposes that development of the socioemotional system surges ahead of the regulatory systems of the prefrontal cortex until mid-adolescence and then plateaus, staying consistent into adulthood (Casey et al., 2008). In the imbalance model, the risk- and reward-seeking impulses do not decline, but rather the cognitive control/regulatory systems catch up as humans develop and are then able to modulate those impulses (Shulman et al., 2016). The imbalance model stresses the role of dopamine in the adolescent brain (Galván, 2012). In this model, two cognitive and neural changes are critical during adolescence: (1) improved cognitive control thanks to the maturation of the prefrontal cortex, and (2) over-exaggeration of neural activation in brain areas that respond to dopamine production (Galván, 2012). The imbalance model is supported by fMRI imaging studies that demonstrate an over-activation of the ventral striatum, a key component of the socioemotional system highly sensitive to dopamine production, as well as animal and postmortem human studies that suggest a higher number of dopamine receptors in adolescents (Padmanabhan & Luna, 2014).

However, some offer critiques of the both the dual systems and imbalance models (Telzer, 2016). Telzer notes that, in both models, the overactivation of the ventral striatum is portrayed primarily as a deficit in adolescent neurobiology (Telzer, 2016). She acknowledges that the increased sensitivity to dopamine in the ventral striatum does lead to more risk-seeking behaviors but notes that there are several cases in which this was of benefit to adolescents rather than an impairment. She notes that adolescent sensitivity to reward can be activated in response to prosocial actions, such as supporting the family, and that the positive feelings generated by the dopaminergic reward system can reinforce positive actions and behaviors (Telzer, 2016). Some research supports her hypothesis: one study found that the experience of ventral striatum activation in response to prosocial events lessened the activation of the ventral striatum in response to risk-taking tasks, which consequently reduced the likelihood that the adolescent would engage in a risky behavior (Tezler, Fuligni, & Galván, 2015). Thus, while the dopaminergic reward system based in the ventral striatum may increase the likelihood of risk-seeking behavior for some teens, for others the very same system could decrease their propensity toward risk depending on their familial and cultural environment (Telzer, 2016). Indeed, there is significant individual variation when it comes to the level and timing of risk-seeking behavior in adolescence (Shulman et al., 2016). Environmental factors play a significant role in whether or not an adolescent is more likely to engage in risk-seeking behaviors.

Environmental Factors: The Influence of Peers on Adolescent Risk Seeking

Research identifies the presence of peers as a significant predictor of risk-seeking behaviors in adolescents (Galván, 2012). For example, adolescents who spend time with peers who use drugs are more likely to use drugs themselves (Galván, 2012). Research associates adolescents' beliefs about how many of their peers are using with their likelihood to try substances (Galván, 2012).

Evidence suggests that this increased susceptibility to risky behaviors in a peer-based context may have a neurodevelopmental basis (Galván, 2012). Research shows that the presence of peers can elicit emotions which activate the ventral striatum in adolescents more than other age groups (Galván, 2012). The ventral striatum is an important component of the socioemotional system and is highly sensitive to dopamine during adolescence. Further, activation of the ventral striatum is predictive of risk-taking behaviors (Galván, 2012). Given that an adolescent is primed to experience more activation of the ventral striatum in the presence of peers and that such activation can trigger risk-taking behavior, the presence of peers can increase the likelihood to engage in risk-taking behavior.

In the case of John (presented earlier in this chapter), peer behavior strongly contributed to his motivation toward drug use and risky behaviors. Many adolescents present to treatment similarly to John, describing that they engage in drug use or risky behavior primarily in the company of peers. Many adolescents label their behaviors as reasonable because their peers do the same things. Many will say, "But my friend does more drugs than I do" as a rationalization for why their behavior is appropriate or their own treatment is not needed. Such statements highlight the importance of peers in adolescent decision making, pointing to the necessity for clinicians to explore an adolescent's peers, peer behaviors, and peer risk taking in assessment.

Environmental Factors: The Relationship Between Adolescent Brain Development and Sleep

Research identifies the impact of sleep on adolescent brain development and cognitive functioning (Telzer, Goldenberg, Fuligni, Lieberman, & Gálvan, 2015). Several negative outcomes are associated with poor sleep in adolescence. For example, poor sleep can negatively impact neural functions involved in memory formation and has been linked to gray matter loss in both cortical and subcortical areas of the brain (Jan et al., 2010). Greater volume of gray matter is associated with better short- and long-term memory (Taki et al., 2011). Therefore, poor sleep in adolescence can result in poorer academic performance and less competence in other memory-based tasks.

While lack of sleep can lead to significant impairment in adolescent brain development, sleep variability also plays a role. Sleep variability refers to differences in sleep schedules such as the time an adolescent falls asleep, when they wake up, or the total number of hours spent asleep (Telzer et al., 2015). Larger differences in time in bed, wake up time, or total time spent asleep, constitutes greater sleep variability (Telzer et al., 2015). One longitudinal study used brain imaging to show that adolescents with greater variability in sleep duration one year prior to receiving a brain scan had lower white matter integrity than adolescents without that sleep variability (Telzer et al., 2015). White matter should be increasing during adolescence through the process of myelination. This association was demonstrated only in those with sleep variability a year prior to the scan versus sleep variability just several months prior (Telzer et al., 2015). The authors interpret this finding to mean that the negative impacts of poor sleep may impact adolescent cognitive functioning in the short term, while greater sleep variability over the course of a year or more may lead to long-term negative effects on adolescent brain development (Telzer et al., 2015).

Such findings illustrate how screening for sleep hygiene, both duration and variability, when working with adolescents is critical to effective assessment. Further, providing psychoeducational materials and feedback on adolescents' sleep can help clients and their families to promote consistent sleep routines that support healthy brain development and functioning.

Implications for Treatment

The recent findings in neuroscience described in this chapter serve to inform both assessment and treatment of adolescent clients. One frequent challenge for clinicians and parents alike is the adolescent propensity toward risk- and reward-seeking behavior (Steinberg, 2007). Since the areas of the brain primed for reward seeking develop before the impulse-regulating systems such as those in the prefrontal cortex (Shulman et al., 2016), risk- and reward-seeking behavior is normal, even healthy. Thus, clinicians need to balance educating adolescents on the consequences of their risk taking (Dahl & Gunnar, 2009), while honoring the social and emotional developmental needs that this behavior serves (Telzer, 2016). For example, risk- and reward-seeking behavior can widen an adolescents' social network and prepare them to leave the family home (Padmanabhan & Luna, 2014). However, these benefits do not always outweigh the severe consequences associated with risks such as reckless driving, substance abuse, and unprotected sex (Dahl & Gunnar, 2009).

In adolescent treatment, a combination of psychoeducation and family engagement may help mitigate these risks. For example, a family intervention that creates experiences in which teens are rewarded for positive actions or choices can redirect the energy of the incentive-motivational behavior from risks toward more positive behaviors. Activation of the dopaminergic system in response to positive behaviors, especially in the family environment, can stimulate the incentive-motivational system in the same way as risks (Telzer, 2016). Over time, this stimulation may motivate an adolescent to engage in positive actions and fewer risks. Clinicians should encourage parents to create systems at home through which adolescents can be rewarded for positive actions. For example, parents who set rules about an adolescent's chores, participation in family meals, help with siblings, or homework completion, could reward a week of strong behavior in one or more areas with increased freedoms for the adolescent, such as access to the family car, later curfews, and so forth.

The role of peers is also important in the context of risk- and reward-seeking behaviors. Since adolescents are more vulnerable to an overactivation of the socioemotional or limbic system when they are with peers (Galván, 2012), assessment should include inquiry into adolescents' peer relationships. This inquiry allows the clinician to understand the types of activities adolescents engage in and the pressures they experience. This inquiry becomes especially important when substance abuse is involved, as teens are more likely to use when their peers use (Galván, 2012). One possible intervention is to encourage adolescents to spend more time with peers who do not use substances and who avoid risky behaviors. Such guidance might include seeking out peers engaged in sports or other positive extracurricular activities. Telling an adolescent not to spend time with a friend who exhibits more risky behavior is likely to elicit resistance and resentment. However, clinicians can help adolescents identify qualities of healthy peer relationships and encourage them toward those kinds of relationships.

Adolescents undergo periods of rapid and dramatic neurodevelopment. Clinicians who incorporate knowledge of the incentive-motivational system, assess peers and family, and address sleep quality and variability will conduct more effective treatment of adolescents. Adolescence is a time of great self-discovery, learning, and exploration. With knowledge of adolescent neurobiological development, clinicians can help adolescent clients to explore in a way that respects their personal growth while safeguarding their well-being.

References

Atkins, S. M., Bunting, M. F., Bolger, D. J., & Dougherty, M. R. (2012). Training the adolescent brain: Neural plasticity and the acquisition of cognitive abilities. In V. F. Reyna, S. B. Chapman, M. R. Dougherty, & J. Confrey (Eds.), *The adolescent brain: Learning, reasoning, and decision making* (pp. 211–241). http://dx.doi.org/10.1037/13493-008

Berridge, K. C., & Robinson, T. E. (1998). What is the role of dopamine in reward: Hedonic impact, reward learning, or incentive salience? *Brain Research Reviews, 28*, 309–369. doi:https://doi.org/10.1016/S0165-0173(98)00019-8

Casey, B. J., Getz, S., & Galván, A. (2008). The adolescent brain. *Developmental Review, 28*, 62–77. doi:10.1016/j.dr.2007.08.003

Dahl, R. E., & Gunnar, M. R. (2009). Heightened stress responsiveness and emotional reactivity during pubertal maturation: Implications for psychopathology. *Development and Psychopathology, 21*, 1–6. doi:http://dx.doi.org/10.1017/S0954579409000017

Galván, A. (2012). Risky behavior in adolescence: The role of the developing brain. In V. F. Reyna, S. B. Chapman, M. R. Dougherty, & J. Confrey (Eds.), *The Adolescent brain: Learning, reasoning, and decision making* (pp. 267–289). Washington, DC: American Psychological Association.

Montgomery, A. (2013). *Neurobiology essentials for clinicians.* New York, NY: Norton.

Jan, J. E., Reiter, R. J., Martin, C. O. B., Urs, R., Freeman, R. D., & Wasdell, M. B. (2010). Long-term sleep disturbances in children: A cause of neuronal loss. *European Journal of Pediatric Neurology, 14*, 380–390.

Johnson, S. B., Blum, R. W., & Giedd, J. N. (2009). Adolescent maturity and the brain: The promise and pitfalls of neuroscience research in adolescent health policy. *Journal of Adolescent Health, 45*, 216–221. doi:10.1016/j.jadohealth.2009.05.016

Padmanabhan, A., & Luna, B. (2014). Developmental imaging genetics: Linking dopamine function to adolescent behavior. *Brain and Cognition, 89*, 27–38. doi:http://dx.doi.org/10.1016/j.bandc.2013.09.011

Shulman, E. P., Smith, A. R., Silva, K., Icenogle, G., Duell, N., Chein, J., & Steinberg, L. (2016). Dual systems model: Review, reappraisal, and reaffirmation. *Developmental Cognitive Neuroscience, 17*, 103–117. doi:http://dx.doi.org/10.1016/j.dcn.2015.12.010

Steinberg, L. (2007). Risk taking in adolescence: New perspectives from brain and behavioral science. *Current Directions in Psychological Science, 16*, 55–59.

Taki, Y., Kinomura, S., Sato, K., Goto, R., Wu, K., Kawashima, R., & Fukuda, H. (2011). Correlation between gray/white matter volume and cognition in healthy elderly people. *Brain and Cognition, 75*, 170–176. doi:10.1016/j.bandc.2010.11.08

Telzer, E. H., Fuligni, A. J., & Galván, A. (2015). Identifying a cultural resource: Neural correlates of familial influence on risk taking among Mexican-origin adolescents. In J. Y. Chiao, S.-C. Li, R. Seligman, & R. Turner (Eds.), *The Oxford Handbook of Cultural Neuroscience* (pp. 209–221). New York, NY: Oxford University Press.

Telzer, E., Goldenberg, D., Fuligni, A. J., Lieberman, M. D., & Galván, A. (2015). Sleep variability in adolescence is associated with altered brain development. *Developmental Cognitive Neuroscience, 14*, 16–22. http://dx.doi.org.10.1016/j.dcn.2015.05.007

Telzer, E. (2016). Dopaminergic reward sensitivity can promote adolescent health: A new perspective on the mechanism of ventral striatum activation. *Developmental Cognitive Neuroscience, 17*, 57–67. http://dx.doi.org/10.1016/j.dcn.2015.10.010

Van Leijenhorst, L., Moor, B. G., Op de Macks, Z.A., Rombouts, S. A. R. B., Westenberg, P. M., & Crone, E. A. (2010). Adolescent risky decision-making: Neurocognitive development of reward and control regions. *Neuroimage, 51*, 345–355. doi:10.1016/j.neuroimage.2010.02.038

Wahlstrom, D., Collins, P., White, T., & Luciana, M. (2010). Developmental changes in dopamine neurotransmission in adolescence: Behavioral implications and issues in assessment. *Brain and Cognition, 72*, 146–159. doi:https://doi.org/10.1016/j.bandc.2009.10.013

4

Assessment in Adolescent Treatment

Joanna E. Bettmann

When you meet with a new adolescent client, what do you ask first? How should you ask about difficult topics? What information should you collect and how should you organize it? This chapter answers all these questions, presenting how to conduct an initial assessment with an adolescent client. The chapter describes what information to collect, how to ask, and how to organize what you collect effectively.

To begin, what information you collect will depend to some extent on the setting in which you are working. Certain settings will need more detail on aspects of adolescent functioning: school performance, substance use, and so forth. However, this chapter will present information that you should collect no matter what setting you are working in. Assessments can be structured into 10 sections. What belongs in each section will be detailed below.

Sections of an assessment
- Identifying Information
- Presenting Problem
- Substance Use History
- Treatment History
- Medical Information
- Family History
- Social History
- Mental Status
- Summary

To begin, the Identifying Information section includes the client's name, age, gender, race/ethnicity, sexual orientation, disability, referral information, etc. This section should be 1–2 sentences long and sounds like a list. For example, "Amy is a 15-year-old Caucasian girl who identifies as lesbian. She reports no physical disability and is referred to treatment by her primary care physician who is concerned about her recent weight loss." This information can be collected from written forms that the client fills out prior to coming to your office or from medical records. If you don't have either of these, you will need to ask your client for this information.

Presenting Problem

The Presenting Problem section is typically the longest section in any assessment. In an initial session with a client, this is the information that your client most wants to talk about: what has been going wrong. This section includes symptoms the client is experiencing or problems she is facing. Make sure you ask about the history of the problem(s) and the solutions the client has undertaken to address it. This section is typically a few paragraphs long. Here is an example of one paragraph from this section: "Evan reported a long history of depression. He stated that he couldn't remember a time when he wasn't sad or down. He explained that he felt sad most of the time, nearly every day, and that he had contemplated suicide at times. He reported passive suicidal ideation, denying any history of attempts or current suicide plan. He stated that he often wished his life would end, but that his parents would be devastated and that his religion asserted that dying by suicide meant you were going to hell for all eternity. He described that he had been on a few different anti-depressants, he couldn't remember their names, but that none were particularly helpful. He reported that he was not taking any psychiatric mediations at the present time. He stated that nothing he did seemed to help his sadness, except being with his girlfriend. He reported that he and his girlfriend of 2 years recently broke up after she began showing interest in another boy." The Presenting Problem section of an assessment report should tell the story of what the client believes is wrong and how she has tried to work it.

In the Presenting Problem section, you should make sure to screen for the most likely psychiatric disorders in your clients. These will always include depression, anxiety, and substance use disorders because of the prevalence of these conditions. But you should also include screening tailored to your client's presenting problem or setting. For example, if your client reports lots of problems at school, screen for learning disorders and ask about current ADHD symptoms.

Additionally, you should always screen for suicidality, homicidal ideation, and psychotic processes. Ask every client: "Are you feeling suicidal now?" "Have you ever felt suicidal?" "Have you ever made a suicide plan or attempted suicide? If so, please tell me about that." "Do you have any current thoughts about suicide?" "Do you have any current thoughts about hurting yourself?" Make sure to distinguish between active and passive suicidal thoughts, assessing whether the client has a current suicide plan and access to the means to carry out the plan. Assess whether the client is in any high-risk groups for suicide completion: if your client is a gay adolescent, does he knows someone who has completed suicide, does he have history of suicide attempts or a history of major psychiatric illness in immediate family, is he impulsive, does he have current substance use disorder, and so forth. Screen for homicidality by asking your client if they have any feelings about or plans to hurt someone. Screen for psychosis by asking your client: "Do you have any beliefs that other people would think are strange?" "Do you ever see or hear anything that others don't see or hear, when you weren't on drugs?" If yes to either of these screening questions, then you will need to delve in depth, screening for psychotic thought content and processes.

One effective way of assessing suicidality is to use a standardized measure. I recommend the Columbia Suicide Severity Rating Scale, which is an empirically validated, widely used instrument for assessing suicidality (available free here: http://cssrs.columbia.edu/). There are shorter screening versions of the scale, as well as longer versions meant to be used in healthcare settings. The website listed above provides free, brief training for the scale, but all versions of the instrument are quite user friendly. You do not need to use an instrument to screen for suicidality; you can simply use the screening questions listed previously. But if you are new to mental health assessment, you may feel more confident using an empirically validated measure that lists all the important questions to ask.

Related to suicidality is the client's self-harming behaviors. Some adolescents cut, burn, or harm themselves in other ways. You should always asses these self-harm behaviors as they can be common in some groups of adolescents, particularly those who are depressed or who have peers who are self-harming. Ask your adolescent clients: "Do you ever hurt yourself on purpose?" "How often do you do that?" "How does it make you feel when you do?" With this last question, you are assessing the aim of the behavior; oftentimes, adolescents physically hurt themselves in order to displace psychological distress or difficult emotions.

For the Presenting Problem section of your assessment, you should also include what your client endorses as his goals for treatment. Ask: "What are you hoping to get out of meeting with me?" "How are you hoping that I can help?" Your client may phrase their treatment goals as "I want my parents to get off my back." If so, ask them to clarify: "How are you hoping that I can help with that?" Help your client to set specific treatment goals. The more specific the goal, the more likely you are able to help your client with it. If your client wants relief from her depressive symptoms, ask her how she will know that she is free from depression or feeling better? Inquire of your client: what will be the markers that you and she will use to gauge that?

Substance Use History

In the Substance Use History section, you will describe the clients' current and past drug and alcohol use. Specify the client's drug of choice and the method and frequency of use. Also note any legal problems that were the result of substance use, such as arrests for illegal drug use or driving under the influence, school suspensions for smoking on campus, and so forth.

Substance	Age at first use	Last use	Frequency of use	Amount of use (each time)	Problems because of use	Tolerance/ withdrawal symptoms
Alcohol	10 years old	yesterday	2 x week	3–5 beers	Parents got angry	Grounded by parents for stealing their beer
Marijuana	13 years old	today	3 x day	1 joint	Hard to get up in morning, late to school	Anxious when not stoned, hard to deal with school sober

For each client, you will need to collect a lot of information for each drug used. This is because the DSM-5 instructs clinicians to diagnose substance use disorder specific to each substance. I have worked with adolescent clients who had four different substance use disorder diagnoses. For such a client, the diagnosis list might read like this:

303.90 Alcohol Use Disorder, Moderate
304.20 Cannabis Use Disorder, Mild
305.50 Opioid Use Disorder, Mild

You will order your diagnostic list from most impairing to least impairing. At the top of the diagnostic list, you will list the substance whose use has caused the client the most trouble. So you will need to ask every client a lot of specific information about each substance used. Refer to the table above which specifies all the information you need to collect about each substance your client used, even if the client only used it once. Collecting a substance use history draws a picture of your client's habits regarding substance use. Will your client use anything available to get high if his drug of choice is not available or will he go to extraordinary lengths to obtain his preferred drug? Ask your client: "how do you obtain your drugs/alcohol?" Clinicians can find additional useful tools for substance use assessment at samhsa.org.

Treatment History

In the Treatment History section, you will need to list all of the previous diagnoses your client has received from other practitioners. You should also list all previous mental health treatment your client has received: inpatient, outpatient, residential, and so forth. This section should include dates of diagnoses and treatment and whether or not the client felt the treatment was effective. Note what the client reports was helpful or not helpful about each previous course of treatment. These descriptors will prove very helpful for you as you move forward in treating the client. Your client is telling you here what not to do or what he found unhelpful in treatment before. This is extremely useful information for you.

Medical Information

In the Medical Information section of the assessment, you will describe all relevant medical information from your client. This should include any major surgeries your client had, head injuries (whether the client lost consciousness or not, whether they received treatment or not), any chronic illnesses, and any major accidents. You should also include current medications (prescription and over the counter) for all medical and mental health conditions. List the client's current medical issues and how the client describes her general health.

In this section you will also need to collect information on your client's current eating and sleeping habits, as well as physical activity level. How often is your client physically active or exercising (breaking a sweat)? For how long each time and how many days a week, on average? Also, you should ask how many meals and snacks your client eats a day and what these meals consist of. You also need to assess your client's sleep. How many hours of sleep does your client get a night? How many hours of sleep does your client need to feel rested? What is the quality of that sleep? Does the client wake feeling rested and refreshed or tired and down? Does the client find it easy to fall asleep and stay asleep or does the client wake in the night and ruminate or wake early and wish he was still sleeping? Sleep patterns impact and correlate with mental disorders. Specifically, lack of sleep can contribute to irritability and inattentiveness, while lack of exercise can contributes to difficulty focusing and concentrating for extended periods of time (McKinney & Morse, 2012). So all of this information is crucial to collect in an initial assessment.

Family History

In the Family History section of the assessment, you will describe your client's family of origin. You will need to ask your client: "Who raised you?" and "Can you give me a few words/adjectives to describe each of those people?" Ask the client: "Who is a part of your family now?" "Who lives with you?" You will also need to ask about history of abuse and trauma. Ask: "Did anything really terrible happen to you when you were younger or more recently?" "Did anyone ever touch you in a way that you didn't like?" "Did anyone ever touch you in a way that made you uncomfortable?" Also ask: "Are there any major events from your childhood that I should know about?" You should also try to get information from the client's parents on any notable events in terms of the client's gestation, birth, and timing of all developmental milestones (such as smiling, sitting up, crawling, walking, speaking words, etc.).

Social History

In the Social History section, you will need to describe your client's socioeconomic status (that of their family), whether or not they hold a job, whether or not they go to school, and how school is going. What grade are they in, and what kind of grades do they typically get? Do they have any problems at school with any teachers, kids, suspension, or expulsions? You should also ask about the client's current important relationships and social supports. Who does the client call when things are difficult? How supportive or helpful is that relationship to the client? How available is that person to the client? Ask about hobbies. "What do you do with your free time?" "Who do you like to spend time with?"

You will also need to collect information in this section about the client's cultural and religious background and affiliations, criminal history, and sexual history. Make sure to ask questions about your clients' sexuality that don't presume heterosexuality. Don't ask a female client, "Do you have a boyfriend?" Instead, ask "Are you dating anyone right now?" Phrase questions in a gender-neutral way. Ask clients explicitly the gender identity and sexual orientation of their partners and themselves.

In this Social History section, make sure you inquire about screen time and social media involvement. How many hours a day is your client in front of a smart phone, computer, television, or tablet? What social media platforms are they on? How do they experience social media: helpful and connecting, difficult and rejecting?

Mental Status

The Mental Status section of an assessment is typically a paragraph long. It includes your observations about the client's mood, demeanor, behavior, and presentation. Include the following: description of client's appearance (level of cleanliness, clothing, hygiene, and any noticeable physical abnormalities); behavior (agitated, restless, teary, or acting in an odd manner); mood (how they have been feeling recently: happy, hopeful, sad, depressed); affect (what feelings they show in session with you: anxious, expressionless, angry, or overly aroused); speech (within normal ranges, talkative, fast, slow). You will also list whether the client is positive for suicidal ideation, homicidal ideation, and psychotic thought process or content.

In the mental status section, you should also report on your client's cognitive functioning. Clinicians often use a standardized measure for this section of an assessment, such as the Mini-Mental State Examination (MMSE; Folstein, Folstein, & McHugh, 1975). This 30-question screening tool is widely used to measure cognitive impairment in clients. The first edition of this instrument is widely available free online and does not require any specialized training to administer. However, to use the second version published in 2010 requires the purchase of a license. Also commonly used to measure cognitive functioning is the Montreal Cognitive Assessment test (MoCA: Nasreddine et al., 2005). This widely used measure requires no specialized training to administer. This instrument is free and available online: www.mocatest.org. Both the MMSE and the MoCA are helpful tools to assess cognitive functioning. Both have easy-to-use instructions and simple scoring, which makes these ideal for new clinicians.

Summary Section

The Summary section of the assessment presents your written interpretation of all the information you collected and how all of the elements contributed to the client's presenting problem. You will need to describe your client's strengths and weaknesses. For example, the client's strengths may be his or her desire to work on the presenting problem, strong insight into problems, and having a support system in place. Your client's weaknesses include past mental health and medical issues as well as financial problems that will make completion of treatment difficult for the client. This section should include diagnoses from the DSM-5 (if warranted), along with narrative justification for your diagnoses. You will need to make sure to explain how your client's symptoms map onto each of the diagnostic criteria (including duration of symptoms). In this section, you can summarize what you found and list your opinions on what is needed. This section should include the disposition of the case (what should happen with the client at your agency) and any appropriate referrals you have made or will make.

Continuum of Care

Following your summary section, you will likely need to make recommendations for treatment or referral. You will need to decide what level and intensity of care your client will need, given that client's current mental state, severity of symptoms, existing supports, and financial and familial resources. The continuum of psychotherapeutic care spans a multitude of treatment programs and services available (American Academy of Child & Adolescent Psychiatry, 2008). This spectrum of care includes less restrictive interventions like one-on-one outpatient therapy and group therapy sessions to more intensive interventions like residential treatment and hospitalization (American Academy of Child & Adolescent Psychiatry, 2008).

Continuum of Care for Adolescent Treatment

The intensity and cost of treatment increases with each step away from outpatient therapy, but so does the restrictiveness of the treatment (Russell & Gillis, 2017). More restrictive settings are typically locked and deprive clients of significant freedoms, while less restrictive interventions provide clients with maximal freedoms but potentially greater risks if they are suicidal, for example. As a general rule, a client should be placed in the least restrictive environment possible (Association for Children's Mental Health).

Clinicians can determine the least restrictive environment by considering treatments that will provide for their client's individual mental health needs without needlessly restricting freedom and autonomy (Taylor, 2004). One study comparing adolescent day treatment to residential treatment found that day-treatment participants reported ambivalence about their treatment setting and sometimes felt overwhelmed with the requirements of going between treatment and home (Nikendei et al., 2016). By contrast, residential treatment participants were more likely to report relief when in their treatment environment, citing the controlled environment and the activities they engaged in together (Nikendei et al., 2016). Since both day treatment and residential treatment have comparable success rates (Nikendei et al., 2016), individual clinicians must determine which setting best fits each client's individual needs.

Confidentiality Concerns

You may encounter clients who are reticent to give you information regarding their substance use. Here is the arrangement that I make with my adolescent clients: I tell them that I will keep their information confidential, with a few exceptions. These exceptions include if they tell me about a child or vulnerable person who is being mistreated, if they let me know they are going to hurt themselves or someone else, or if I feel that they are putting their safety at risk. I tell them that, if I am concerned about their safety, I will always give them a chance to tell their parents first. I tell them that I am not interested in ratting them out to their parents. I am interested in facilitating dialogue between them and their parents; my primary interest is keeping them safe. I explain that, if they won't tell their parents about some risky behavior within a given time period that we decide together (typically a week or two, depending on the behavior), then I will tell the parents myself. This kind of arrangement tends to satisfy most adolescent clients. These clients want confidentiality and they want to feel in control of their own information. But they also need to know that I will do everything I can to keep them safe, that I am concerned for their well-being.

Documenting Your Assessment

Make sure you note when any information is missing in any assessment. Maybe you forgot to ask your client about their substance use history and experience of concussions. In this case, you will need to add this sentence to your assessment: "Client was not asked about his substance use history or history of head trauma/concussions." Or maybe your client refused to answer questions about substance use. In this case, you will add this sentence to your assessment: "Client refused to answer any questions about substance use, current or historical." If you don't list what information isn't provided, then the reader of that material will assume that the client was not asked about it. This makes your assessment look amateurish. You should always note what information is missing and why.

When you are writing an assessment, you will need to note that your client "stated" or "reported" something, rather than writing it as if you know it to be true. Think about the difference between these two sentences:

- Evan was sexually abused by his older sister nightly for 3 years.
- Evan reports that he was sexually abused by his older sister nightly for 3 years.

Remember that you may be in a position to defend what you write down about your client. You could be called to a court of law or questioned by your client's parents, parents who generally have the legal right to see the medical records of their children. How do you know that what Evan reports is true? It may be; it may not be. Writing that your client "reported" or "stated" something sticks to what you know to be true. You know what your client told you and *that* is what you should write down in an assessment.

When you are writing down your assessment, write only what your client told you. The only place you put your *opinions* is in the summary section, where you will be summarizing and making meaning of everything your client told you.

Special Considerations in Assessment

You should think about how your culture, ethnicity, age, sexual orientation, and so forth will impact your client and the information you get from him. What assumptions is your client likely to make about you based on how you look, how you present yourself to the client, how you dress, and how your office looks? What messages are these things sending to your clients? Are they likely to think that you are like them or that you are completely different and may not be able to understand them? Watch out for countertransference here. Are you likely to think, "I don't know anyone like this client. I'll never be able to help her."

You should also give thought to what meaning you make of your clients' cultural identities. What cultures/ethnicities does your client identify with? Are these groups that you have any familiarity with? There can be strong countertransference for you here too. Are you likely to think, "This person is so much like me. I know exactly what they are going through"? This is your countertransference and is not likely to be accurate. What was helpful to you as an adolescent may not be helpful to your client. You do not know exactly what they have been going though, even if you went through similar experiences, because your client is not you.

In assessment, you will be on solid ground if you use your client as your informant. Ask your client what role their cultural affiliations play in their lives. How important are their ethnic identities in their daily lives? Don't make assumptions about this; ask your client how it is for him. I highly recommend the book *Interviewing Clients Across Cultures* (Fontes, 2008) as a terrific resource for these issues.

Calling Clients by Their Labels

Please remember not to call your clients by the names of their diagnoses, not even when talking about your clients with other clinicians. For example, your client is not "an addict"; your client is "a person with an addiction" or "a person with a substance use disorder." Your client is not "a borderline," but "an adolescent with borderline personality disorder traits." Your client may not want to be referred to as "a refugee," but rather "a person from a refugee background." Clients might be sensitive to being called their parents' "adopted child," rather than just their parents' "child." Be attentive to your client's potential sensitivities to the various labels that we and others put on them. Let your clients tell what terms you should use when you talk *about* them or *to* them.

Assessing Ego Functioning

One factor you may assess in your clients is ego functioning. Both ego functions and defense mechanisms are important components to assess. *Ego functions* include reality testing (defined as the ability to understand and accept socially constructed reality), judgment, impulse control, affect regulation, self-esteem regulation, and mastery (which refers to the successful advancement of the ego when an individual masters successive developmental challenges; Schamess & Shilkret, 2016). Defense mechanisms within the ego attempt to respond and adapt to intrapersonal conflicts that arise in the context of the surrounding environment (Danzer, 2012; Schamess & Shilkret,

2016). Some examples of defense mechanisms include denial, introjection, projection, acting out, repression, intellectualization, and humor. Clinicians should consider assessing how healthily an adolescent's ego is responding to their environment. For example, a clinician might consider: What defense mechanisms is an adolescent client utilizing? Are these defense mechanisms enhancing functioning (as in the case of more mature defensive processes such as humor or sublimation) or are they lowering functioning (as in the case of more primitive defense mechanisms such as denial or projection)? Is the adolescent successfully employing ego functions such as affect regulation or mastery to adapt to challenges in the environment? Asking these questions may indicate your client's strengths challenges to consider in treatment.

Using Standardized Measures for Assessment

Many clinicians utilize standardized measures in the assessment process. These measures can form the structure for a clinical interview or provide symptom checklists to screen for specific disorders. Originally developed by medical doctors William Chambers and Joaquim Puig-Antich, the K-SADS-PL is a semi-structured diagnostic interview to screen for psychopathology in children and adolescents. The K-SADS-PL yields severity ratings for symptomology and screens for the presence of most major mental disorders. The instrument is free and in the public domain, available here: https://www. kennedykrieger.org/sites/default/files/library/documents/faculty/ksads-dsm-5-screener.pdf. Using an instrument such as the K-SADS-PL provides assessment interview structure for new clinicians, which can be enormously helpful. The instrument includes questions to ask at each stage of the interview and clear scoring guidelines for psychiatric disorders, which can help new clinicians to make diagnoses with more confidence. While lengthy, the K-SADS-PL can give new clinicians confidence that they are covering all critical material and doing it thoroughly.

The authors of the DSM-5 have collected numerous standardized measures for assessment and posted them here: https://www.psychiatry.org/ psychiatrists/practice/dsm/educational-resources/assessment-measures. There is an entire section listing measures for adolescent assessment of psychiatric disorders, which includes measures for somatic symptoms, sleep disturbance, depression, anger, irritability, mania, anxiety, substance use, and repetitive thoughts/behaviors. All the instruments listed here are free for clinicians' use. I strongly encourage new clinicians to become familiar with these screening tools. These tools can help you to feel more confident in making diagnoses.

There are three websites that offer hundreds of assessment tools that measure cognition, emotion, sensation, and motor ability. These are the National Institutes of Health (NIH) Toolbox, Patient-Reported Outcomes Measurement Information System (PROMIS), and Grid-Enabled Measures Database (GEM). Many of these assessment tools are free, have versions adapted for age and developmental level, and can be translated into other languages upon request if not already translated. In addition to access to assessment tools, these websites offer demonstration videos and test administration trainings.

1. The NIH Toolbox (http://www.healthmeasures.net/explore-measurement-systems/nih-toolbox/intro-to-nih-toolbox) offers a comprehensive set of neurobehavioral measurement tools to assess cognitive, emotional, sensory, and motor functions. The tools have been empirically validated and can be administered on computers or in paper formats. The website also lists online training tools and workshops to help ensure proper administration of the measurement tools.
2. The PROMIS website (http://www.nihpromise.org) provides a set of measures to evaluate mental, social, and physical health in children and adults. All the measures offered have been empirically validated and are free to use.
3. The GEM website (https://www.gem-beta.org/) lists highly regarded social science, behavioral, and other scientific measures at no cost and is offered through the National Cancer Institute.

Concluding Thoughts

When you are meeting with a client for the initial session, you will feel lots of pressure to collect a ton of information. Remember this: your client will not want to tell you much unless she feels that you like her and might be able to help her. You will not be able to collect good information unless you give attention to the therapeutic alliance you are forming. Make time to connect with your client. Don't bury your face in your notebook or your computer screen. Make eye contact and connect with what your client is saying. Help them to feel that you understand what they are saying and want to help.

Your initial session is also likely to go more smoothly if you explain to your clients at the beginning of the session how the time will be spent in the assessment session(s). For example, "This first time we are meeting will be different than all the other times in the future. This first time, I want to learn a lot about all different parts of your life. So I will be asking you lots of questions and I may interrupt you sometimes because we have a lot of things to cover in this first meeting. But the next time we meet, it will be your time to talk about whatever you want. Does that make sense?" Some of your clients may never have been in mental health treatment before. You will need to explain to them how it goes, why you are asking what you are asking, what you will do with the information you collect, and so forth. When you take the time to connect with your clients and explain the process, you are far more likely to collect accurate information from your clients and they are more likely to return to see you.

Conducting an assessment can be hard to do at first. Many clinicians say that they simply don't have enough time in 50 minutes to collect all the information they need to. Also, there is so much information to collect and it can be hard to remember all of it. If your agency doesn't use a computerized assessment format or a structured paper assessment form, you might consider making notes on the side of your notebook prior to the session. These notes can list categories or specific information you need to collect so that you don't get anxious in session and forget something. When I was learning to conduct assessments, I sometimes forgot important big pieces, like sleep habits or substance use history. I typically wouldn't remember what I forgot until after the client left my office. Make it easier by creating lists before the client arrives. Remember that it takes time to learn this skill. Completing assessments will get easier every time you do it. You can do this.

Sample Assessment

Nearly all agencies will ask you to utilize their specific assessment forms. However, the sample below will show you what one completed assessment looks like, if you are utilizing the format described in this chapter:

Identifying Information

William is a 15-year-old adolescent, who identifies himself as hetero-sexual and African-American. William states that he is able bodied and has no diagnosed disabilities. He is referred by his school social worker, who recommended that he seek treatment for impulsivity in the classroom.

Presenting Problem

William described that the biggest problem in his life revolved around school. He stated that he was failing most of his classes at his public high school and was frequently suspended from school. He explained these in detail, noting that he often got in trouble because he found it difficult to stay in his seat in class, often interrupted his teacher and classmates, and sometimes failed to follow his teachers' directions. He stated that he wanted to be a good student, but had difficulty keeping his focus on his schoolwork in his loud and busy classrooms. He described that his teachers frequently got angry at him and sent him to the principal's office because they thought he was deliberately not following rules. William stated that he wasn't trying to disobey, but simply had trouble following directions because he would get distracted and start talking to his peers. He stated that he had always had trouble in school, from his earliest memories of school environments. He described that he had less trouble following directions at home, explaining that it was quieter there and that his mother knew how to set him up for success (writing down steps of tasks to be completed, following up with him during task processes, and creating quiet places for him to focus). William stated that he believed he was "stupid" because he was unable to succeed in school environments, reporting that his peers seemed to find school easy.

Treatment History

William stated that he had never been in any kind of treatment before. He stated that he had never received any mental health diagnoses from any provider.

Medical History

In a phone interview, his mother stated that William met all major developmental milestones on time and within normal age ranges. William himself stated that he was in good health. He described that he had never had a concussion or head trauma, surgeries, major medical issues, or injuries. He stated that he broke his arm falling off a skateboard when he was 7. He stated that currently he was not taking any medications for health or mental health issues. He denied any historical psychiatric medication use. He described that he typically slept about 8 hours a night, sleeping well in a bedroom with both his siblings. He stated that it was sometimes hard for him to fall asleep, but that he typically slept deeply and well once asleep. William described his eating habits as "mostly junk food." He stated that, because his mother and stepfather worked long hours, he and his siblings generally prepared their own food, relying on prepackaged foods like pop tarts, canned fruit in syrup, McDonald's burgers, and freezer entrees. He described his favorite food as "candy—I would eat it every day, all day, if I could." He stated that he typically ate three meals a day, plus a snack in the afternoon when he got home from school.

Family History

William described that he lived in an apartment in a large city with his mother, stepfather, and two younger brothers. He described his mother as "loving, never around, would do anything for me." He described his stepfather, who joined his family 10 years ago, as "strict, loves football, quiet." He stated that he is oldest of his siblings: he reported that his brother Eli is 9 and his brother Bob is 6. He described his brothers as "annoying," but noted that they often played sports together in the neighborhood. He denied any history of abuse, neglect, or trauma, but noted that his biological father "is an angry guy." He stated that his parents split up when he was 3 and that his father was incarcerated shortly after that for a drug-related offense. He stated that he had memories of his parents yelling at each other from his early childhood. He stated that he has not had contact with his biological father in years and doesn't know where he is now.

Social History

William stated that he is currently in the 10th grade. He denied any criminal history, but noted that the police had questioned him numerous times as he played on the sidewalk or in the park in his neighborhood. He described himself as heterosexual, stating that he did not have a girlfriend currently. He described his support system as consisting of a group of boys who lived in his neighborhood and had "known each other forever." William described his family as "Christian," noting that his mother liked to have the whole family attend church every Sunday. He described his family's ethnicity as "African American, but a mix"—explaining that his maternal grandmother emigrated to the United States from Haiti, while his paternal great-grandmother emigrated from the Dominican Republic. William stated that his family struggled to pay their bills, but seemed to do okay. He stated that his mother always seemed stressed about having enough money to pay the rent on their apartment. He stated that his mother worked as a preschool teacher and his stepfather as a part-time, evening security guard. His mother reported that no one in the family had health insurance.

Mental Status

William appeared to be of average height and build; he was well-groomed and cleanly shaven. During the session, William manifested psychomotor agitation, as evidenced by looking around the room frequently, tapping his foot repeatedly, and showing an inability to sit still. His eye contact ranged from good to sporadic; he often appeared distracted. William's attitude was cooperative; he appeared eager to answer questions. His speech was of normal rate, rhythm, and volume. William described his mood as anxious and hopeful. His affect was within normal ranges and was appropriate to the context. William's thought processes were coherent and logical. He denied current or historical suicidal and homicidal ideation. His though content did reveal anxiety and a severe phobia of crowds and leaving his home. William exhibited normal perception; symptoms such as delusions, hallucinations, and depersonalization were not elicited. William was oriented to person, time, place, and situation. William displayed fair insight, as he appeared to be aware of his troubles in school, but confused about their origin. His judgment appeared good. William was not assessed for cognitive functioning or abstraction.

Summary

William appears to be a smart adolescent who is eager to succeed in school, but hampered by his ADHD symptomology. William's strengths include a strong support system in his family and friends and a wish to do well in school. His challenges include his family's low socio-economic status which may make accessing treatment and educational resources difficult. William appears to meet criteria for attention-deficit/hyperactivity disorder, combined presentation. His symptoms include failing to give close attention to tasks or making careless mistakes, frequent difficulty sustaining attention on tasks, often failing to follow through on instructions, often fidgeting or squirming in his seat, leaving his seat in the classroom often, and running around in his classroom when he is supposed to stay put. He reports that these symptoms have been present since he began school. William reports that he has never received treatment for these symptoms before. Referrals at this time will include a psychiatric evaluation for the purposes of medication appropriateness, as well as initiating an Individualized Education Plan to set up appropriate educational resources for him at school. Individual weekly psychotherapy should begin at this time at this clinic, with the focus on building skills for him to manage his symptoms in his school environment, as well as offering coaching for his parents in how best to support him at home. Notably, his mother appears to have set up a strong support system in the home environment in order to best manage his tasks at home.

F90.2 Attention-Deficit/Hyperactivity Disorder, Combined presentation
Z59.6 Low Income

References

Academy of Child & Adolescent Psychiatry. (2008). Continuum of mental healthcare [Information sheet]. *Facts for Families, 42.* Retrieved from https://www.aacap.org/

aacap/families_and_youth/facts_for_families/fff-guide/The-Continuum-Of-Care-For-Children-And-Adolescents-042.aspx

Association for Children's Mental Health. (n.d.). Types of treatment. Retrieved from http://www.acmh-mi.org/get-information/childrens-mental-health-101/treatments-supports/

Danzer, G. (2012). Integrating ego psychology and strengths-based social work. *Journal of Theory Construction & Testing, 16*, 9–15.

Folstein, M. F., Folstein, S. E., & McHugh, P. R (1975). Mini-mental state: A practical method for grading the cognitive state of patients for the clinician. *Journal of Psychiatry Research, 12*, 189–198.

Fontes, L. A. (2008). *Interviewing clients across cultures: A practitioner's guide.* New York, NY: Guilford Press.

McKinney, C., & Morse, M. (2012). Assessment of disruptive behavior disorders: Tools and recommendations. *Professional Psychology: Research and Practice, 43*, 641–649.

Nasreddine, Z. S., Phillips, N. A., Bédirian, V., Charbonneau, S., Whitehead, V., Collin, I., . . . Chertkow, H. (2005). The Montreal Cognitive Assessment, MoCA: A brief screening tool for mild cognitive impairment. *Journal of the American Geriatrics Society, 53*, 695–699.

Nikendei, C., Haitz, M., Huber, J., Ehrenthal, J. C., Herzog, W., Schauenburg, H., & Dinger, U. (2016). Day clinic and inpatient psychotherapy of depression (DIP-D): Qualitative results from a randomized controlled study. *International Journal of Mental health Systems, 10, 41.* doi:10.1186/s13033-016-0074-6

Russell, K. C., & Gillis, H. L. (2017). Experiential therapy in the mental health treatment of adolescents. *Journal of Therapeutic Schools and Programs*, 47–79.

Schamess, G., & Shilkret, R. (2016). Ego Psychology. In J. Berzoff, L. M. Flanagan, & P. Hertz, *Inside Out and Outside In* (4th ed., 64–99). London, UK: Rowman & Littlefield.

Taylor, S. J. (2004). Caught in the continuum: A critical analysis of the principal of the least restrictive environment. *Research & Practice for Persons with Severe Disabilities, 29*, 218–230. doi:https://doi.org/10.1177/154079698801300105

5

Building Therapeutic Alliance
With Adolescents

Joanna E. Bettmann

Building therapeutic alliance with your adolescent client is critical to the work you do together. Alliance means that there is a productive relationship between the therapist and client, a relationship in which there is agreement on both sides about what will be worked on and how to work on it. Horvath and Greenberg (1989) defined *working alliance* as agreement between the therapist and client on the *goals* of treatment and the necessary *tasks* to achieve those goals, as well as the quality of the *bond* between therapist and client.

The quality of the therapeutic alliance links strongly to psychotherapeutic outcome (Horvath, Flückiger, & Symonds, 2011). So it is critical that your client believes that you are on his side and that you will able to help him. How do you accomplish this? In this chapter, we will address how adolescents' developmental trajectory impacts therapeutic alliance and how goals for treatment impact alliance, and we will explain some tools you can use to build therapeutic alliance with your adolescent clients. We will use an understanding of transference and attachment to help us conceptualize these alliance processes, as well as explain the critical role of routine outcome monitoring in alliance building.

Adolescent Development

Adolescence has often been described as a period of storm and stress. Anna Freud (1958/1975) wrote that psychoanalysts did not work well with adolescents because "we fail to recover [in the analytic work]. . . the atmosphere in which the adolescent lives, his anxieties, the height of elation or depth of despair, the quickly rising enthusiasms, the utter hopelessness, the burning . . . intellectual and philosophical preoccupations, the yearning for freedom, the sense of loneliness, the feeling of oppression by the parents" (p. 126). Anna Freud detailed here the emotional turmoil which many adolescents experience, the widely swinging emotions and poor emotion regulation which can characterize adolescent psychology. Developmentally, the distance between adults and adolescents is significant. Adolescent clients often see their adult therapists as being too distant from adolescence to understand them, being on the side of their parents, being on the side of the school, being too adult to get it.

Developmental theory offers a useful lens here. Erik Erikson's life stage model posited its fifth stage of development as addressing the conflict *identity versus role confusion*. Erikson believed that adolescents at this life stage were exploring their identities, trying on different peer groups, and experimenting with new roles and responsibilities (Santrock, 2018). An adolescent client might conclude that her therapist, by virtue of how that therapist dresses, talks, or communicates, can't understand her—that their identities are too different. Adults have typically worked through identity conflicts at earlier ages, consolidating their identities into an adult identity that fits with their current relationships, communities, work environment, and so forth. An adolescent might look at the pictures on my walls or my clothes and say to himself, "She won't understand me. We're just too different." I am no longer an adolescent. An adolescent client might perceive me as too far from their developmental conflicts to understand their internal works. Writing about alliance, Shirk and Karver note, "The developmental press towards autonomy, the increasing centrality of peer relationships, and growing doubts about adults' capacity for understanding youth experiences can contribute to alliance difficulties" (2011, p. 83). An adolescent's developmental stage can make forming therapeutic alliance difficult, but not impossible.

Using the lens of Piaget's cognitive development theory, adolescents in the *formal operational* stage are beginning to think abstractly of the future and dream of life possibilities (Santrock, 2018). But younger adolescents might still be in the Piagetian stage of *concrete operations*. At the *concrete operational* stage, your clients might not understand some treatment approaches commonly used. For example, many intensive outpatient and residential programs use level systems, a behavioral intervention, to indicate how clients are progressing in the program. But if this system uses metaphors to help clients understand what level they are on ("you are now at the elephant stage in our program—how are you like an elephant?"), this is likely to be confusing to your client.

These adolescents at earlier developmental stages in terms of cognition are likely to be more present-focused and more ego-centric. You might build alliance by asking your older adolescent client: "Where do you see yourself in a year? Five years? How do you get there?" But a developmentally younger adolescent will need questions like, "What are your favorite things to do each day?" "What are your favorite parts of every weekend?" "Do you have anything that you are looking for to?" Understanding your clients in terms of their developmental trajectory will enhance your ability to adjust treatment to where they are at, helping your clients to feel understood.

Addressing Adolescents' Goals in Treatment

Adolescent clients often enter treatment because their caregivers want the adolescent to get help or change something—not because the adolescent himself wants help with something. Thus, the clinician often must form a strong alliance with an adolescent client who does not want help. The clinician must negotiate that alliance with the adolescent while maintaining alliance with the caregivers who are often paying for that treatment. The clinician must help both the adolescent and her caregivers to feel that the goals of both are being worked on. How can you build a strong therapeutic alliance with both your adolescent client and her caregivers? You do this by helping both to feel that you on their side, working on their goals.

I'll give an example of a time that this commitment to both an adolescent's and a parent's goals did not go so well. Some time ago, I was contacted by a father who wanted his 18-year-old daughter to receive outpatient therapy. He was interested in finding a new therapist for her because he felt that her outpatient therapist of 3 years wasn't keeping him apprised of the daughter's progress in treatment adequately. I explained to him how I worked with adolescents' privacy and confidentiality (see the section "Confidentiality Concerns" in Chapter 4, "Assessment in Adolescent Treatment"), noting that I wouldn't be able to release significant information about treatment to him unless his daughter consented because she was now a legal adult. He stated that he understood my approach and limitations, and that he wanted me to begin meeting weekly with his daughter. I met with his daughter, April, for weekly sessions for approximately 3 months. She came on time to each weekly session, sharing readily about her life and issues she faced. However, she was clear that she did not want me to share any of this information with her father. Every few weeks, the father would call me and ask for an update on treatment. Because the daughter had agreed to some small disclosures, I detailed for the father the number and timing of sessions that the daughter attended and described treatment as beginning well. I explained the importance of therapeutic alliance in early treatment and that the daughter seemed to be forming some alliance with me. The father seemed comfortable with this limited information on our first treatment update call. But in subsequent calls, he pressed to get more information from me about what the daughter was discussing in treatment. About 3 months into treatment, he pressed harder for this information. When I flatly refused, he stated that the treatment was over and that he would not pay for any subsequent sessions. I never heard from the father or daughter again.

Clearly here, the father had some goals for treatment which included me providing a window into his daughter's life. I think he believed that it was the proper role of a therapist to provide that window and that information to him. The daughter's goals for treatment were substantively different. She wanted to explore relational issues that were presenting in her current life, none of which involved her father. I think treatment ended prematurely because I failed to help the father see how his goals were being met. Treatment with an adolescent almost always involves their caregivers. As clinicians for adolescent clients, we need to help both the adolescent client *and* their caregivers to experience that both sets of goals are being met. The adolescent's goals for treatment and their caregivers' goals for treatment are rarely the same.

Tools to Build Therapeutic Alliance

Clinicians have numerous tools that they can use to build alliance and break down the notion that they are too adult to understand adolescent concerns. Clinicians can focus first on what the adolescent wants to discuss or what she is passionate about. Ask your clients what they like to do in their free time. Ask what they most enjoy doing. When or where are they happiest? You build alliance by spending time on these topics, expressing interest in your clients as people—not just problems.

A study of mentors and adolescents found that the most successful partnerships were those in which the mentor first devoted their energies toward developing a strong relationship based on trust, openness, lack of judgment, and emotional bonding (Morrow & Styles, 1995). After a strong relationship was established, it then became possible to work toward mentoring goals with more efficacy (Morrow & Styles, 1995). Relationships that jumped directly to the mentoring work without time spent on establishing the relationship were dramatically less successful (Morrow & Styles, 1995).

Focus on building rapport by finding things that you have in common with your adolescent client. Is it a favorite sports team? A common hobby? You can share benign things about yourself: your favorite sports team, your childhood pet, your fondness for the beach—but stay away from disclosing your own trauma or difficult history. Avoid talking about your own parents or your childhood experiences. You are trying to build a relationship with an adolescent by allowing them to see you as human—but you are not equal. You have much more power and influence that your adolescent client does. Do not equate your experiences with their own.

I'll give another example of the importance of therapeutic alliance from one of my graduate students:

"Conrad" was a 16-year-old adolescent male, a client in a wilderness therapy program for his Oppositional Defiant Disorder and low-frequency marijuana use. Upon arrival in wilderness therapy, Conrad was initially pleasant to all, but somewhat apathetic. After two-and-a-half years of involuntary treatment in various settings, he had a strong dislike for therapy and adults in positions of authority. I met him on his first day in the wilderness therapy program. As a new staff member at the program, I was excited to help him and get to the bottom of why he was in the program. We exchanged some basic pleasantries that first morning. Later in the afternoon as we were backpacking, I decided that I would walk next to him and try to help him adjust to the program and work on his issues. Very quickly, Conrad understood what I was doing as I politely probed him with questions about his past and treatment history. He first became resistant and then enraged; he dropped his backpack and began swearing at me, refusing to go another step. He refused to speak to me for the next several days, until a blizzard forced us to take shelter in a tent, where we were confined for days. Forced into confined quarters, Conrad and I began getting to know one another. We shared stories about our experiences, interests, and hopes. We played games together. We saw each other as people, and I treated him as an adult with whom I was comfortable sharing some information or playing cards.

The turnaround in the therapeutic relationship was magical. After several days of this, he voluntarily began bringing his concerns to me; I didn't have to ask. Within days, we had begun working towards his therapeutic goals, and he became excited about the future. He made tremendous progress and left our program two months later. Conrad explained that, in previous settings, he had never felt heard or appreciated for who he was. He told me that he felt like a victim of a therapeutic assembly line. I think he was. Building the therapeutic alliance was key to connecting with Conrad. (J. Yates, personal communication, 2018)

Adolescent transference often manifests, as it did for Conrad, in the form of negative transference. Conrad experienced previous treatment as an environment in which he was not seen or heard. He experienced treatment in which no one wanted to know him; they only wanted to change him. When he encountered a staff person who was interested in listening to him and sharing with him, he became engaged in the therapeutic relationship and began building therapeutic alliance.

Use open-ended questions to get to know your clients and their thoughts. "What happened with _____? Why do you think that occurred? Is there anything that you could do differently if it happened again?" Learn from your clients slowly. Building relationship takes time. When your adolescent client sees that you are genuinely interested in him, he will begin to see you as a partner in the therapeutic process, as someone who supports him in working toward what he sees as important.

Understanding Adolescent Transference

Anna Freud (1958/1975) described adolescent treatment as particularly challenging due to adolescents' tendency to resist parental figures, who, thanks to transference, may include the clinician. How then are adult clinicians to build therapeutic alliance with adolescent clients? One of the best tools clinicians have in their toolbox to build therapeutic alliance is an understanding of adolescent clients' transference.

Drawn from psychodynamic theory, the concept of transference refers to feelings adolescents have had in previous relationships (often with caregivers or other important adults in their lives) which they transfer onto the therapeutic relationship. Transference is sometimes triggered by something the therapist does or some way that the therapist presents herself. But often transference evolves simply from the adolescent client's previous experiences with important adults in their lives. Adolescents expect their therapists to be similar to the other authority figures in their lives: available, responsive and attentive, mean, rejecting, and cold, or somewhere in between. Adolescents expect clinicians to support them or to reject them. Adolescents may think clinicians will disbelieve them or lie to them. All of these transference feelings arise due to adolescents' previous relationships with important adults.

Notably, transference occurs entirely out of the client's awareness. An adolescent client may simply think, "this therapist is so annoying," without realizing the ways in which the therapist seems like the client's own mom. Transference is an entirely unconscious process. However, clients can become aware of transference by talking about the therapeutic relationship. A therapist might ask, "how are you feeling about our work together?" "What feelings have you been having when you leave my office?" "How do you feel when you think about coming to my office?" "How did it feel to you when you just shared that with me?" All of these open questions can begin a conversation about the working relationship between therapist and client.

An example from my own clinical experience illuminates this concept of transference. Aimee, a 14 year-old cisgender Latina adolescent, presented to the outpatient community mental health clinic where I worked. After completing an initial assessment session with a different mental health worker, she was referred to me for individual psychotherapy. In our first session together, she described herself as a willing participant in psychotherapy, interested in getting help to manage the anxiety she was feeling at school. In this first session, she gave long descriptions of her friends, her school environment, and her family at home. She cried occasionally as she talked about the burden of the anxiety she carried. Aimee talked on and on, and I contributed little other than attentive non-verbal behavior and occasional verbal responses like "that sounds so hard for you." I was attempting to build therapeutic alliance by showing her that I was willing to sit with her in her difficult emotions, that I wanted to hear her concerns and her distress. Aimee scheduled a second session for the following week.

When Aimee arrived at that second session, she was furious at me from the moment she walked in. She stared at me angrily and told me that she was unhappy with therapy so far. When I probed to find out what she was unhappy with, she explained that I hadn't helped her the previous week. "You didn't make it better," she said. We then spent significant time going over her goals for our psychotherapy, the expectations she had of me specifically, and the things she wanted to do in that session. Our exploration of the *tasks, bond,* and *goals* of treatment (Horvath & Greenberg, 1989) began to build our therapeutic alliance. Aimee clearly had expectations of how I should have responded to her distress during our initial session together. I didn't meet those expectations because I didn't know them. When we explored these expectations, she began to trust that I was interested in her, that I might be an available and responsive adult to her. Her transference toward me, her unconscious feelings about me, was striking and intense. I had never had a client respond so negatively after an initial session. Her transference was: "you should save me from these feelings. You should make it better for me. You shouldn't empathize, you should fix it." She must have had feelings with other important adults or caregivers whose message to her was: "you don't need to feel those feelings. I'll make it all better for you." Unconsciously, she transferred those expectations onto me. Without knowing what her expectations were, I failed her. We could only build a stronger therapeutic alliance when we explored what she expected from me, what she wanted from therapy, and how she wanted to work on her problems in therapy. Our discussion of those things and our eventual agreement on them enabled us to build a solid therapeutic alliance that lead to a productive working relationship.

Understanding Attachment Theory to Build Therapeutic Relationship

Another lens for thinking about how to build strong therapeutic alliance comes from attachment theory. John Bowlby (1969), the founder of attachment theory, believed attachment relationships served as the basic foundation for human development and relationships. He believed we form mental representations of attachment figures and ourselves based on our earliest relationships. Bowlby labeled these internalized relational representations "internal working models." Internal working models include expectations of relationships, how we expect others to treat us based on how we have been treated in the past. We rely on these representational models to guide our decisions about how to interact with specific people in specific situations. Similar to transference, these internal working models drive clients' expectations of how we will treat them in therapy and what they can expect from us.

An individual uses their internal working models built by early attachment relationships as a model for future relationships (Delgado, Strawn, & Pedapati, 2014; McCarthy & Maughan, 2010). An example of this phenomena is the case of a sexually abused child who seeks attention through overly sexualized behavior. Examined through the lens of attachment theory, it is possible that this child has learned this behavior through early relationships and believes it to be the only way to develop new relationships with possible caregivers or loved ones.

Ainsworth, Blehar, Waters, and Wall (1978) furthered Bowlby's ideas by creating a classification system for attachment representations. Their classification system named three categories of attachment: *secure, insecure-anxious,* and *insecure-avoidant* (Hesse, 2008). In this model, *secure* children are those who trust their caregivers and, by extension, are more willing to trust others and develop close relationships. *Insecure-anxious* children demonstrate intense distress and often cling in relationships out of fear that a loved one doesn't care about them (Ainsworth et al., 1978). *Insecure-avoidant* children either avoid or dismiss close relationships, over-regulating their emotional distress and keeping it to themselves. Ainsworth et al. (1978) hypothesized that these *insecure-avoidant* infants learned to hide or repress feelings of alarm through past experiences when they were unable to get the care they needed from a parent or other close relationship (Ainsworth et al., 1978), sometimes because the infants' own distress dysregulated the caregiver.

A fourth attachment category later defined by Main and Solomon (1986) was *disorganized* attachment. Main and Solomon found that some infants did not fit neatly into any of the three other attachment classifications. Children display *disorganized* attachment through unpredictable or contradictory behaviors that indicate a possible conflict between the desire to reunite with the caregiver and a desire to flee or fear (Duschinsky, 2015; Hesse & Main, 2000; Main & Solomon, 1986). Of the four attachment types, children labeled with *disorganized* attachment are the most likely to have been abused or neglected.

Notably, securely attached adolescents tend to have healthier peer relationships, are better able to manage stress, and are less likely to develop mental health issues (Delgado et al., 2014; Laible, 2007; Seiffge-Krenke, 2006; Shoshani, Nakash, Zubida, & Harper, 2014). Conversely, adolescents with insecure attachment classification are more likely to manifest mental health symptomology, particularly those with trauma histories (Joubert, Webster, & Hackett, 2012; Nilsson, Holmqvist, & Jonson, 2011).

Attachment theory offers us a useful lens through which to consider adolescent behavior, especially in a psychotherapeutic setting. In clinical settings, many adolescent clients evidence signs of insecure attachment representations. Based on their previous relationships with caregivers, adolescent clients may expect clinicians to leave them, not to care about them, to reject them. These feelings can be conceptualized either as clients' transference or manifestations of their internal working models.

Clinicians can use an understanding of attachment theory to build therapeutic alliance with adolescent clients. An adolescent whose internal working model includes the messages, "People will be available to help me, people love me, I am loveable" is likely to have an easier time connecting with and trusting their therapist. By contrast, an adolescent whose internal working model includes the messages, "I am an unlovable person. If you really knew me, you wouldn't want to be near me. I'm likely to upset you or freak you out or depress you. You better stay away from me" is likely to distance their therapist, to build walls between them, to ensure that the therapist never really knows them or knows what is going on. Yet another adolescent might have an internal working model whose messages include, "I better stay close to you. If you go too far away from me, I might lose you or you might forget about me. Staying close and in conflict is the only way I can feel safe." This adolescent is likely to want to merge with their therapist and to create conflict in the relationship. Whatever caregiver relationships existed in the adolescent's early life, he likely will seek to recreate in the therapeutic relationship.

Such behavior does not make logical sense, but it makes sense using the lens of attachment theory. We all exist within a web of relationships that feel safe and familiar to us. You might think that an adolescent who experienced an abusive caregiver in childhood would seek nurturing and supportive relationships to help heal him later in life. But instead, that adolescent will unconsciously seek out relationships which make him feel the same way: belittled, abused, shamed. When we are mistreated as children, we internalize that mistreatment and blame ourselves. An abused child doesn't blame his caregiver, but instead thinks of himself as at fault for the abuse. "I'm too loud, I'm too much, I get into trouble, I made my parents mad, that's why they hit me." Children carry those internalized messages into adolescence. They show up in therapy with you believing that they are at fault, that they are unlovable, that to know them is to want to reject them or hurt them. Not all our adolescent clients have been abused or neglected, but many have experienced trauma, difficult circumstances, or caregivers with their own mental health issues. Our adolescent clients are often in our offices because their behavior is out of control and they don't have strong support systems or emotion regulation skills to weather those storms. They come into our offices often with insecure attachment schema, with beliefs that we won't care about them and that they are unlovable.

While some research has supported Bowlby's assertion that early attachment schemas would remain relatively stable from infancy through adulthood (Waters, Merrick, Treboux, Crowell, & Albersheim, 2000), other research has found just the opposite (Groh et al., 2014). Research does suggest that chaotic and negative life events such as trauma, divorce, and immigration, can prompt a transition from secure to insecure patterns of attachment (Beijersbergen et al., 2012; Sroufe, 2005). While secure attachment in childhood may predict secure attachment in some adolescents, it does not necessarily guarantee it. But having a strong therapeutic alliance in a clinical relationship may impact adolescents' internal working models. Adolescents may begin to develop internal schema which allow them to trust some adults and to believe that they are lovable people in some circumstances. This shift is called "earned secure attachment" (Roisman, Padrón, Sroufe, & Egeland, 2002). This shift, accomplished in part by building a strong therapeutic alliance, forms a core part of my treatment goals with adolescent clients.

Case Study: Teresa

A case example will illustrate how an adolescent's internal working model impacts the therapeutic relationship and how a clinician can work to address these attachment schemas in treatment. Teresa was a 15-year-old Caucasian adolescent who presented for treatment at an all-girls adolescent residential treatment program at her parents' referral. She had recently been transferred from another residential treatment program (her second residential placement) where she had been living for the previous 8 months. That program stated that she had been sneaking out at night, passing letters to her boyfriend at home by convincing program staff to mail these for her, and calling her boyfriend at home by convincing night program staff to let her. They were frustrated with her rule-breaking and suggested she might flourish elsewhere.

Teresa had been in and out of psychotherapeutic treatment for the previous 3 years. She had participated in multiple courses of outpatient psychotherapy, none of which had resulted in the significant behavior change her parents sought. Upon her arrival to the residential treatment center at which I was working, she was now in her third residential treatment placement.

Teresa was a bit of mystery to me. Her symptoms were not enormously severe, but they were confusing. Teresa was the second biological child born to heterosexual, married parents residing in a large Western state. Her older sister was four years older, now in college near the family home. Her father was a doctor and her mother engaged in volunteer work. The family lived an upper middle-class life style, filled with social engagements and private schools. Teresa was bright and capable at school, but neglected her schoolwork to the point of failing grades. She had a habit of dating much older men—dating a 29-year-old when she was 13. Often these men had criminal records for felony assault or fraud or substance-related charges. But she didn't engage in substance use herself and wasn't doing the things that most other adolescents in residential treatment were doing: being oppositional with adults, running away, or getting suspended from school for behavioral infractions. Teresa's parents were baffled by her behaviors and so was I.

When I met Teresa, she engaged in banter with me but didn't reveal much about herself. During the months that we worked together, I often felt that I didn't know her well. She kept me at a distance emotionally, revealing as little as possible about herself while still coming to our individual psychotherapy sessions. She preferred joking to speaking about herself. She changed topics if I raised the issue of her problematic boyfriends at home. She claimed that they were "good guys" despite their criminal behaviors. She claimed that her parents' resistance to her boyfriends was an example of their prejudice against people from lower socioeconomic groups. I felt that I was not building a strong therapeutic alliance with Teresa, but I was baffled as to why. What made me such a dangerous object that I couldn't be permitted to know her? Further, what drove Teresa to repeatedly choose boyfriends who not only had criminal histories but predated on her by stealing her credit cards, lying to her, and committing identity fraud using her information? What made Teresa's judgment so poor in the arena of romantic relationships? What was I missing?

Teresa's parents came for a visit to the residential treatment facility after she had been with us for 4 months. I still felt like I barely knew her. In psychotherapy, she had shown little interest in exploring the roots of her behavior and demonstrated no insight about her choice of boyfriends or failing school grades. She was generally compliant with rules at the treatment center, but none of the staff felt they knew her at all. She was funny and smart, sweet with other girls, but still a mystery.

After they had been on campus for 24 hours, Teresa's parents met with Teresa and me for a family therapy session. The point of the session was to explore Teresa's progress toward her treatment goals and explore ways that her parents could support her in modifying problematic behaviors. The session dragged on for 2 hours as her parents asked questions to which Teresa claimed not to know the answers. They wanted to know the same things I did: why did you choose those boyfriends? Why did you trust people who were untrustworthy? Why aren't you applying yourself at school? Why is someone so smart not doing well in her academics? The session felt unproductive and long. I struggled to feel connected to Teresa, who still seemed to regard me as dangerous. Finally, more than 2 hours after the session began, Teresa shared something important. She began crying and said, "I have never told you this before. . . ." She detailed a pattern of sexual abuse by her paternal uncle which began when she was 5 and continued until the present day, whenever she was home as he lived nearby. She described herself as a willing participant in the sexual abuse, believing that the sexual activity was consensual. Her sense of shame and discomfort was strong. She didn't conceptualize herself as a victim. She begged her parents and me not to speak to the uncle or to "get him into trouble."

Analysis of the Case Study

Teresa provides us with an example of an adolescent who has learned from the age of 5 that the world is not safe, that adults can't be trusted, that her caregivers won't be able to protect her from harm. She has learned to keep the adults in charge at a safe psychological distance. She may have had the unconscious belief, "you won't be able to help me or protect me, so I will just stay away from you. I'll stay here in my shell." She had little ability to form a therapeutic alliance because, based on her lived experience, her unconscious belief was that I, as therapist, would hurt her or fail to protect her. In relationships with older men who took advantage of her, we can see her attempt at mastery: trying to gain control over an interpersonal situation with a dangerous older male. Teresa's breakthrough in the family session when she disclosed the sexual abuse was the beginning of her productive therapeutic work. Once she trusted that adults would hear her and respond to keep her safe, she could begin to process her feelings related to the abuse.

Working with Teresa reinforced for me the notion that adolescent behavior always has meaning and reason. Teresa's insistence on staying superficial in our therapeutic relationship had enormous meaning. It meant: you are too dangerous, you might hurt me too. Her superficiality had reason too: you will probably be like those other people who failed to protect me, so I won't tell you anything of importance or let you get close to me. Given her history of sexual abuse and particular relationships, Teresa's behavior in the therapeutic relationship seems now both reasonable and rationale.

New clinicians often get frustrated at clients' resistance to getting close with their therapists, at adolescents' unwillingness to engage in productive therapeutic relationships. However, many adolescents are in treatment at their parents' request or urging. Many adolescents participate in treatment unwillingly or involuntarily. Their resistance has meaning. Sometimes an adolescent's resistance in treatment might mean, "I didn't choose this treatment and I don't want it. My parents' decision to enroll me in this treatment violates my sense of my autonomy and independence." Other times, an adolescent's resistance might mean, "I believe that my life is fine right now. It works for me. I don't want you to change it—that would be too scary for me." Recognize that your adolescent client's resistance to you has meaning and reason. There are very good reasons why they do what they do, just as Teresa's behavior makes sense in the context of her internal working model, her history, and her relationships.

Understanding and Using Countertransference

Sigmund Freud wrote, "I have good reasons for asserting that everyone possesses in his own unconscious an instrument with which he can interpret the utterances of the unconscious in other people" (S. Freud as cited in Ladame, 1996). He was speaking here of countertransference. Countertransference is the unconscious feelings that clinicians have about their clients. In countertransference, we find an incredibly useful tool for building therapeutic alliance.

Recognizing your own countertransference—your feelings toward the client—can be difficult. Like transference, countertransference is an unconscious process. You can begin to detect your own countertransference by surveying your internal landscape while you are in session with any given client. Ask yourself: "How do I feel when I am with this client? What do I notice about my emotions or my physical self? Am I bored, tired, turned on, happy, excited, or something else entirely?" Sometimes your countertransference really has only to do with you—your own life, your own tiredness, your own availability for your professional obligations that day. But more often, your countertransference is elicited by your interactions with the client. You are feeling a particular way because of your reaction to a client.

Your adolescent clients might treat you the way they treat their mother, father, stepmother, stepfather, sister, brother, teacher, coach, grandparent, religious leader, and so forth. Your clients do not do this deliberately or consciously, but rather unconsciously and automatically. This is their transference. Similarly, your clients will evoke in you echoes of your previous or current relationships. Is your client like your younger brother or sister, like your annoying roommate, or your ex-girlfriend? This is your countertransference. In it, you can find important clues to what your client is trying to tell you (Malove, 2014). Maybe you feel annoyed by your client because he is not revealing anything intimate or authentic. Maybe he evokes in you a sense of failure that you can't connect with him, a sense of inadequacy or impotence that you can't figure out what is going on. Maybe you feel anxious because his parents or teachers are anxious for therapy to "work," for therapy to "fix" him. Maybe you worry that you will fail as a therapist, that everyone will know you can't do this work.

By understanding your own countertransference and naming it in session, you can help your clients to recognize dynamics from their own lives that they are recreating with you (Malove, 2014). Once you and the client recognize the dynamic, you can both work toward creating new patterns in the therapeutic relationship. In this situation, you might name your countertransference for your client. "I notice that I am feeling anxious when I'm with you. I'm feeling that way because I feel like I don't know you well at all, even though we've spent months meeting weekly. Your parents keep calling me because they are worried about you. So now, I'm sitting here feeling anxious. How does all of that sound to you?" Your authenticity with your own emotions models emotional intimacy for your client. It shows her what authentic sharing looks like. It creates a space for her to recognize her own withholding and distance from you, if that is what's happening. It creates a space for her to say, "I don't know if I can trust you. That's why I don't want to tell you anything. Are you going to tell my parents everything I say?"

Sharing your countertransference with your client is not always the best strategy for building therapeutic alliance. It may not be helpful for you to share with your client that you feel bored around her or depressed by her depression or turned on by her attractiveness. However, it is always productive for you to share your countertransference in supervision or consultation with professional colleagues. Unpacking your countertransference in supervision or consultation allows you to understand your own reactions more deeply, to delve into what is being evoked in you and why. Understanding your own countertransference can help you to plan treatment, to figure out what would be the most helpful next steps with your client. Whether you choose to share it with your client or not, recognizing your own countertransference will always be a useful tool for you in building therapeutic alliance with your clients.

Building Trust With an Adolescent Client

A core component of building therapeutic alliance with your adolescent clients includes building trust in that relationship. In order to build trust, acknowledge when you have messed up. We are all fallible beings and we make mistakes. Predict to your adolescent clients that you won't be perfect at your job, regularly ask them to give you feedback, and embrace your mistakes. Being a perfect therapist is impossible. Our aim is to do the best we can and then to acknowledge our errors when they occur.

Ruptures in the therapeutic alliance are common, but repair of the rupture is critical. Practitioners must be attuned to the therapeutic alliance ruptures, taking initiative to explore what happened when they detect that a rupture may have occurred (Safran, Muran, & Eubanks-Carter, 2011). Did you notice that your client became more withdrawn or more reticent to speak with you? Did you accidentally say something insensitive or hurtful? Inquire of your clients: "What is happening right now? Did I hurt your feelings?" "I want to help you, but I'm worried that I made a mistake here and said something that was hurtful." "Can you help me to understand what's happening with you right now? I wonder if I said something insensitive or wrong." Your attention to potential ruptures and attempt at repair is critical in ensuring strong treatment outcomes.

Routine Outcome Monitoring

Routine outcome monitoring means collecting data from your clients every session or at regular intervals. A significant body of research links routine outcome monitoring in psychotherapy with better client outcomes (Lambert, 2007; Lambert, Hansen, & Finch, 2001; Lambert et al., 2003). But strengthening therapeutic alliance is another important reason for utilizing routine outcome monitoring.

There are many measures clinicians can use to assess therapeutic alliance and client outcomes. Some empirically validated and free tools for individual clinicians are available here: www.scottdmiller.com. The Session Rating Scale (Duncan et al, 2003) and the Child Session Rating Scale, both developed under the auspices of the International Center for Clinical Excellence (www.centerforclinicalexcellence.com), can be used with adolescent clients for routine outcome monitoring. The instruments ask about whether clients feel heard, if material important to the client was covered, if the client felt good about what was covered. With simple scoring mechanisms, these tools are useful for every clinician.

Your client might have feedback for you which they feel too uncomfortable to say aloud, but may be willing to write down on a form. I have often received feedback from clients filling out the Session Rating Scale which they declined to give me in person, even when I invited and welcomed their verbal feedback. If you don't know how your clients are perceiving the treatment, you are unable to ensure that treatment is maximally relevant for them. You need their feedback to build alliance, and session rating scales can help provide you with that feedback.

Conclusion

When you are sensitive to your client's emotional states, when you are attuned to their feelings toward you and the treatment, when you set clear treatment goals in a collaborative process with your client and work toward those goals using methods that you both have agreed upon, you increase the chances of strong psychotherapy outcomes for your adolescent clients. Work with your clients on the *tasks, bonds,* and *goals* of treatment (Horvath & Greenberg, 1989). Be attentive to transference and countertransference. Notice potential ruptures in the therapeutic alliance and strive to repair those. Survey your clients on how you are doing each session. When you do these things, you are building a strong therapeutic alliance and increasing the likelihood that the treatment you are delivering will be effective.

References

Ainsworth, M., Blehar, M., Waters, E., & Wall, S. (1978). *Patterns of attachment: A psychological study of the Strange Situation.* Hillsdale, NJ: Erlbaum.

Beijersbergen, M. D., Juffer, F., Bakermans-Kranenburg, M. J., & van IJzendoorn, M.H. (2012). Remaining or becoming secure: Parental sensitive support predicts attachment continuity from infancy to adolescence in a longitudinal adoption study. *Developmental Psychology, 48,* 1277–1282. doi:10.1037/a0027442

Bowlby, J. (1969). Attachment and loss (Vol. 1). London, UK: Hogarth Press.

Delgado, S. V., Strawn, J. R., & Pedapati, E. V. (2014). *Contemporary psychodynamic psychotherapy for children and adolescents: Integrating intersubjectivity and neuroscience.* New York, NY: Springer.

Duncan, B. L., Miller, S. D., Sparks, J. A., Claud, D. A., Reynolds, L. R., Brown, J., & Johnson, L. D. (2003). The session rating scale: Preliminary psychometric properties of a "working" alliance measure. *Journal of Brief Therapy, 3,* 3–12.

Duschinsky, R. (2015). The emergence of the disorganized/disoriented (D) attachment classification, 1979–1982. *History of Psychology, 18,* 32–46. doi:http://dx.doi.10.1037/a0038524

Freud, A. (1958/1975). Adolescence. In A.H. Esman (Ed.), *The Psychology of Adolescence: Essential Readings* (pp. 122–140). New York, NY: International Universities Press, Inc.

Groh, A. M., Roisman, G. I., Booth-LaForce, C., Fraley, R. C., Owen, M. T., Cox, M. J., & Burchinal, M. R. (2014). The Adult Attachment Interview: Psychometrics, stability and change from infancy and developmental origins: IV. Stability of attachment security from infancy to late adolescence. *Monographs of the Society for Research in Child Development, 79,* 51–66. doi:http://dx.oi.ezproxy.lib.utah.edu/10.1111/mono.12113

Hesse, E. (2008). The Adult Attachment Interview: Protocol, method of analysis, and empirical studies. In J. Cassidy, P. R. Shaver, J. Cassidy, & P. R. Shaver (Eds.), *Handbook of attachment: Theory, research, and clinical applications* (2nd ed., pp. 552–598). New York, NY: Guilford Press.

Hesse & Main (2000). Disorganized infant, child, and adult attachment: Collapse in behavioral and attentional strategies. *Journal of the American Psychoanalytic Association, 48,* 1097–1127. doi:http://dx.doi.org.ezproxy.lib.utah.edu/10.1177/00030651000480041101

Horvath, A. O., Flückiger, C., & Symonds, D. (2011). Alliance in individual psychotherapy. In J. C. Norcross (Ed.) *Psychotherapy relationships that work* (pp. 25–69). New York, NY: Oxford University Press.

Horvath, A. O., & Greenberg, L. S. (1989). Development and validation of the Working Alliance Inventory. *Journal of Counseling Psychology, 36,* 223–233.

Joubert, D., Webster, L., & Hackett, R. K., (2012). Unresolved attachment status and trauma-related symptomatology in maltreated adolescents: An examination of cognitive mediators. *Child Psychiatry & Human Development, 43,* 471–483. doi:10.1007/s10578-011-0276-8

Ladame, F. (1996). The transference mirage and the pitfalls of countertransference (with special emphasis on adolescence). In J. Tsiantis, A. Sandler, D. Anastasopoulos, & B. Martindale (Eds.), *Countertransference in psychoanalytic psychotherapy with children and adolescents* (pp. 87–94). Madison, CT: International Universities Press.

Laible, D. (2007). Attachment with parents and peers in late adolescence: Links with emotional competence and social behavior. *Personality and Individual Differences, 43,* 1185–1197.

Lambert, M. (2007). Presidential address: What we have learned from a decade of research aimed at improving psychotherapy outcome in routine care. *Psychotherapy research, 17,* 1–14.

Lambert, M. J., Hansen, N. B., & Finch, A. E. (2001). Patient-focused research: Using patient outcome data to enhance treatment effects. *Journal of Consulting and Clinical Psychology, 69,* 159–172. doi:http://dx.doi.org/10.1037/0022-006X.69.2.159

Lambert, M. J., Whipple, J. L., Hawkins, E. J., Vermeersch, D. A., Nielsen, S. L., & Smart, D. W. (2003). Is it time for clinicians to routinely track patient outcome? A meta-analysis. *Clinical Psychology: Science and Practice, 10,* 288–301.

Main, M., & Solomon, J. (1986). Discovery of a new, insecure disorganized/disoriented attachment pattern. In T. B. Brazelton & M. Yogman (Eds.), *Affective development in infancy* (pp. 95–124). Norwood, NJ: Ablex.

Malove, S. C. (2014). Using relational theory to treat adolescent girls victimized by social aggression. *Clinical Social Work Journal, 42,* 1–12. doi:10.1007/s10615-012-0424-z

McCarthy, G., & Maughan, B. (2010). Negative childhood experiences and adult love relationships: The role of internal working models of attachment. *Attachment and Human Development, 12,* 445–461. doi:10.1080/14616734.2010.501968

Morrow, K. V., & Styles, M. B. (1995). *Building relationships with youth in program settings: A study of Big Brother/Big Sister ventures.* Philadelphia, PA: Public/Private Ventures.

Nilsson, D., Holmqvist, R., & Jonson, M. (2011). Self-reported attachment style, trauma exposure and dissociatve symptoms among adolescents. *Attachment & Human Development, 13,* 579–595.

Roisman, G. I., Padrón, E., Sroufe, L. A., & Egeland, B. (2002). Earned secure attachment status in retrospect and prospect. *Child Development, 73,* 1204–1219. doi:10.1111/1467-8624.00467

Safran, J. D., Muran, J. C., & Eubanks-Carter, C. (2011). Repairing alliance ruptures. In J. C. Norcross (Ed.), *Psychotherapy relationships that work* (pp. 224–238). New York, NY: Oxford University Press.

Santrock, J. W. (2018). *Essentials of life development* (5th ed.). New York, NY: McGraw-Hill Education.

Seiffge-Krenke, I. (2006). Coping with relationship stressors: The impact of different working models of attachment and links to adaptation. *Journal of Youth and Adolescence, 35,* 25–39.

Shirk, S. R., & Karver, M. S. (2011). Alliance in child and adolescent psychotherapy. In J. C. Norcross (Ed.), *Psychotherapy Relationships That Work* (pp. 70–91). New York, NY: Oxford University Press.

Shoshani, A., Nakash, O. Zubida, H., & Harper, R.A. (2014). Mental health and engagement in risk behaviors among migrant adolescents in Israel: The protective functions of secure attachment, self-esteem, and perceived peer support. *Journal of Immigrant & Refugee Studies, 12,* 233–249. doi:10.1080/15562948.2013.827769

Sroufe, L. A. (2005). Attachment and development: A prospective, longitudinal study from birth to adulthood. *Attachment & Human Development, 7,* 349–367.

Waters, E., Merrick, S., Treboux, D., Crowell, J., & Albersheim, L. (2000). Attachment security in infancy and early adulthood: A twenty-year longitudinal study. *Child Development, 71,* 684–689.

SECTION II
TREATING MENTAL HEALTH ISSUES

6

Evidence-Based Interventions
for Adolescent Anxiety

Joanna E. Bettmann, Anthony D. Bram, and Taylor Berhow

Anxiety disorders are one of the most common psychiatric disorders in adolescents (Cartwright-Hatton, McNicol, & Doubleday, 2006; Fonagy, Target, Cottrell, Phillips, & Kurtz, 2002; Merikangas, 2005; Pine, Cohen, Gurley, Brook, Ma, 1998). Research suggests that anxiety disorder prevalence in those under 20 may be as high as 30% (Fonagy et al., 2002; Merikangas et al., 2010; Simon & Bögels, 2009) and appears to be increasing (Merikangas et al., 2010; Pine et al., 1998). Although adolescent anxiety often presents within developmentally normal ranges, approximately half of those with anxiety symptoms experience functional impairment severe enough to qualify for a diagnosis (Fonagy et al., 2002; Merikangas et al., 2010).

Anxiety disorders are more prevalent among young females than young males (Costello, Egger, Copeland, Erkanli, & Angold, 2005; Merikangas et al., 2010; Moffitt et al., 2007): In one study, 38% of teen girls met criteria for anxiety disorders while only 26.1% of teenage boys did (Merikangas et al., 2010). Anxiety disorders typically onset between the ages of 10 and 12 (Merikangas et al., 2010). Anxiety manifests differently in younger teenagers than older teenagers (Merikangas, 2005; Pine et al., 1998). For example, younger adolescents are likely to develop social anxiety, whereas older adolescents are more likely to develop panic disorders, which have a media age onset of 17–18 years (Merikangas, 2005). In a U.S. study of more than 10,000 adolescents, 22.1% qualified for a Specific Phobia, 11.2% for a Social Anxiety Disorder, 8% for PTSD, and 9% for Separation Anxiety Disorder (Merikangas et al., 2010).

Anxiety disorders are prevalent throughout the lifespan, but the majority of adult anxiety disorders begin in adolescence (Hollander, 2007; Simon & Bögels, 2009). Some theorize that adolescents experience increased stress levels and that their developing brains are more prone and susceptible to mood changes, leading to the development of adolescent anxiety disorders

(Midgley, Hayes, & Cooper, 2017). Notably, the earlier anxiety onsets, the more destructive and debilitating it tends to be; thus, adolescents are at particularly high risk of experiencing lifelong, disabling anxiety (Essau, Conradt, & Petermann, 2000; Simon & Bögels, 2009). Anxiety disorder treatment constitutes large portions of state and private healthcare costs (Simon & Bögels, 2009). For example, one study found that families who support clinically anxious children can spend up to 20 times more in healthcare costs than families who do not (Simon & Bögels, 2009).

In the DSM-5, there are seventeen disorders characterized by symptoms of severe anxiety (American Psychiatric Association, 2013). This chapter will focus on those anxiety disorders that are most common in adolescents.

Risk Factors for Adolescent Anxiety

Some adolescents appear predisposed to anxiety (Bennet & Stirling, 1998), perhaps due to family dynamics, medical conditions, cultural influences, genetics, or other factors. Research does suggests links between certain parental demographics and adolescent anxiety disorders: anxiety disorders manifest more frequently in adolescents whose parents are divorced or separated compared to adolescents whose parents cohabitate (Merikangas et al., 2010).

Some parenting styles appear to increase the likelihood of adolescents' anxiety disorders (Wong & Rapee, 2015). Specifically, adolescents whose parents tend to be overprotective and controlling or low-warmth are more likely to experience anxiety (Wong & Rapee, 2015). Additionally, certain types of attachment styles contribute to an increased likelihood of adolescent anxiety. For example, insecure parental attachment is associated with social anxiety disorder in adolescents (Wong & Rapee, 2015). Other research suggests a link between a mother's overprotective behavior and child/adolescent anxiety disorders (Merikangas, 2005). Parental anxiety or fear also appears associated with adolescent anxiety (Merikangas, 2005).

Medical illness is another risk factor that appears linked to adolescent anxiety (Pao & Bosk, 2011; Merikangas, 2005). Research shows that adolescents who experienced chronic physical illness throughout childhood are more likely to develop an anxiety disorder later in life (Pao & Bosk, 2011; Merikangas, 2005). Richardson et al. (2006) observed the relationship between asthma and anxiety in adolescent populations, noting that adolescents experienced increased levels of anxiety on higher-asthma symptom days (Richardson et al., 2006). Researchers also link anxiety disorders with severe head injuries, finding an increase in anxiety symptoms post-head injury (Merikangas, 2005). Anxiety disorders also appear to have genetic links. Some suggest that certain types of anxiety disorders, like social anxiety disorder and generalized anxiety disorders, have strong genetic components (Merikangas, 2005; Wong & Rapee, 2015).

Traumatic events also appear to contribute to vulnerability for adolescent anxiety disorders (Heim & Nemeroff, 2001; Suliman et al., 2009). Adolescents exposed to early adverse and traumatic experiences, such as child abuse, are at increased risk for developing anxiety (Heim & Nemeroff, 2001; Merikangas, 2005). Additionally, adverse childhood experiences appear to alter adolescents' neurobiology (Heim & Nemeroff, 2001). Specifically, Heim and Nemeroff (2001) found that adverse experiences may alter the production of neurotransmitters in the regulation of stress responses.

Another risk factor for adolescent anxiety is low socioeconomic status (Merikangas, 2005). One study found that adolescents of lower socioeconomic status tended to experience greater emotional distress—as measured by negative mood, social anxiety, and psychological anxiety—than their wealthier adolescent peers (Ansary, McMahon, & Luthar, 2011). Researchers postulated the correlation between low socioeconomic status and increased emotional distress likely was related to poorer school quality, safety problems characteristic of low-income urban areas, and lack of social and educational resources (Ansary et al., 2011). Another study found adolescents who resided in lower-income households experienced worse mental and physical health compared to their peers from high- or middle-income households (Vine et al., 2012). Authors of that study suggested that low socioeconomic status might increase adolescents' daily stress as a result of fewer community resources, increased number of household moves, and greater likelihood of neighborhood violence (Vine et al., 2012). Additionally, children whose parents have not completed a college degree experience increased risk of developing some kind of anxiety disorder (Merikangas et al., 2010). This correlation could be related to familial income and education levels, both of which are risk factors for the development of adolescent anxiety (Merikangas et al., 2010).

Notes for Assessment of Anxiety Disorders
1. When assessing for adolescent anxiety, clinicians should screen for the possibility of adverse childhood events and, if necessary, incorporate a trauma-informed or trauma-focused care model (Merikangas, 2005).
2. Clinicians should also screen for parenting styles (such as over-protective, controlling, or low warmth) that might contribute to or exacerbate adolescent anxiety.

Obsessive-Compulsive Disorder

While the DSM-5 presents Obsessive-Compulsive Disorder (OCD) in its own distinct chapter separate from other anxiety disorders, OCD and its related disorders are characterized by symptoms of anxiety and are considered to be anxiety disorders (Hollander, 2007). For these reasons, this chapter will include a discussion of adolescent OCD.

OCD is one of the more functionally debilitating anxiety disorders and often runs a chronic course from adolescence into adulthood (Essau et al., 2000; Hollander, 2007). Like other anxiety disorders, OCD is often comorbid with depression; the combination of the two disorders often constitutes a lifelong presentation of psychiatric symptoms (Hollander, 2007). The World Health Organization ranks OCD among the top 10 most debilitating mental illnesses; some literature suggests the disabilities associated with OCD are equal to those with schizophrenia (Hollander, 2007). Some of these impairments include difficulty maintaining personal relationships, low self-esteem, poor academic performance, and interference with employment and higher education completion (Hollander, 2007). Additionally, OCD significantly increases suicide risk (Hollander, 2007).

In cases of OCD, there is typically a delay between symptom onset and treatment, a delay which can be more than 15 years (Hollander, 2007; Nakatani, Mataix-Cols, Micali, Turner, & Heyman, 2009). Troublingly, longer gaps between symptom onset and initial treatment may hinder treatment efficacy (Hollander, 2007). But the earlier OCD is diagnosed and treated, the more likely clients will experience symptom reduction (Hollander, 2007). Thus, early detection is critical.

OCD symptomology is commonly assessed with the Childhood Yale-Brown Obsessive Compulsive Scale (C-YBOCS). The C-YBOCS is a semi-structured, clinician-administered questionnaire available free on the International OCD Foundation (IOCDF) website (iocdf.org). The instrument assesses OCD symptoms in four categories: symmetry, sex/aggression, hoarding, and washing/checking. Using a developmentally appropriate measurement tool is important because research suggests there are key differences in how OCD symptomology manifests in adolescence compared to adulthood (Geller et al., 2001; IOCDF, 2018). Notably, adolescents and adults appear to differ in their obsessions and compulsions. For example, religious and sexual obsessions, as well as hoarding compulsions, are more common in adolescent OCD patients compared to adult patients (Geller et al., 2001).

Comorbidity

As many as 70% of adolescents with anxiety disorders manifest with a psychiatric comorbidity (Lewinsohn et al., 1997). Anxiety comorbidity rates are higher in adolescent populations than in adult populations (Costello et al., 2005; Lewinsohn et al., 1997). Comorbid cases tend to be more severe and intractable than anxiety-only cases (Moffitt et al., 2007). Similarly, many adolescents present with symptoms of multiple anxiety disorders and many qualify for more than one (Lewinsohn et al., 1997).

Adolescent anxiety disorders often present comorbid with mood disorders, substance use disorders, and eating disorders (Fonagy et al., 2002; Kim-Cohen et al., 2003). Research suggests that depression is 8 times more likely in adolescents diagnosed with an anxiety disorder compared to adolescents without (Costello et al., 2005). Additionally, adolescents with both depression and anxiety are more likely to attempt suicide, as well as to experience difficulty in school (Lewinsohn et al., 1997). While many anxiety disorders are comorbid with depression, there is an especially strong correlation between generalized anxiety disorder (GAD) and major depressive disorder (Moffitt, et al., 2007). GAD and major depressive disorder also manifest cumulative comorbidity: individuals often experience both diagnoses over the course of their lifespan, but not necessarily simultaneously (Moffitt et al., 2007). Clinicians should consider comorbidities when developing a treatment plan to manage with anxiety, as these teenagers may be experiencing depression as well (Hollander, 2007).

Some research suggests an association between substance use and anxiety: adolescents who use substances often present with significant anxiety

(Merikangas, 2005). Other research suggests that 7–40% of adolescents who use substances experience clinically distressing anxiety (Horigan et al., 2013). Approximately 15% of teenagers with a substance abuse disorder will manifest clinically significant anxiety over a lifetime (Lewinsohn et al., 1997). Notably, adolescents with social anxiety disorder or generalized anxiety disorder are at increased risk for alcohol and cigarette use (Zehe, Colder, Read, Wieczorek, & Lengua, 2013). The existing literature reports mixed results on which comes first: the substance abuse or the anxiety (Merikangas, 2005). Given these high comorbidities, clinicians who detect an anxiety disorder in their adolescent clients should carefully assess for the presence of other psychiatric disorders, including other anxiety disorders, mood disorders, and substance use disorders.

Assessment

Screening carefully for adolescent anxiety is critical. Both self-report questionnaires and clinical interview protocols are effective in detecting anxiety (Beesdo, Knappe, & Pine, 2009; Simon & Bögels, 2009). However, make sure you are using an adolescent-specific anxiety assessment tool, as adolescent anxiety can manifest differently than adult anxiety (Costello et al., 2005).

The Diagnostic Interview Schedule for Children and Adolescents can be administered by individuals who are not clinically trained, but days-long training in the instrument is strongly recommended (Columbia University DISC Development Group, 2006; Merikangas, 2005). The instrument is not anxiety specific; it measures 34 common psychiatric diagnoses (Columbia University DISC Development Group, 2006). It is available online, free of charge, at www.cdc.gov.

The Kiddie-Schedule for Affective Disorders and Schizophrenia (K-SADS; Kaufman et al., 2016) is another commonly used instrument, also available free of charge, but must be administered by someone with clinical mental health training. K-SADS specific training is not required (Merikangas, 2005). This semi-structured interview is designed to measure anxiety and its common comorbidities (Kaufman et al., 2016); a DSM-5 version is available online at https://www.kennedykrieger.org/sites/default/files/community_files/ksads-dsm-5-screener.pdf.

Though diagnostic interviews are valuable, clinicians can also assess for anxiety without them. Assessing for risk factors like socioeconomic status, familial mental health patterns, parental discipline techniques, family relationship, and common comorbidities is important in developing a complete biopsychosocial picture of your client (Merikangas, 2005).

In order to screen for anxiety, you can ask clients: "Do you feel worried or anxious a lot of time?" This screens for generalized anxiety disorder. After asking an open question such as that, you can then follow up with specific questions asking about the specific symptoms of each anxiety disorder. Other broad anxiety screening questions might include: "Are there specific things you are afraid of or nervous about?" "Do you often find that there are thoughts in your head that you can't get rid of?" "Do you have trouble controlling or managing your worries?" Using broad screening questions such as these can help you determine whether you need to do more in-depth, specific screening for certain anxiety disorders.

You can also ask adolescents to rate themselves on a "fear thermometer" or other visual analogue tool, assessing adolescents' anxieties for different types of worries or anxiety under different conditions. Using visual analogue tools can help adolescents, particularly younger ones, to understand a range of anxious feelings or strength of those feelings. You might draw a thermometer where "10" is labeled "extremely anxious—can't think about anything else," "5" is labeled "thinking anxious thoughts a lot," and "1" is labeled "barely worried at all." For example, you might ask an adolescent with a fear of flying, "When you think about flying, where on the thermometer is your anxiety level?"

Treatment of Adolescent Anxiety

There are several evidence-based psychotherapeutic treatment approaches for adolescent anxiety. Cognitive behavior therapy (CBT) is the most well-established treatment protocol for adolescent anxiety disorders which include generalized anxiety disorder, specific phobia, and OCD (Cartwright-Hatton, Roberts, Chitsabesan, Fothergill, & Harrington, 2010; Fonagy, Allison, & Ryan, 2017; Fonagy et al., 2002). CBT appears to significantly decrease both short- and long-term symptoms of adolescent anxiety (Barrett, Duffy, Dadds, & Rapee, 2001; Cartwright-Hatton, McNicol, & Doubleday, 2006; Cartwright-Hatton et al., 2004). Research suggests that, because CBT requires clients to develop complex emotional and cognitive skills, it begins its effectiveness with clients aged 10–11 (Cartwright-Hatton et al., 2006).

CBT aims to modify adolescents' thinking by identifying thought patterns which may not be aligned with reality (Kumara & Kumar, 2016). Adolescents who experience anxiety often suffer from irrational thought patterns which can lead to dysfunctional learning processes, as well as an inability to cope with intense emotions (Kumara & Kumar, 2016). While CBT is widely used and its efficacy confirmed in numerous studies, CBT has been adapted for adolescents who experience some forms of anxiety by emphasizing different components of CBT (Barrett, Duffy, Dadds, & Rapee, 2001; Cartwright-Hatton et al., 2004; Cartwright-Hatton, McNicol, & Doubleday, 2006; Kumara & Kumar, 2016). Kumara and Kumar (2016) adapted CBT to treat adolescent anxiety and depression, finding strong outcomes. The main goal of their approach is to facilitate the necessary insight required to produce behavior change so that adolescents can control their thoughts, feelings, and actions (Kumara & Kumar, 2016). In this CBT model for adolescents, clinicians use more concrete examples, rather than theoretical ones, to illustrate points and concepts. Other minor adaptations include a specific focus on the adolescent's thinking errors, emotional shifts during session, and ability to self-regulate, solve problems, and use effective social skills (Kumara & Kumar, 2016).

In Kumara and Kumar's (2016) model, the initial sessions of adolescent CBT address the client's thoughts and cognitive distortions. These sessions provide the adolescent with psychoeducation about how thoughts can affect emotions and mood. The concept of thoughts, that they are not innately tied to emotions themselves, should be defined in the first session (Kumara & Kumar, 2016). In subsequent sessions, clinicians introduce the concept of thinking errors and assist adolescents in identifying situations in which they use thinking errors (Kumara & Kumar, 2016). Clinicians draw from each adolescent's situation, providing concrete examples of thinking errors (Kumara & Kumar, 2016). In the first few sessions, clinicians also discuss confidentiality; presenting the scope and limitations of confidentiality can facilitate trust and rapport between the clinician and adolescent client (Kumara & Kumar, 2016).

In sessions five through eight of Kumara and Kumar's CBT model, clinicians teach adolescent clients about the effects of anxiety and depression and these disorders' impact on the ability to enjoy life (Kumara & Kumar, 2016). Clinicians help adolescents identify activities that they appreciate, as well as how the symptoms of anxiety and depression are obstacles in the enjoyment of these (Kumara & Kumar, 2016). Identifying real-life experiences helps the client and clinician develop and define specific goals to help manage anxiety (Kumara & Kumar, 2016). Education about effective goal-setting is also provided during these sessions. The established goals should include reducing cognitive distortions and establishing ways to improve the client's mood (Kumara & Kumar, 2016). Clinicians using this model might also introduce relaxation techniques to help with emotional regulation and effective communication about emotion (Kumara & Kumar, 2016).

The last three sessions of this CBT approach focus on the adolescent's relationships and how these relationships impact mood and emotions (Kumara & Kumar, 2016). These sessions explore how to have a healthy social support system, how to develop and strengthen that support system, and what effective communication looks like (Kumara & Kumar, 2016). In the final session, clinicians help clients to evaluate their own experience with therapy, exploring their own strengths and weaknesses, and highlighting skills developed during therapy. Clinicians might consider sharing these goals and other experiences with the adolescent's parents, teachers, family members, and other relevant care-giving parties (Kumara & Kumar, 2016).

While using CBT, clinicians may utilize exposure therapy, a behavioral technique, to help adolescents become more comfortable with tolerating their anxious thoughts when presented with an anxiety trigger. Because anxiety disorders are often characterized by avoidance of anxiety triggers, exposure therapy can be enormously useful in helping adolescent clients to reduce their avoidance.

Research suggests that exposure therapy is effective in treating various types of anxiety disorders, including specific phobias and OCD (Berman, Weems, Silverman, & Kurtines, 2000; Fonagy et al., 2002). Specifically, exposure-based CBT shows efficacy in treating several adolescent anxiety disorders (Berman et al., 2000; Kendall et al., 2005). In the exposure-based CBT model, the clinician provides psychoeducational preparation before coaching the client to begin a series of exposures to gradually more anxiety-provoking situations (Kendall et al., 2005). Kendall et al. (2005) describe their exposure-based CBT adaptation as divided into two segments, the first focusing on skill training and the second focusing on skill practice. The clinician uses information gathered throughout treatment to design and build a fear hierarchy or fear thermometer which is used to implement exposure tasks to be completed by the adolescent (Kendall et al., 2005). The development of this hierarchy is a collaborative effort between the therapist and the adolescent and should represent a scale of events or situations which gradually increase in intensity—the least anxiety-provoking situation at the bottom and the most anxiety-provoking at the top (Kendall et al., 2005). In this approach, levels of anxiety are measured in subjective units of distress/ discomfort (SUDs; Kendall et al., 2005). Once the hierarchy is completed and the necessary education provided, the therapist and adolescent can explore the situations on the hierarchy as a way of safely exposing the adolescent to situations which might trigger anxiety symptoms (Kendall et al., 2005). The Figure 6.1 illustrates this hierarchy (Kendall et al., 2005):

CBT is also an evidence-based treatment for OCD, often used in conjunction with the administration of selective serotonin-reuptake inhibitor medications; this combination treatment protocol has been validated by several randomized control trials (Hollander, 2007; Nakatani et al., 2009). The American Psychiatric Association recommends CBT as a first line treatment for adolescents with OCD (Nakatani et al., 2009).

A smaller body of research shows that psychodynamic psychotherapy evidences efficacy for the treatment of adolescent anxiety, particularly when administered to adolescents in conjunction with their families or when there is trauma or maltreatment within the family system (Fonagy, Allison, & Ryan, 2017; Midgley & Kennedy, 2011). Psychodynamic psychotherapy involves techniques that focus on the expression of a client's emotion, as well as his/her attempt to avoid upsetting thoughts and emotions (Shedler, 2010). With a treatment goal to explore clients' interpersonal relationships, past experiences, and fantasies, psychodynamic psychotherapy seeks to impact clients beyond symptom reduction, effecting personality and behavioral shifts (Shedler, 2010).

Case Examples

Though it is essential for practitioners to be familiar with the research literature on disorder-specific treatments for adolescents with various kinds of anxiety disorders, devising a treatment plan for an individual requires evidence-based practice in a more nuanced way than extrapolating only from randomized controlled trial (RCT) research (American Psychological Association Presidential Task Force, 2006). This nuanced approach to practice means accounting for how a client is similar to and different from those formally studied in RCTs (Westen & Morrison, 2001), cultural factors, stages of change, treatment preferences, capacity for therapeutic alliance, coping

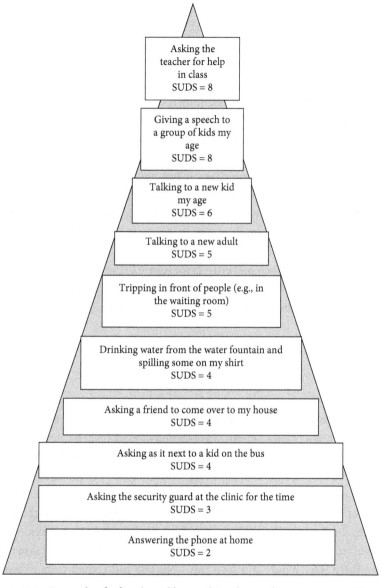

Figure 6.1. Example of a fear-based hierarchy to be used in treatment with an adolescent who experiences social anxiety triggers. Reprinted from Kendall, P. C., Robin, J. A., Hedtke, K. A., Suveg, C., Flannery-Schroeder, E., & Gosch, E. (2005). Considering CBT with anxious youth? Think exposures. *Cognitive and Behavioral Practice, 12*, 136–150. Copyright © 2005, with permission from Elsevier.

style, comorbid conditions, and other client and family characteristics (see Bram, 2013 for a review of many of these variables). Thus, two adolescents with the same DSM-5 anxiety disorder may require very different approaches to treatment. In clinical practice—despite what may be portrayed in professional associations (e.g., Society of Clinical Psychology, 2018) and the media (e.g., Brown, 2013)—treatment planning is often more complex than moving from DSM-5 diagnosis to a treatment package identified as effective in RCTs for that specific disorder. Of course, such research should and does inform decisions about an individual's treatment. However, the link between DSM-5 diagnosis and treatment modality is not always straightforward. In this portion of the chapter, we aim to illustrate why and how adolescents who share the same anxiety disorder diagnosis require and benefit from disparate treatment courses, one involving the more narrowly defined evidence-based modality and the other a different approach. Specifically, we present two adolescents who each met criteria for severe OCD but whose treatments were quite different. Our premise is that both treatments can be considered evidence-based in the broader and more nuanced way.

Case 1: Abbie

Abbie was an exceedingly bright 15-year-old high school sophomore who was referred by her pediatrician for a psychological consultation because her heightened anxiety about germs was creating difficulties at home and school. At home, she was becoming increasingly anxious and avoidant when her parents and siblings touched her things and went into her room, resulting in conflict and arguments. At school, she was often late to classes if there were no other students around to open doors because she feared touching the handles. In the initial consultation, Abbie was distraught by her symptoms, recognized that her fears were unrealistic, but expressed helplessness to overcome them. Her hands and forearms were red and chafed from excessive washing which was the clue that led her pediatrician to inquire and make the mental health referral. Though distressed by her predicament, Abbie engaged readily with me (ADB), was articulate, made good eye contact, and expressed eagerness about working with me to get relief. She described a stable home life with supportive parents, a number of friends including a best friend, and participation in school sports and other extra-curricular activities. Her grades in her mostly Advanced Placement curriculum had fallen from A/A−/B+ to B/B−/C+ the previous semester as her symptoms exacerbated. She described some of her teachers as attuned and concerned and wanting to help her.

Assessment of her symptoms with the Children's Yale-Brown Obsessive-Compulsive Scale (CY-BOCS) clarified that Abbie met criteria for OCD in the severe range. Although she reported some depressive symptoms—lower energy and mild social withdrawal and anhedonia—she did not meet criteria for a full-blown depressive disorder. She also did not meet criteria for any other anxiety disorders. Inquiry using the CY-BOCS Symptom Checklist revealed that her obsessions primarily were organized around contamination fears, but, more specifically, preoccupation that contamination would result in "brain damage" that would rob her of her intelligence and future achievement. For Abbie, this meant that she was particularly fearful of people with intellectual disabilities and objects with which they had come in contact (such as door handles, lunch tables). As Abbie was otherwise invested in social justice causes, revealing the nature of her contamination fears was a source of shame. So she did not reveal these fears until our third and final pre-arranged consultation session. Abbie's compulsions predominantly involved excessive washing of herself (such as multiple showers per day and changes of clothes) and washing objects (such as demanding her mother clean her laundry and bed sheets frequently; vacuuming her rug daily) as well as avoidance of potential contamination (rules about others' not entering her room). She also engaged in compulsive reassurance-seeking from her parents: "I'll be okay, right?"

In the third consultation session, I shared with Abbie and her parents my understanding that her symptoms appeared to meet criteria for severe OCD. I offered them basic psychoeducation about OCD and its treatment. I emphasized the neurobiological/genetic basis of OCD, including showing contrasting brain scans of people with and without OCD (March & Mulle, 1998). I explained that OCD is nobody's fault and that it is considered a chronic illness that can be managed similar to asthma or diabetes. Abbie and her parents responded with relief that her condition could be named and treated, but they also shared some shock and sadness at Abbie's diagnosis. I described the treatment options of CBT and/or pharmacotherapy, presenting pros and cons of each. Her parents expressed that they would do "whatever it takes" to help Abbie, communicating guilt that they had been so angry and yelled at Abbie for her rules about who could go where and touch what in the household which they now understood as symptomatic of her illness. I empathized with her parents that they could not have known then what they knew now. I also introduced the narrative element of CBT for OCD, which involved externalizing OCD as an enemy to be fought against by the team of client, family, and therapist (Chansky, 2000; March & Mulle, 1998).

Abbie indicated that she preferred the CBT but not the medication option, even though the latter might provide more immediate relief. Much later, I would learn that this preference was driven by her obsessive fears that medication might contaminate and damage her brain. We all agreed that Abbie and I would begin meeting for weekly individual sessions of CBT with intermittent family meetings for the purpose of providing further education about OCD and how her parents could best support Abbie's exposure assignments at home.

Before describing the course of treatment, I believe it is valuable to discuss my thought process in recommending CBT. Obviously, Abbie clearly met criteria for OCD. CBT utilizing exposure with response prevention (ERP) is the psychosocial treatment for OCD with the most research evidence. But there were other reasons that I viewed this as an optimal fit for Abbie. First, I did not foresee any concerns with her ability to form a therapeutic alliance: She was thoughtful and collaborative in our consultation. In the consultation sessions, her representations of relationships (in her descriptions of family, friends, and teachers) were benevolent and trusting (Peebles, 2012). Thus, I believed she could "take in" me and my CBT interventions without much intrapsychic or interpersonal conflict. Second, she exhibited reasonable insight that her obsessive worries were unrealistic and could ally with me around this. Third, Abbie's symptoms were highly distressing and disruptive and needed to be addressed directly therapeutically, especially if she were reluctant to try medication. Fourth, she was clearly bright and able to readily cognitively grasp the psychoeducational elements of treatment. From her academic history, I could see that she was a gritty, conscientious, hard worker who would not back down from the rigor of this treatment and would engage in between-session assignments. Fifth, I recognized that she had a family who appeared able and willing to support the treatment, getting Abbie to attend appointments reliably and attending family sessions. These collective strengths are not always present in treatment, but they increase the likelihood of treatment engagement and positive outcomes.

Early therapy sessions with Abbie involved in-depth psychoeducation which provided her with essential information that would later be applied in exposure work and served to enhance our collaborative alliance (Bram & Bjorgvinnson, 2004). I made sure that Abbie could define obsessions and compulsions, as well as explain and draw the habituation curve which provided a rationale for later exposures. Not surprisingly, Abbie learned fast. We worked together to be aware of the difference between Abbie's own thoughts and "OCD thoughts." When OCD was "bossing her around," I taught her to practice "bossing it back" (March & Mulle, 1998). I also introduced the analogy of obsessions being like junk mail or spam thoughts (Chansky, 2000). This psychoeducational intervention attenuated some of her shame and guilt about her contamination fears about students with intellectual disabilities.

Additionally, these interventions set the stage for role plays where I would portray the OCD and Abbie's job was to tell me/OCD to shut up and leave her alone. This experiential intervention helped her develop the mindset and narrative that she was not her OCD. It also reinforced the idea that she needed to be vigilant and assertive to resist OCD's demands. Abbie was able to play along and we had some fun with this. She shared that it was fun to have some sense of control and give the OCD a "piece of my mind."

I also introduced the tool of a "fear thermometer," rating scale from 1 to 10 denoting lowest to highest anxiety levels (March & Mulle, 1998). Abbie and I used this tool to construct a hierarchy of situations that evoked obsessions and compulsions/avoidances. I explained that the hierarchy would be our road map for exposure work and that we would start with situations that were mild/moderate (such as 4–5) on our scale and gradually build toward those evoking higher levels of anxiety. Although Abbie expressed concern that this might be difficult for her, she also communicated trust that we would take it slowly even while I would "nudge" her toward trying each exposure. I explained that it was ultimately up to her whether she was ready for exposures. If a specific exposure seemed too difficult for her, I suggested that we could find another exposure for which she felt more prepared. I also let her know that I would not ask her to do any exposure that I would not do myself and that I would be willing to do the exposures alongside her (March & Mulle, 1998).

Toward the lower end of her hierarchy (situations evoking mild to moderate anxiety), Abbie ranked touching objects that had briefly contacted the floor at school. These included items such as her backpack, school binder, and school books. Midrange on the hierarchy was touching objects that more regularly touched the floor at school, such as her shoes and boots. The highest and most anxiety provoking was directly touching the floor and door handles at school, especially near the classrooms frequented by students receiving special education. To maximize the benefit of ERP, it is essential to help the patient to approach and endure the anxiety-evoking/avoided situation and prevent the compulsions (response prevention), but also to zero in on exposure to the specific obsession (Foa & Wilson, 2009). For Abbie, the obsession was usually a variant of: "Because I'm touching this _____ and not washing, I'm becoming contaminated and it is causing me brain damage." To make exposures gradually more challenging, she and I would eat M&M's or similar candies after touching the object. The purpose here was to modify the obsession: ". . . and now I'm eating the contamination and it's going right to my brain and damaging my brain." Throughout each exposure, I encouraged her to repeatedly focus on and repeat the obsession. The therapeutic task was to help her learn that she could handle the feared thoughts. I further aimed for her to experience that her thoughts were harmless and even boring with repetition. I was also hoping that she would begin to see that thinking the thoughts would not cause the feared outcome, meaning there was no evidence Abbie was becoming brain damaged.

As we worked our way up her hierarchy, we typically spent each session on one or more of such ERPs. In the earlier and middle phase of our year-and-a-half of weekly meetings, these ERPs were all conducted in the office. Between sessions, Abbie agreed to various homework ERPs such as touching the same objects at home or, later, moving them to her room, while agreeing to not wash herself or the objects. We set goals for reducing the frequency and duration of showering and handwashing. There were some weeks where Abbie was more successful in completing these at-home ERPs than others. When she had more difficulty, we subsequently problem-solved about what was getting in the way and/or modified the assignment for the next week. I scheduled parent meetings bimonthly to discuss how her mother and father could best support her with at-home ERPs and stay allied with her in the "us vs. OCD" battle plan. Some of this work involved helping her parents to refrain from offering reassurance that she would be "okay" if she completed the exposures. Reassurance-seeking is actually a form of compulsion, aimed at neutralizing the obsession of contamination/brain damage and thus reducing Abbie's anxiety. I explained this to Abbie and her parents so that they could understand the rationale and agree to this arrangement, despite its seemingly being counterintuitive to supportive parenting.

As Abbie experienced mastery of in-session and at-home ERPs, we focused on the remaining tasks in her fear hierarchy: direct contact with door handles and floors at school. More than 6 months into treatment, it was now the summer. At this point, Abbie was experiencing less anxiety, both because of her progress in therapy, but also because she did not have to face the OCD triggers at school. But I suggested that, in order to help her be ready for the next school year, it would help to conduct ERPs at school. With hesitation, she agreed to this. We created a mini-hierarchy of the different doors that she feared and avoided at school. We began ERPs with those that were less anxiety provoking. Abbie would hold on to the door handles, verbally repeating her obsession about contamination and brain damage. After six sessions of this, she had worked her way up to the top of the hierarchy, touching and opening doors in the special education building, as well as touching the outside door handles of the program's vans. By the time the school year started, Abbie reported that she was able to touch and open all the doors. She reported that her anxiety at school was much reduced. A repeat administration of the CY-BOCS yielded a score that placed Abbie in the low–moderate range of OCD, down from her initial score in the severe range. Her mood and activity level had also improved and she was more engaged with friends and sports over the summer and into the fall.

We continued weekly individual sessions, now returned mostly to the office, for another 4 months, designing ERPs and problem-solving strategies to reduce her showering at home and to allow family and friends to enter her room. She gradually chipped away these symptoms, so we tapered to biweekly and then monthly sessions over her remaining years in high school. The task in these later years was to maintain her gains, to construct exposures to address OCD symptoms as they flared up, and to solidify her understanding of CBT/ERP, so she would be prepared to handle symptoms as they flared up in her life. We can think of this work as akin to how someone with asthma knows how to use an inhaler or someone with diabetes knows how to monitor and maintain blood sugar. In these later years of therapeutic work, we had established a trusting and helpful relationship so Abbie felt free to talk with me about her concerns with relationships and college options. Despite our history of doing more directive/psychoeducational work together, the shift to more traditional talk/reflective therapy met her developmental needs.

Abbie's treatment demonstrates how effective CBT for OCD can be when the conditions line up: an adolescent who (a) has a supportive family system and no socioeconomic barriers; (b) is readily able to engage in a collaborative alliance; (c) is cognitively capable of grasping the CBT concepts and methods; (d) is highly motivated; and (e) is not afflicted by complicating comorbid conditions. Under such optimal conditions, CBT can proceed in a more textbook way, as it is applied in RCTs, beginning with alliance-building psychoeducation and moving into systematic ERPs to feared and avoided thoughts and situations. In clinical practice, though, Abbie's ability to engage fully and successfully in the CBT/ERP protocol with minimal glitches is often more the exception than the rule with adolescents. The next case presentation will be more illustrative of the challenges and complications involved in treating an adolescent with OCD or other anxiety disorders. Finally, it is important to acknowledge that Abbie's OCD symptoms flared up in college in another state. So she sought CBT therapy there. Even the successful implementation of an "evidence-based" treatment in the narrow sense of the term (as CBT/ERP for OCD is considered) does not mean that further treatment will be unnecessary.

Case 2: Leah

Leah was a 14-year-old high school freshman referred for consultation by a colleague of mine (ADB) who was a friend of Leah's family. Leah took AP classes in school, but her parents were concerned about her precipitous drop in grades from middle school to high school, her increasing refusal to complete homework, her low energy, her withdrawal from friends, and her dropping off the soccer and basketball teams and other extracurricular activities. Her most recent physical exam did not offer a medical explanation for her symptoms. Leah's parents were concerned that she might be depressed. Leah had been an intellectually gifted, diligent, and high-achieving student. Her family strongly valued academic success. In our multi-session initial consultation, Leah was easily engaged and articulate, but highly self-deprecating and self-critical. She stated that her recent academic difficulties were the result of being "lazy" and "entitled." She shared that two teachers recently confronted her for "not taking responsibility" when she failed to turn in papers on time. Leah explained that she "just needed to be more responsible." I often find explanations of academic difficulties in terms of irresponsibility and laziness to be oversimplified and unhelpful. So I focus on ruling out a number of possible contributing factors including previously unidentified learning disabilities, problems of attention and/or executive functioning, depression or other mood disorders, and/or various forms of anxiety including OCD. I recommended Leah's parents seek neuropsychological and psychological testing for her to assess the role of these and other possible etiological factors. But in the interim before the testing was scheduled, I used the CY-BOCS to assess whether OCD might be present. When presenting problems include slowness or failure to complete schoolwork, one of my routine rule-outs is OCD, especially of the type marked by paralyzing perfectionism.

Based on an interview using the CY-BOCS symptom checklist and associated rating scales, I found that Leah did meet criteria for OCD. Her OCD symptoms then might account for her academic decline and depressed mood. Notably, Leah did struggle with perfectionistic obsessions and compulsive needs to redo tasks that did not meet her exacting, obsessional standards. Thus, reading and writing assignments were painfully slow for her. Reading was fraught by obsessions that she "missed something" or did not "completely understand" and then associated compulsions to reread. Writing assignments were difficult to even begin because she was scared she might not choose the right topic or phrase her ideas perfectly. She neutralized these obsessions with compulsions of constant deleting and rewriting. If there was any diagramming, drawing, or graphing required, Leah could only manage her perfectionistic obsessions by erasing and redoing again and again.

Leah recalled that, in middle school, she was typically awake until midnight or later completing her homework. With the increased workload at her city's competitive public high school, she could not finish her assignments unless she stayed up very late in the evenings, sacrificing her sleep. Months into high school, she reported that she felt burned out by years of having to work so hard. She described that, out of a sense of helplessness, she decided to give up on her homework and spend her time online, playing videogames, and sleeping. Rather than cope with her obsessions through compulsiveness, Leah now chose massive avoidance.

Not surprisingly, Leah's grades further deteriorated. We would later explore in treatment her longstanding, underlying fear of failing to live up to her own and others' expectations. Previously, this fear was a motivator in her diligence around schoolwork. But now she was actually experiencing the failure that she had feared, reinforced by feedback from teachers that she was not taking responsibility, was wasting her potential, and was lazy. She internalized this feedback, feeling that she was letting her parents and teachers down. But she still could not bring herself to do the schoolwork. She became more withdrawn from peers at school and increasingly depressed.

I reviewed the findings of the OCD assessment with Leah and her parents. Her mother and father were saddened and felt guilty that they had pressured

Leah with their own high expectations. They wondered whether they had caused Leah's OCD. I provided psychoeducation that OCD is nobody's fault and has a significant neurobiological basis (March & Mulle, 1998). This comforted her parents. However, Leah had difficulty believing that her academic difficulties reflected anything other than deep personal flaws.

Over time, Leah staunchly held on to this view of herself as deeply flawed, in a way that exemplifies the diagnosis of OCD *with poor insight* (American Psychiatric Association, 2013). Thus, when we discussed treatment options, Leah was not interested in CBT that would help her directly with her symptoms and was not amenable to the idea that the obsessions were meaningless "brain hiccups." Rather than wanting a didactic, skill-building focus in sessions, Leah wanted to share the many things on her mind—specifically her relationships with family, peers, and teachers—which fueled her distress. She stated that she wanted to use therapy to think and talk about these. Taking her preferences into account in treatment planning (Swift, Callahan, & Vollmer, 2011), I agreed to this treatment focus on her relationships, noting that if she wanted to address OCD symptoms more directly at a later time, we could. Thus, our primary therapeutic modality would be a relational, reflective, and psychodynamic process. Moreover, I conceptualized therapy as aiming to address Leah's underlying maladaptive character patterns (Peebles, 2012) which included entrenched, rigidly held, negative views of herself.

The neuropsychological testing revealed that Leah suffered from attention-deficit/hyperactivity disorder with associated executive functioning weaknesses, as well as some unexpected cognitive unevenness (specifically superior verbal, but poorer nonverbal capacities). I used this diagnostic data to deepen my understanding of Leah's academic difficulties, to help her parents advocate for an Individualized Education Plan (IEP) at school, and to connect her with an executive function coach to assist with completing her homework assignments. Although her OCD symptoms were not a primary direct target of our outpatient therapy, I made sure that they were taken into account in the IEP by attending meetings at her school. Thus, her IEP included such accommodations as encouragement of "good enough" work products, focus on concept mastery rather than volume of output, opportunities for verbal rather than written evaluation, addition of more structure to open-ended assignments (e.g., providing fewer choices of writing topics, as Leah could obsess about choosing the "right" one), and reduction in the volume of take-home work. She now had access to daily one-on-one resource room support. As clinicians working with adolescents, our therapeutic impact transcends our in-session interventions. As with Leah, IEPs can be an essential component in addressing symptoms of OCD and other forms of anxiety.

In individual psychotherapy, I focused on helping Leah to reconsider and modify her entrenched, harsh self-perceptions and judgments. Leah had enormous difficulty accepting my explanations about the role of OCD, as well as her attentional and executive functioning challenges, on her academic functioning. She didn't want to accept her IEP accommodations or the medication consult I was recommending. While she could intellectually understand the psychoeducation I provided that OCD is a neurobiological condition that is not her (or anybody's) fault, she was not able to accept at a deeper, emotional level this explanation that her needs for support and accommodation were justified. Instead, she clung to rigid beliefs that her academic struggles were manifestations of her laziness, irresponsibility, and badness. She stated again that she was letting everyone down. While not imminently suicidal, Leah expressed a belief that she would never feel better, never amount to anything, and would end up letting people down and killing herself eventually.

My own anxiety and urgency to help her feel better led to efforts to weave in some formal psychoeducation and worksheet exercises involving cognitive-restructuring. For example, I worked to help her recognize how her automatic negative thoughts did not match up with the evidence and how those thoughts drove her anxiety, depression and avoidance. We used "thought record" worksheets that involved a series of steps aimed at modifying her maladaptive thoughts, such as identifying "thinking errors," looking for evidence to refute such thoughts, and so forth.

But these cognitive interventions were not compelling to Leah: she did not appreciate my more didactic role in our individual sessions. She said that this approach made sessions "feel like school," which she already hated. I backed off of this cognitive approach, focusing more on listening, empathizing, and clarifying her point of view. I became less didactic at this point in treatment, casting aside the school-like worksheets and pushing her less to reflect on discrepancies between her beliefs and feedback about herself she was getting from other people. She soon agreed to a medication consult, then a trial of antidepressant, and later a psychostimulant. Her mood improved a bit. She was now better able to accept help from her executive function coach to get some difficult assignments completed. However, Leah continued to refuse some IEP accommodations. For instance, she could not accept that she was allowed to complete every other problem on a math assignment. Leah did not like the idea that she needed special accommodations, insisting in black-and-white fashion that it was not fair to her classmates who were required to complete all of the problems.

Leah's movement from this absolutist position was slow. Her attitude shifted in fits and starts over more than 3 years of individual therapy. Over these years, she began to share about new online friendships she developed with other teenagers who were struggling with various emotional and physical disabilities. Leah expressed great compassion for her friends and their plights. Often, she used their traumatic life circumstances to minimize her own difficulties. But often she encouraged them to seek and accept help. In therapy, Leah and I wrestled with the inconsistency between her advice to her friends and her attitude toward her own needs. Her rigid thinking about herself as a lazy failure destined to commit suicide gradually began to change. She increasingly viewed herself in a more balanced way, envisioning a future for herself as a helper/advocate for members of disadvantaged groups.

After about 18 months of therapy, Leah expressed greater hope for her future and our therapeutic alliance felt solid. At this point, Leah was amenable to my suggestion of some circumscribed CBT for one of her OCD symptoms. Leah enjoyed and had a talent for math, but was beginning a high school calculus course that would require a fair amount of homework involving graphing. She was concerned that her perfectionistic obsessions would lead to compulsive erasing and redrawing, rendering a torturous process where she might decide to completely avoid and not even try. I explained to Leah the rationale for exposure with response prevention (ERP) to break the link between obsessions and compulsions. She seemed to understand this.

In subsequent sessions, I assisted Leah to complete sets of graphing problems with the task of making her drawings imperfect. She then would sit with the anxiety in session, learning that she could survive the anxiety and her work would still be good enough. Leah's calculus teacher agreed to look at these practice graphs; he corroborated for her that this level of precision was acceptable in his class. From these exercises, Leah internalized that she could tolerate imperfection and that imperfection would not have catastrophic consequences. These interventions, combined with a highly skilled, warm, and accepting math teacher, contributed to Leah's calculus class of being one of her most rewarding and conflict-free academic experiences in high school.

The above description of a successful symptom-focused CBT intervention to reduce OCD symptoms might imply that Leah's therapy was becoming more straightforward and her progress linear. The reality was messier than that. Getting through high school continued to be challenging for Leah and fraught with anxiety, avoidance, and occasionally deeper depression. High school for Leah involved not only completing required coursework, but navigating relationships with peers and teachers who varied in their ability to accept her IEP and understand Leah's difficulties using more nuanced explanations than "not taking responsibility." Many teachers are not familiar with OCD. Even with some education about mental illness, some teacher struggle to understand that, when a bright student is not completing their schoolwork, it may not be a motivational problem.

In our sessions, Leah was remarkably open about her fears and vulnerabilities. Although not as pronounced as earlier, Leah still expressed worries that she would never be what she and others expected her to be, that she could never be truly happy. She focused on her online relationships, some of which became romantic. I now had opportunities to help her reflect on her anxieties evoked by closeness and to think about what constituted healthy ways of having intimate relationships.

In considering her anxiety about how to be genuine with a partner, Leah began to open up with me, explaining that, since the onset of puberty, she had experienced significant gender dysphoria which made it difficult to let her guard down and be vulnerable. It became clearer that much of her anxiety and anguish about meeting others' expectations was entwined with a sense that she could never be the girl or young woman that others believed and expected her to be. The source of her anxiety-fueling negative thoughts about herself ran much deeper than I realized. At this phase of treatment, we focused on Leah's anxiety and disdain for her developing feminine body, her subjective sense of maleness, and whether and how to come out to family and friends as "Leo." Through our therapeutic work, connecting online with a community of transgender teenagers, and later engaging an in-person support group, Leo did decide to come out. He experienced his parents and other family members as surprisingly supportive and his anxiety was meaningfully reduced. He continued to use psychotherapy to address concerns about gender (including possibilities of hormone treatment and surgery), relationships, growing up, and ways that OCD-driven perfectionism can interfere with task completion. Our therapy continued to involve occasional ERP in order to target recurrent OCD symptomology.

At this point in treatment, our psychotherapy helped him navigate developmental tasks of young adulthood. But Leo's OCD and other symptoms had improved significantly and his depression resolved. He was more engaged with peers, had resumed recreational sports, and was able to graduate high school with his class. Leo began attending college part-time and took a leadership role with a local agency serving young people struggling with gender dysphoria.

Conclusions From Case Examples

The cases of Abbie and Leah/Leo illustrate how adolescents with the same DSM-5 diagnosis, in this case severe OCD, may require very different treatments. Both treatment plans were informed by evidence from RCTs about the efficacy of CBT using ERP, but only Abbie's involved ERP as the primary modality. Abbie's difficulties were mostly OCD-specific, and her work ethic and ready capacity for trust was conducive to a straightforward application of ERP. For Leo, OCD-specific psychoeducation and ERP was applied judiciously and in circumscribed ways in accord with his insight, preferences, state of the therapeutic alliance, and acute needs.

But Leo benefited from a treatment package that entailed so much more than this. Over time, his treatment involved the space to tell his story and articulate his concerns, relational/reflection-promoting interventions, parent and family sessions (psychoeducational interventions, planning at-home exposures, processing dynamics associated with Leo's coming out as transgender), medication, an IEP that took into account his OCD and executive function weaknesses, private executive skills coaching, and participation in support groups. I included each of these approaches thoughtfully, based on a nuanced understanding of my client and rooted in many forms of evidence (such as neuropsychological test findings, alliance factors, client treatment preferences, pharmacological research, and clinical experience). If I had insisted on an only OCD-focused ERP treatment, I doubt that Leo would have remained in treatment.

Psychotherapy research tells us that a "Procrustean bed" approach to treatment is associated with greater risk of drop out and poor outcome (Norcross & Wampold, 2011; Owen & Hilsenroth, 2014). "Procustean bed" is a metaphor for forcing someone or something to fit a pre-existing model. So in psychotherapy, a "Procrustean bed" refers to imposing a particular therapeutic modality regardless of the characteristics, needs, and preferences of individual patients. Research- and clinically informed flexibility in therapeutic approach allowed the space for Leah/Leo to share and address underlying gender dysphoria. His gender dysphoria likely played a significant role in his anxiety, but I didn't know about it and thus couldn't have planned for it at treatment onset.

In our current mental health climate, a DSM-5 diagnosis is often conflated with understanding a person. Sometimes as clinicians, we believe that because a person meets criteria for a particular diagnosis, we know who the person is and exactly what the person needs therapeutically. Further, "evidence-based treatment" is often defined in overly restrictive ways, often limited to findings from disorder-specific RCT research. This narrow definition is typically used in lists of "evidence-based treatments" such as those offered by the Society of Clinical Psychology (2018). Such lists stand in contrast to the broader conceptualization of what constitutes evidence, outlined by the APA Presidential Task Force on Evidence-Based Practice (2006). In keeping with this broader definition, the cases presented here remind us of the wisdom of Shevrin and Shectman (1973): in the process of diagnostic understanding and planning treatment, "the clinician does not have a 'problem' to deal with; rather [the clinician] has a *person* with a problem to deal with" (p. 458, italics added). The two case examples illuminate complex clinical presentations of adolescents with anxiety, as well as integrative approaches for treatment. The cases highlight both the complexities of adolescent anxiety and the importance of tailoring treatment to adolescent individualities.

References

Ansary, N. S., McMahon, T. J., & Luthar, S. S. (2011). Socioeconomic context and emotional behavioral achievement links: Concurrent and prospective associations among low- and high-income youth. *Journal of Research on Adolescence, 22,* 14–30. doi:10.1111/j.1532-7795.2011.00747.x

American Psychiatric Association. (2013). *Diagnostic and statistical manual* (5th ed.), Washington, DC: American Psychiatric Press.

APA Presidential Task Force on Evidence-Based Practice. (2006). Evidence-based practice in psychology. *American Psychologist, 61,* 271–285.

Barrett, P. M., Duffy, A. L., Dadds, M. R., & Rapee, R. M. (2001). Cognitive-behavioral treatment of anxiety disorders in children: Long-term (6-year) follow-up. *Journal of Consulting and Clinical Psychology, 69,* 135–141. doi:10.1037//0022-006X.69.I.135

Beesdo, K., Knappe, S., & Pine, D. S. (2009). Anxiety and anxiety disorders in children and adolescents: Developmental issues and implications for DSM-V. *Psychiatric Clinics of North America, 32*, 483–524. doi:10.1016/j.psc.2009.06.002

Bennet, A., & Stirling, J. (1998). Vulnerability factors in the anxiety disorders. *British Journal of Medical Psychology, 71*, 311–321. doi:10.1111/j.2044-8341.1998.tb00994.x

Berman, S. L., Weems, C. F., Silverman, W. K., & Kurtines, W. M. (2000). Predictors of outcome in exposure-based cognitive and behavioral treatments for phobic and anxiety disorders in children. *Behavior Therapy, 31*, 713–731. doi:10.1016/s0005-7894(00)80040-4

Bram, A. D. (2013). Psychological testing and treatment implications: We can say more. *Journal of Personality Assessment, 95*, 319–331.

Bram, A., & Bjorgvinnson, T. (2004). A psychodynamic clinician's foray into cognitive-behavioral therapy utilizing exposure-response prevention for obsessive-compulsive disorder. *American Journal of Psychotherapy, 58*, 304–320.

Brown, H. (2013). Looking for evidence that works. *New York Times.* Retrieved from https://well.blogs.nytimes.com/2013/03/25/looking-for-evidence-that-therapy-works/

Cartwright-Hatton, S., McNicol, K., & Doubleday, E. (2006). Anxiety in a neglected population: Prevalence of anxiety disorders in pre-adolescent children. *Clinical Psychology Review, 26*, 817–833. doi:10.1016/j.cpr.2005.12.002

Cartwright-Hatton, S., Roberts, C., Chitsabesan, P., Fothergill, C., & Harrington, R. (2004). Systematic review of the efficacy of cognitive behaviour therapies for childhood and adolescent anxiety disorders. *British Journal of Clinical Psychology,43*, 421–436. doi:10.1348/0144665042388928

Chansky, T. E. (2000). *Freeing your child from obsessive-compulsive disorder.* New York, NY: Three Rivers Press.

Columbia University DISC Development Group. (2006). *Interviewer manual.* Retrieved from www.cdc.gov

Costello, E. J., Egger, H. L., Copeland, W., Erkanli, A., & Angold, A. (2005). The developmental epidemiology of anxiety disorders: Phenomenology, prevalence, and comorbidity. *Anxiety Disorders in Children and Adolescents, 14*, 631–648. doi:10.1017/cbo9780511994920.004

Essau, C. A., Conradt, J., & Petermann, F. (2000). Frequency, comorbidity, and psychosocial impairment of anxiety disorders in German adolescents. *Journal of Anxiety Disorders, 14*, 263–279. doi:10.1016/s0887-6185(99)00039-0

Foa, E. B., & Wilson, R. (2009). *Stop obsessing: How to overcome your obsessions and compulsions.* New York, NY: Bantam Books.

Fonagy, P., Allison, L., & Ryan, A. (2017). Therapy outcomes: What works for whom? In N. Midgley, J. Hayes, & M. Cooper (Eds.), *Essential research findings in child and adolescent counseling and psychotherapy* (pp. 79–118). London: SAGE.

Fonagy, P., Target, M., Cottrell, D., Phillips, J., & Kurtz, Z. (2002). *What works for whom? A critical review of treatments for children and adolescents.* New York, NY: Guilford Press.

Geller, D. A., Biederman, J., Faraone, S., Agranat, A., Cradock, K., Hagermoser, L., . . . Coffey, B. J. (2001). Developmental aspects of obsessive compulsive disorder: Findings in children, adolescents, and adults. *The Journal of Nervous and Mental Disease, 189*, 471–477.

Heim, C., & Nemeroff, C. B. (2001). The role of childhood trauma in the neurobiology of mood and anxiety disorders: Preclinical and clinical studies. *Biological Psychiatry, 49*, 1023–1039. doi:10.1016/s0006-3223(01)01157-x

Hollander, E. (2007). Anxiety and OC spectrum disorders over life cycle. *International Journal of Psychiatry in Clinical Practice, 11*, 5–10. doi:10.1080/13651500701388468

Horigian, V. E., Weems, C. F., Robbins, M. S., Feaster, D. J., Ucha, J., Miller, M., & Werstlein, R. (2013). Reductions in anxiety and depression symptoms in youth receiving substance use treatment. *The American Journal on Addictions, 22*, 329–337. doi:10.1111/j.1521-0391.2013.12031.x

International OCD Foundation. (2018). Retrieved February 02, 2018, from https://iocdf.org/

Kaufman, J., Birmaher, B., Axelson D., Perepletchikova, F., Brent, D., & Ryan, M. (2016). *Kiddie-schedule for affective disorders and schizophrenia* (K-SADS-PL DSM-5). Retrieved from https://www.kennedykrieger.org/sites/default/files/community_files/ksads-dsm-5-screener.pdf

Kendall, P. C., Robin, J. A., Hedtke, K. A., Suveg, C., Flannery-Schroeder, E., & Gosch, E. (2005). Considering CBT with anxious youth? Think exposures. *Cognitive and Behavioral Practice, 12*, 136–148. doi:10.1016/s1077-7229(05)80048-3

Kim-Cohen, J., Caspi, A., Moffitt, T. E., Harrington, H., Milne, B. J., & Poulton, R. (2003). Prior juvenile diagnoses in adults with mental disorder. *Archives of General Psychiatry, 60*, 709–717. doi:10.1001/archpsyc.60.7.709

Kumara, H., & Kumar, V. (2016). Impact of cognitive behavior therapy on anxiety and depression in adolescent students. *Journal of Psychological Research, 11*, 77–85.

Lewinsohn, P. M., Zinbarg, R., Seeley, J. R., Lewinsohn, M., & Sack, W. H. (1997). Lifetime comorbidity among anxiety disorders and between anxiety disorders and other mental disorders in adolescents. *Journal of Anxiety Disorders, 11*, 377–394. doi:10.1016/s0887-6185(97)00017-0

March, J. S., & Mulle, K. (1998). *OCD in children and adolescent: A cognitive-behavioral treatment manual.* New York, NY: Guilford Press.

Merikangas, K. R. (2005). Vulnerability factors for anxiety disorders in children and adolescents. *Child and Adolescent Psychiatric Clinics of North America, 14*, 649–679. doi:doi:10.1016/j.chc.2005.06.005

Merikangas, K. R., He, J., Burstein, M., Swanson, S. A., Avenevoli, S., Cui, L., . . . Swendsen, J. (2010). Lifetime prevalence of mental disorders in U.S. adolescents: Results from the national comorbidity survey replication—adolescent supplement (NCS-A). *Journal of the American Academy of Child & Adolescent Psychiatry, 49*, 980–989.

Midgley, N., & Kennedy, E. (2011). Psychodynamic psychotherapy for children and adolescents: A critical review of the evidence base. *Journal of Child Psychotherapy, 37*, 232–260. doi:10.1080/0075417x.2011.614738

Moffitt, T. E., Harrington, H., Caspi, A., Kim-Cohen, J., Goldberg, D., Gregory, A. M., & Poulton, R. (2007). Depression and generalized anxiety disorder: Cumulative and sequential comorbidity in a birth cohort followed prospectively to age 32 years. *Archives of General Psychiatry, 64*, 651–660.

Nakatani, E., Mataix-Cols, D., Micali, N., Turner, C., & Heyman, I. (2009). Outcomes of cognitive behaviour therapy for obsessive compulsive disorder in a clinical setting: A 10-year experience from a specialist OCD service for children and adolescents. *Child and Adolescent Mental Health, 14*, 133–139. doi:10.1111/j.1475-3588.2008.00509.x

Norcross, J. C., & Wampold, B. E. (2011). What works for whom: Tailoring psychotherapy to the person. *Journal of Clinical Psychology, 67*, 127–132.

Owen, J., & Hilsenroth, M. J. (2014). The importance of therapist flexibility in relation to therapy outcomes. *Journal of Consulting Psychology, 61*, 280–288.

Pao, M., & Bosk, A. (2011). Anxiety in medically ill children/adolescents. *Depression and Anxiety, 28*, 40–49. doi:10.1002/da.20727

Peebles, M. J. (2012). *Beginnings: The art and science of planning psychotherapy* (2nd ed.). New York, NY: Routledge.

Pine, D. S., Cohen, P., Gurley, D., Brook, J., & Ma, Y. (1998). The risk for early-adulthood anxiety and depressive disorders in adolescents with anxiety and depressive disorders. *Archives of General Psychiatry, 55*, 56–64.

Richardson, L. P., Lozano, P., Russo, J., McCauley, E., Bush, T., & Katon, W. (2006). Asthma symptom burden: Relationship to asthma severity and anxiety and depression symptoms. *Pediatrics, 118*, 1042–1051. doi:10.1542/peds.2006-0249

Shedler, J. (2010). The efficacy of psychodynamic psychotherapy. *American Psychologist, 65*, 98–109. doi:10.1037/a0018378

Shevrin, H., & Shectman, F. (1973). The diagnostic process in psychiatric evaluations. *Bulletin of the Menninger Clinic, 37*, 451–494.

Simon, E., & Bögels, S. M. (2009). Screening for anxiety disorders in children. *European Child and Adolescent Psychiatry, 18*, 625–634. doi:10.1007/s00787-009-0023-x

Society of Clinical Psychology. (2018). Treatments. Retrieved 2/10/18 from https://www.div12.org/psychological-treatments/treatments.

Suliman, S., Mkabile, S. G., Fincham, D. S., Ahmed, R., Stein, D. J., & Seedat, S. (2009). Cumulative effect of multiple trauma on symptoms of posttraumatic stress disorder, anxiety, and depression in adolescents. *Comprehensive Psychiatry, 50*, 121–127. doi:10.1016/j.comppsych.2008.06.006

Swift, J. K., Callahan, J. L., & Vollmer, B. M. (2011). Preferences. *Journal of Clinical Psychology, 67*, 155–165.

Vine, M., Stoep, A. V., Bell, J., Rhew, I. C., Gudmundsen, G., & McCauley, E. (2012). Associations between household and neighborhood income and anxiety symptoms in young adolescents. *Depression and Anxiety, 29*, 824–832. doi:10.1002/da.21948

Westen, D., & Morrison, K. (2001). A multidimensional meta-analysis of treatments of depression, panic, and generalized anxiety disorder. An empirical examination of the status of empirically supported therapies. *Journal of Consulting and Clinical Psychology, 69*, 875–899.

Wong, Q. J. J., & Rapee, R. M. (2015). The development psychopathology of social anxiety and phobia in adolescents. In K. Ranta, A. M. La Greca, L.-J. Garcia-Lopez, & M. Marttunen (Eds.), *Social anxiety and phobia in adolescents: Development, manifestation, and intervention strategies* (pp. 11–37). Switzerland: Springer International.

Zehe, J. M., Colder, C. R., Read, J. P., Wieczorek, W. F., & Lengua, L. J. (2013). Social and generalized anxiety symptoms and alcohol and cigarette use in early adolescence: The moderating role of perceived peer norms. *Addictive Behaviors, 38*, 1931–1939. doi:10.1016/j.addbeh.2012.11.013

7

Evidence-Based Interventions
for Adolescent Depression

Joanna E. Bettmann and Bryan Casselman

Adolescents are currently more depressed than at any time in modern American history, with rates consistently rising since the 1930s (Twenge et al., 2010). In 2015, 12.5% of the U.S. adolescent population reported a depressive episode in the previous year (Center for Behavioral Health Statistics and Quality, 2016). The numbers of adolescents diagnosed with clinical depression increased by 37% in the past decade (Mojtabai, Olfson, & Han, 2016). Moreover, depression is the largest psychiatric risk factor for adolescent suicidality, increasing the risk for suicide 6 fold (Auerbach, Stewart, & Johnson, 2017; Nock et al., 2013). As a result, suicide is the second leading cause of adolescent deaths (Center for Disease Control, 2016). However, only 40.3% of depressed adolescents receive treatment (Mojtabai et al., 2016). Thus, clinicians need to know what contributes to adolescent depression, how to assess for it, and how to treat it. This chapter will address all of those components.

Depression rates tends to spike just after puberty, peaking at age 13 and stabilizing in early adulthood (Sallis et al., 2017). Consequences from adolescent depressive episodes include academic failure (McCarty, 2008; McLeod, Uemura, & Rohrman, 2012), poor peer relations (Eberhart & Hammen, 2006; Prinstein, Cheah, & Guyer, 2005), behavioral problems (Silk, Steinberg, & Morris, 2003; Wolf & Ollendick, 2006), low self-esteem (Orth, Robins, Meier, & Conger, 2016), substance abuse (Edlund et al., 2015; Kilpatrick et al., 2003), loneliness and social isolation (Matthews et al., 2016), and developmental problems in cognitive functioning in areas such as verbal fluency, sustained attention, and memory (Wagner et al., 2015). Further, youth with depressive episodes are more likely to be viewed as "dangerous" (Pescosolido et al., 2007) or to be teased and mocked by their peers for receiving mental health treatment (Moses, 2009).

Relapse after treatment is also a serious concern, as research suggests depression can recur in as many as 70% of depressed adolescents (Curry et al., 2011; Peters et al., 2015). Research also suggests that depressive episodes in adolescence are predictive of future depressive episodes in adulthood (Monroe & Harkness, 2005). Some research on adult depression which originated in childhood show recurrence rates as high as 76% (Kessler, Berglund, & Demler, 2005; Kim-Cohen et al., 2003). Thus, addressing and ameliorating adolescent depression should be of critical concern to clinicians.

Contributing Factors to Adolescent Depression

Depression in adolescents appears influenced by both genetic and environmental contributors. However, the primary influence of either is difficult to untangle. There is substantial evidence of early-onset depression aggregating within families, but research does not explain to what extent genetics or shared environmental factors are responsible for common familial symptoms (Rice, 2010). Currently, there is only one twin study on the heritability of adolescent clinical depression, reporting an average heritability rate of 40% (Glowinski et al., 2003). A large study of adopted-in-infancy and nonadopted adolescents found that adolescents manifested elevated levels of depression if their mothers were depressed, suggesting strong environmental relationship (Tully, Iacono, & McGue, 2008). In that study, adopted adolescents experienced higher risk of depression if their adoptive mothers were depressed, and nonadopted adolescents experienced higher risk of depression if their biological mothers were depressed, showing the significant contribution of environment to adolescents' depression risk. A follow-up study using the same sample found similar results (Marmorstein, Iacono, & McGue, 2012).

Neurological Contributors

However, there are genetic biomarkers associated with depression in adolescents (Xia & Lao, 2015). These biomarkers are largely associated with the serotonergic system (Eley et al., 2004), dopaminergic system (Xia & Lao, 2015), and the synthesis of brain-derived neurotrophic factor (Cruz-Fuentes et al., 2014), suggesting these neurochemical systems may play a role in early-onset depression. Current research suggests hypothalamic-pituitary-adrenal (HPA) dysfunction may be involved in adolescent depression, but more research needs to confirm HPA's relationship to depressive symptoms (Rudolph, Troop-Gordon, Modi, & Granger, 2018). No current literature confirms HPA axis dysregulation as a causal factor in the development of depression (Guerry & Hastings, 2011).

Notably, the brains of depressed adolescents look different compared to their nondepressed peers. There are differences in cortical surface area (Kelly et al., 2013), occurring in the lower anterior cingulate and orbitofrontal cortex surface area in females and in lower right orbitofrontal cortex surface area in males (Schmaal et al., 2017). Larger left-hippocampal size appears to correlate with greater mediation of social contributors to depression in adolescents, suggesting that while neurobiological factors may play a role in the expression of depressive symptoms, the manifestation of depression may depend upon the adolescent's perception of her environment's stability (Schriber et al., 2017).

Environmental Contributors

There also appear to be strong environmental contributors to adolescent depression. For example, research suggests a link between stressful and traumatic events and adolescent depression, finding that those exposed to multiple traumatic incidents experienced more significant depression than those exposed to a single trauma (Suliman et al., 2009). Severe stress or chronic trauma may leave an adolescent with lifelong depression, kindled through adulthood into enduring illness (Monroe & Harkness, 2005).

Maternal depression also links to higher rates of depressive symptoms in their children (Tully, Iacono, & McGue, 2008). Notably, maternal stress regarding finances also appears strongly linked to adolescent depression (Agerup, Lyderson, Wallander, & Sund, 2014). Some literature links paternal depression with adolescent girls' depression: adolescent females who reported significant paternal hostility were particularly at risk of depression if their fathers were depressed (Reeb, Conger, & Wu, 2010). The authors explain their findings by suggesting, "The greater tendency of girls to emphasize or value relationships may translate into risk for depressed mood in the context of paternal depression and hostility" (Reeb et al., 2010, p. 138).

Adolescents raised by single mothers are also at greater risk for depressive symptoms. Specifically, these adolescents report greater amounts of rumination, hyperfocusing on a depressed mood (Daryanani et al., 2017). Relatedly, adolescents in single-mother homes also experience more adverse life events and chronic stressors (Daryanani et al., 2017). Foster care also manifests as a significant risk factor. Youth in foster care are 8 times more likely to be diagnosed with a mental illness than those raised out of the foster care system (Burns et al., 2004). Teenage mothers manifest higher levels of depression than their adult counterparts (Lanzi, Bert, Jacobs, & the Center for the Prevention of Child Neglect, 2009), suggesting yet another link between stress and depression.

Additionally, lower socioeconomic status consistently links to higher rates of adolescent depression (Pino et al., 2018). Adolescents raised in lower income families are more likely to experience stressful situations, such as financial instability, parental divorce or separation, lack of parental support, or residence in higher-crime neighborhoods, which appear correlated with depressive symptoms (Tracy et al., 2008). Adolescents with low socioeconomic status also face significant challenges in accessing mental health services. Barriers to service access include transportation, child care, and even the hours of operation of behavioral health clinics (Borschuk, Jones, Parker, & Crewe, 2015). As a result, children in lower socioeconomic groups are less likely to utilize behavioral health services (Borschuk et al., 2015) and are at greater risk of developing mental illness (Williams, Cunich, & Byles, 2013).

Gender Contributors

Female adolescents are twice as likely to have a depressive episode compared to their male peers (Chuang et al., 2017). However, after treatment and postdepressive episode, adolescent females had no behavioral differences from their peers, while males became more isolated, retained academic and behavior problems, and had lower senses of well-being and self-esteem even after depressive symptoms dissipated (Derdikman-Eiron et al., 2012). The authors state, "When stressed, girls seek support and express their feelings more than boys" (p. 1861). They suggest that adolescent girls' social skills might assist them in getting help and support for their distress, while boys could experience isolation without such skills.

Race as a Risk Factor in Adolescent Depression

Recent data suggest that U.S. adolescents with the highest rate of major depressive disorder are Hispanic adolescents at 8.9%, just above Other race (8.3%), non-Hispanic Black adolescents (8.0%), and non-Hispanic White (7.1%; Avenevoli, Swendsen, He, Burstein, & Merikangas, 2015). However, adolescents from racial minorities appear to utilize mental health services far less than Whites (Avenevoli et al., 2015). A study of suicidal adolescents found that those from ethnic minority groups were far less likely than Whites to utilize inpatient or outpatient mental health services (Wu, Katic, Liu, & Fuller, 2010). Thus, adolescents from racial minority groups are more likely to experience depression, as well as far less likely to be treated for it, issues which should concern us as clinicians.

Technology Use as a Risk Factor in Adolescent Depression

Adolescents' significant use of screen time appears to present a significant risk for depression (Costigan, Barnett, Plotnikoff, & Lubans, 2013; Liu, Wu, & Yao, 2015). One study of young adolescents found that lower levels of leisure-time screen use were associated with lower levels of depression (Kremer et al., 2014). Another study found that the more time adolescents spend on a computer, the poorer their attachment to parents (Richards, McGee, Williams, Welch, & Hancox, 2010). Clinicians should assess all adolescent clients in terms of their screen time, evaluating how technology use influences our clients and may limit their live, not-computerized interpersonal interactions.

Assessing Depression

You can assess depression using standardized measures or your own individual questions. One standardized measure is the Kutcher Adolescent Depression Scale (Zhou et al., 2016), which aims to identify adolescents at risk of depression. The 11- and 6-question forms of the scale are available free at http://teenmentalhealth.org/product/kutcher-adolescent-depression-scale-kads-english/ and do not require specialized training to use. Another standardized measure, the Short Mood and Feelings Questionnaire (Angold, Costello, & Messer, 1995) is a brief screening tool to identify symptom severity. It is available free at https://www.seattlechildrens.org/pdf/PAL/SMFQ-rating-scale.pdf and does not require training to use.

If you are assessing adolescents without standardized measures, ask "How have you been feeling most days, most of the time?" You are trying to see if your client meets criteria for a major depressive episode. Screen for all of the symptoms of major depressive episodes in adolescent-appropriate language. Ask your clients: "Have you noticed that your weight went way up or way down when you weren't trying to make it do that?" "Do you have trouble sleeping? In what way?" "Do you have trouble falling asleep, staying asleep, waking too early, or sleeping too much?" "Do you have trouble keeping your attention on what you are doing or concentrating on what you are trying to do, like at school?" "Have you thought about suicide or ending your life?" "Have you felt hopeless, helpless, or guilty a lot of the time?" "Have you noticed that you have less interest or pleasure in things that you usually enjoy doing?" "Do you feel tired most of the time?" "Do you notice yourself feeling irritated a lot of the time?" Each of these questions is formulated based on DSM-5 symptoms of major depressive episode.

Also, observe your client's motor behavior: does she look agitated or speedy, or slowed down and psychomotor retarded? Psychological symptoms can influence motor behavior, resulting in client's movements looking agitated or slowed. Also, make sure to explore your client's academic functioning, substance use, and disruptive behavior, all of which can be impacted by depression.

When assessing adolescent depression, be aware of the significant diagnostic comorbidities with depression. For example, anxiety and depression frequently co-occur in adolescents, with comorbidity as high as 75% (Garber & Weersing, 2010). Attention-deficit/hyperactivity disorder (ADHD) is commonly comorbid with depression at 20 to 47% (Biederman et al., 2008), as are substance use disorders at 35% (Deas & Brown, 2006), and anorexia nervosa at 34.5% (Bühren et al., 2014). Chronic physical illnesses also link to adolescent depression; this is perhaps not surprising, as those who have chronic medical conditions experience social isolation, activity restriction, treatment side effects, and symptoms of physical illness (Pinquart & Shen, 2011). So be sure to assess for the presence of any significant or chronic medical concerns in each adolescent client.

You will also need to screen carefully for suicidality, as depressed adolescents are at increased risk for suicide attempts and completion (Auerbach et al., 2017; Nock et al., 2013). Review Chapter 4 of this book, which explains in depth how to assess for suicidal risk in adolescents.

Case Studies

Several case examples will illuminate what depression can look like in adolescents. Marian was a 17-year-old adolescent girl who presented to an outpatient community mental health clinic with symptoms of unremitting depression. She identified as a Pacific Islander by ethnicity and detailed her family of origin as low income. She described depression that began when she was 11 and continued unabated to the present day. She explained that her mother had also dealt with severe depression for her entire adult life.

Marian described a pleasant childhood, living with married parents and several siblings. She detailed happy times in her youth and denied any history of trauma or neglect, points which were reinforced by her mother's reports. However, she described that depression descended on her like an enormous wave—pushing her down—when she was 11. She explained that she had near-constant but passive thoughts of suicidality ever since then, anhedonia, difficulty concentrating, difficulty falling and staying asleep while also sometimes sleeping too much, feelings of hopelessness, and overwhelming low mood the majority of the time. She delivered this narrative in a low, slow monotone voice—displaying signs of psychomotor retardation in slowed body movements, as well. Marian was slightly overweight, but explained that her weight had been relatively stable over time.

In terms of family history, Marian detailed significant mental illness in both her parents' families. Within her mother's family, there was severe depression in Marian's mother, as well as bipolar illness in Marian's maternal grandmother. Marian also reported that her maternal great-grandfather committed suicide. In her father's family, there was a history of substance use disorders, as well as trauma and some mood disorders of moderate severity.

Marian reported that she had been taking a tricyclic anti-depressant for months, prescribed by her mother's psychiatrist. Marian's mother explained that she had been helped somewhat by similar medications. However, Marian reported increased fatigue and excessive sleepiness since taking the medication. Marian reported that she was doing okay in school, mostly getting low

B's and high C's, but didn't have much energy to engage with her peers. In session, Marian was cooperative and appeared to answer questions openly.

I assessed Marian as clearly meeting criteria for major depressive disorder, recurrent, severe. In collaboration with both Marian and her parents, I (JEB) developed a treatment plan which included weekly individual therapy, a support group for other adolescent girls with depression, and medication evaluation with a new psychiatrist for consideration of medications with fewer side effects. We agreed to reevaluate Marian's symptoms after 4 weeks of this intensive, multi-pronged treatment approach.

Another adolescent I (JEB) worked with in an outpatient community mental health setting was a 15-year-old African-American boy named Max. His parents sought treatment for his low-grade but long-standing symptoms of depression. Max often looked irritable, instead of depressed. He tended to snap at his parents, siblings, teachers, and peers—particularly when tired or frustrated. He ate little, reported low energy, and had difficulty focusing in class. He and his parents reported that his symptoms began when he was 13, but all denied difficult life events or trauma occurring at that time or previously. He denied current or historical suicidal ideation.

Max appeared irritable in his initial session with me. Everything I said seemed to annoy him. He didn't detail a history of oppositional behavior, but rather reported his frequent feeling that everyone was doing things wrong. He seemed tired and disengaged. He reported little interest in getting to know anything new. He expressed little interest when I tried to engage him in a conversation about his favorite foods and places to visit. Max expressed frustration at having to talk to a therapist and asked if he could go lie down somewhere. In his first few sessions, he showed little engagement or interest in anything, was often frustrated and irritable with small issues, and continued his pattern of eating little at home.

Max appeared to meet criteria for persistent depressive disorder (dysthymia). He manifested a primarily irritable presentation of depression, which sometimes is difficult to disentangle diagnostically from disruptive behavior disorders. However, Max and his parents reported no history of his rule breaking, criminal behaviors, disruptive behaviors, or oppositional behavior specifically with authority figures. All people irritated Max, whether they were authority figures or not. These reports suggest his symptoms map better onto an irritable presentation of a depressive disorder than oppositional defiant disorder. Following a thorough assessment process with both Max and his caregivers, I developed a treatment plan which included weekly individual therapy, medication evaluation with a psychiatrist due to the 2-year duration of his symptoms, and group therapy with depressed peers.

Depression can look very different in different adolescent clients. Youth depression can look more irritable than sad; depression can be a matter of weeks, months, or even years. Some depressed adolescents will be suicidal, while others will manifest simply with low or irritable mood without suicidality. Depression might appear following a difficult life event, trauma, or series of traumas—or it might appear out of the blue with no apparent precipitant. Clinicians screening adolescents for depression need to remember how diverse the presentation of depression will be.

Treatment for Adolescent Depression

Pharmacotherapy

Significant research suggests the efficacy of pharmacotherapy in the treatment of adolescent depression, specifically selective serotonin reuptake inhibitor (SSRI) medications (Usala, Clavenna, Zuddas, & Bonati, 2008). However, before recommending pharmacotherapy, clinicians should carefully assess each adolescent. Some suggest monitoring adolescents for a few weeks before beginning pharmacotherapy (Goodyer et al., 2008). However, each adolescent's treatment plan will vary depending upon the needs and wishes of the client, the wishes of their caregivers, the severity of the client's symptoms, and their suicidality.

Clinicians should be aware of some cautions in pharmacological treatment. Adolescents prescribed tricyclic antidepressants, an older type of antidepressants, can more easily overdose and experience severe medical consequences, compared to SSRIs which are more commonly prescribed (Sheridan, Lin, & Horowitz, 2017). Additionally, the U.S. Food and Drug Administration issued regulations in 2004 requiring manufacturers of antidepressants to include a "black box" warning on labels which stated that the products may increase suicidality for young adults aged 18 to 24 (Food and Drug Administration, 2004). This decision came after a comprehensive review of 372 placebo-controlled trials with more than 100,000 subjects discovered that the suicidality rate of drug-treated subjects was double that of those treated with a placebo, 4 and 2% respectively (Laughren, 2006). While antidepressants appear to evidence protective qualities against suicide in adolescents (Dubicka & Brent, 2017), clinicians should discuss the implications of the black box warning with the adolescent and her family so they can make the best decision regarding medication use (Newman, 2004).

Cognitive Behavioral Therapy

Psychotherapy is an evidence-based approach for treating adolescent depression. Although many forms of psychotherapy for depression exist, cognitive behavioral therapy (CBT) and interpersonal therapy are the psychotherapeutic treatments for adolescent depression with the strongest research support (Sburlati, Lyneham, Mufson, & Schniering, 2012).

A significant body of research has established CBT as an efficacious treatment for adolescent depression (Oar, Johnco, & Ollendick, 2017). CBT also appears to have a small but substantial *preventative* effect toward the development of depression (Hetrick et al., 2016). CBT for adolescent depression is typically delivered in 12 to 15 weekly individual sessions, followed by 2 months of biweekly meetings and gradual termination with monthly sessions (Vitiello, 2009). While CBT is a specific approach, clinicians must modify treatment to the individual circumstances of the adolescent in question, incorporating and responding to their interests, identities, and family dynamics (David-Ferdon & Kaslow, 2008).

Research shows the efficacy of one psychoeducational CBT protocol, Adolescents Coping with Depression (Clarke, Lewinsohn, & Hops, 1990; David-Ferdon & Kaslow, 2008). This CBT approach consists of 16 2-hour group therapy sessions held over an 8-week period, a separate support group for their parents, and a brief individual CBT program for youth on SSRI medications (Rohde, 2017). These interventions do not need to be delivered concurrently. Manuals for these treatments are available for free here: https://research.kpchr.org/Research/Research-Areas/Mental-Health/Youth-Depression-Programs. The Adolescents Coping with Depression CBT protocol focuses on eight core treatment components:

1. Clinician explains depression and how it can be treated by Cognitive Behavioral Therapy.
2. Clinician focuses on modifying client's depressive cognitions, as well as identifying, challenging, and changing negative beliefs and thought processes. For example, a clinician might use the comic strip *Garfield* in

a psychoeducational intervention to illustrate depressotypic behaviors and explain how to generate positive alternative thoughts in response to each adolescent's specific triggers.

3. Clinician provides training in problem solving and communication techniques. These techniques can include problem-solving strategies like brainstorming, evaluating options, defining problems, and specifying an agreement between parties, and communication skills such as active listening and expressing negative and positive thoughts.

4. Clinician provides training in social skills, including basic conversation, making friends, and planning activities.

5. Clinician teaches deep breathing techniques, muscle relaxation exercises, etc. due to depression's frequent comorbidity with anxiety.

6. The adolescent monitors her mood daily in order to create baseline data, noting any changes and improvements from any new skill practices.

7. The adolescent sets realistic goals to increase the frequency and variability of enjoyable activities. These goals are monitored and modified as needed.

8. The intervention concludes with relapse prevention, coalescing the skills learned throughout the treatment with a discussion about possible future problems and a life plan for the adolescent. (Clarke et al., 1990)

Common components of CBT approaches for children and adolescents include providing psychoeducation about depression and its treatment, helping clients to achieve measurable goals, increasing clients' competence in specific life areas, increasing clients' self-monitoring, improving their relationship skills, modifying their negative thoughts, enhancing their problem-solving skills, and improving management of their behaviors (Dietz et al., 2014; Kennard et al., 2009; McCarty & Weisz, 2007).

Some research critiques the CBT approach. Specifically, a manualized CBT treatment (20 individual sessions delivered over 30 weeks) was no better than a brief manualized psychosocial intervention (12 individual sessions plus several family/marital sessions delivered over 20 weeks) or brief manualized psychoanalytic therapy (28 individual sessions delivered over 30 weeks) after 12 months of follow-up (Goodyer et al., 2017). Research also suggests that adolescents whose mothers have significant depressive symptoms may benefit less from CBT in terms of gaining problem-solving skills, so alternative forms of therapy such as systemic behavior family therapy should be considered for these clients (Dietz et al., 2014).

CBT Combined With Pharmacotherapy

Multiple studies document the results of combining pharmacotherapy and CBT with mixed results. The Treatment of Adolescents with Depression Study was the first extensive placebo-controlled study of adolescent depression treatment (March et al., 2006). This study observed 439 adolescents ages 12 to 17 between 13 clinical sites, dividing the subjects into the following treatment groups: fluoxetine (Prozac) only, placebo medication, CBT only, and combined treatment (CBT plus Prozac). After 12 weeks of treatment, the groups with the greatest improvement were combined treatment (73%) and fluoxetine (62%), followed by CBT (48%), and placebo (35%; March et al., 2006). All three nonplacebo groups appeared to continue to improve through the maintenance phase at 36 weeks and follow-up at 52 weeks (Rohde et al., 2008). Some suggest that this study utilized subjects with more severe symptoms and this may account for why CBT was less effective than combined treatment or pharmacotherapy (Daviss, 2010). Some also suggest that the CBT delivered in other studies was more flexible than the model used in this study (Apter, Kronenburg, & Brent, 2005). Notably, the combined treatment group had fewer suicide attempts (8.4%) than the Prozac-only cohort (14.7%). Combined treatment, however, is typically more expensive than pharmacotherapy alone and requires the adolescent to engage regularly with multiple professionals: one who prescribes the medication and one who provides the therapy (Kratochvil & Vitiello, 2008; Vitiello, 2009).

Two other large studies have done similar investigations. The Adolescent Depression and Psychotherapy Trial study observed 208 adolescents treated in the National Health System in the United Kingdom, with grouping identical to the Treating Adolescents with Depression Study (Goodyer et al., 2007). The U.K. study found no difference between combined treatment and pharmacotherapy alone (Wilkinson et al., 2011). But the U.K. study consisted of subjects with more severe symptoms than previous investigations (Vitiello, 2009). Thus, combined treatment may be more effective for adolescents with mild to moderate symptoms (Curry et al., 2006).

The Treatment of SSRI-Resistant Depression in Adolescents study also compared pharmacotherapy alone versus combined treatment, but in adolescents whose symptoms were resistant to previously prescribed SSRI medications (Brent et al., 2008). This study found that combined treatment was more successful than pharmacotherapy alone after the first 12 weeks of treatment (Brent et al., 2008). The researchers found that adolescents whose depressive symptomology persisted after 24 weeks of treatment appeared to have more severe depression, greater family conflict, presence of substance use, and comorbid anxiety disorders (Emslie et al., 2009). In summary, research suggests that CBT alone is an efficacious approach for adolescent depression and that CBT combined with pharmacotherapy should be considered.

Interpersonal Therapy

Research suggests the efficacy of Interpersonal Psychotherapy for Depressed Adolescents (IPT-A; Mufson et al., 2004; Mufson & Sills, 2006; Mufson, Weissman, Moreau, & Garfinkel, 1999). The IPT-A approach frames depression as stemming from interpersonal problems within each adolescent's life and thus focuses on treating clients' poor social support, insecure attachment style, attachment losses, maladaptive communication patterns, and poor problem-solving skills (David-Ferdon & Kaslow, 2008; Mychailyszyn & Elson, 2018; O'Shea, Spence, & Donovan, 2014). IPT-A focuses on four categories: grief, interpersonal role disputes, role transitions, and interpersonal deficits, understanding problems in these areas as linked to adolescents' depression (Mufson, Gallagher, Dorta, & Young, 2004).

The treatment goals of IPT-A fit the needs of adolescent populations: focusing on individuation, establishing autonomy, developing romantic relationships, coping with loss and death, and managing peer pressure (Mufson & Sills, 2006). By helping each adolescent identify and understand problematic triggers and behaviors, the clinician works with each adolescent client to improve his interpersonal interactions (Wolff et al., 2017). An important aspect of IPT-A is the inclusion of the adolescent's parents in the therapy (Gunlicks-Stoessel & Mufson, 2016). When clinicians educate parents about depression's mechanisms, parents are less likely to blame their child for depressive symptoms and more likely to be optimistic about recovery (Mufson & Sills, 2006). IPT-A is delivered in both individual and group approaches (Mychailyszyn & Elson, 2018).

IPT-A typically lasts 12–16 sessions. The following three-phase structure of IPT-A is a guide; the length of the treatment is up to the clinician and centers on the needs and progress of each adolescent (Mufson & Sills, 2006).

Initial Phase of IPT-A Treatment. This phase includes the first one to four sessions (Mufson et al., 2004). In this phase, clinicians meet with the adolescent and her caregivers individually (Mufson & Sills, 2006). These first meetings have three goals. The first goal is to explain the nature, implications, prevalence, and symptoms of depression to the client and her caregivers (Brunstein-Klomek et al., 2017). The clinician also assigns the client to what is known as the Limited Sick Role, in which the clinician defines depression as a medical illness and encourages adolescents to work actively on improving their symptomology (Mufson & Sills, 2006). The clinician explains the adolescent's symptoms as being outside of her control and not due to personal deficits (Brunstein-Klomek et al., 2017). This stance shifts the blame for the adolescent's behavior from herself to the depressive disorder, allowing the family to be more understanding and more encouraging (Mufson & Sills, 2006). Finally, the clinician explains that the treatment will focus on the depressive symptoms and how they affect the adolescent's relationships (Mufson & Sills, 2006). The clinician also asks clients to rank their mood on a scale of 1 to 10 during each visit, something continued throughout the middle phase (Jacobson & Mufson, 2012; Mufson & Sills, 2006).

During the remaining three sessions of the initial phase, the clinician conducts an interpersonal inventory with the adolescent in order to identify problems contributing to the disorder (Mufson et al., 2004). The clinician conducts this inventory by asking the adolescent for basic information regarding the relationships in their life and then more detailed questions in order to determine which existing relationships may be influencing depressive symptoms (Markowitz & Weissman, 2004). The interpersonal inventory is a diagnostic tool through which the clinician can detect relational patterns in the adolescent's life, giving a window into maladaptive interpersonal dynamics (Mufson & Sills, 2006). The clinician uses this tool to help target criteria to focus on in therapy (Mychailyszyn & Elson, 2018). Finally, the clinician establishes a treatment contract with the adolescent (Mufson & Sills, 2006). This contract outlines the roles of the clinician and the adolescent, while setting guidelines for the parents (Mellin & Beamish, 2002). The treatment goals should be attainable and personalized to the adolescent, emphasizing the reduction of depressive symptoms and enhanced interpersonal skills (Mufson & Sills, 2006).

Middle Phase. This phase typically lasts from four to eight sessions (Hall & Mufson, 2009; Mychailyszyn & Elson, 2018). This phase aims to accomplish three goals: (1) further clarification of maladaptive relationship themes; (2) formation of strategies for confronting identified problems; and (3) the implementation of interventions to relieve depressive symptoms (Mufson & Sills, 2006). During this phase, the clinician monitors the adolescent's symptoms while focusing on the problems and critical areas identified in the initial phase (Mufson et al., 2004). The clinician may choose from a number of therapeutic techniques to utilize, including interviewing, supportive acknowledgment, and encouraging the adolescent to discuss difficult topics (Mufson & Sills, 2006).

IPT-A utilizes communicative analysis technique. This approach asks the clinician to walk the adolescent through a recent experience, exploring possible alternative scenarios if different choices were made and what the impact of those choices might have had on the adolescent's feelings regarding the situation (Hall & Mufson, 2009). Clinicians can also use this technique to explore scenarios that have gone poorly so the adolescent has background to handle similar situations in the future (Mufson & Sills, 2006). Clinicians using this technique can discuss the situations with client or role play in session (Mufson et al., 2004). Through these role plays, the clinician emphasizes to clients the importance of experimenting with new interpersonal strategiess (Mufson & Sills, 2006). Most sessions in middle phase will be individual sessions with the adolescents, although parents can be invited to collaborative sessions during this phase in order to review the therapy's progress (Mufson et al., 2004).

Termination Phase. This phase involves the final three to four sessions (Mufson & Sills, 2006; Mychailyszyn & Elson, 2018). During these sessions, the clinician reviews the adolescent's progress on previously identified goals and identifies areas for improvement (Mufson & Sills, 2006). The clinician should explore how positive changes in symptomology may link to improved interpersonal relationships. The adolescent also explores what was most helpful during the therapy (Mufson et al., 2004). Clinicians should be mindful of potential relapse into depressive symptoms and should review with clients and their caregivers the triggers for depressive episodes, suggesting when further treatment might be needed (Hall & Mufson, 2009). This is especially true if the adolescent is still experiencing symptoms or is suffering from another disorder (Mufson & Sills, 2006). The therapist should also meet with the adolescent's caregivers for a termination session, either separately or with their child (Mufson & Sills, 2006). This session should prepare the caregivers to support their child's symptoms at home and to know when symptoms are warning signs of future depressive episodes (Mufson et al., 2004).

Interpersonal psychotherapy shows a medium to large effect size (Gunlicks-Stoessel, Mufson, Jekal, & Turner, 2011). IPT-A may be especially useful with adolescents who have a significant amount of interpersonal conflict with family and friends. Research also suggests that, when provided by school counselors, IPT-A may keep adolescents from leaving school for academic or behavioral reasons (Young, Kranzler, Gallop, & Muffson, 2012). The IPT Institute offers trainings in IPT for clinicians and students; information is available here: https://iptinstitute.com/ipt-training/ipt-training-overview/.

Bibliotherapy and Other Approaches

Bibliotherapy, which is psychological treatment via self-help books or other forms of media, is an accessible and effective psychotherapeutic intervention for adolescents with depression and anxiety, according to meta-analyses (Yuan et al., 2018). Bibliotherapy is appealing, in part, due to its easy access as a form of treatment (Bekker, Griffiths, & Barrett, 2016). While bibliotherapy has poorer outcomes compared to CBT for depressed adolescents (Rohde, Stice, Shaw, & Gau, 2015), clinicians should consider utilizing bibliotherapy adjunctively for clients transitioning out of therapy, those who cannot attend treatment regularly, or in conjunction with other treatment approaches. Regardless of what therapy you utilize, you must evaluate its effectiveness throughout treatment. See the section on "Routine Outcome Monitoring" in Chapter 5, "Building Therapeutic Alliance With Adolescents" for suggestions about instruments you can use to monitor process and outcomes of treatment.

Contributors to Successful Treatment: Familial Factors

Clinicians treating adolescents should consider the adolescents' caregivers' own mental health. Mothers of depressed adolescents in treatment who displayed symptoms of subclinical depression showed symptom improvement similar to that of their child without being in individual therapy, suggesting that adolescent therapy may benefit other family members without their own individual therapy (Perloe, Esposito-Smythers, Curby, & Renshaw, 2014).

Further, treating parents' depression can decrease depressive symptoms in their children, so clinicians should make treatment referrals for adolescent's caregivers when appropriate (Keller & Gottlieb, 2012). One study found that a majority of parents found value in a family-centered CBT session, and it addressed questions and fears they had about their child's care (Asarnow, Scott, & Mintz, 2002).

Providing Culturally Sensitive Treatment for Adolescent Depression

Clinicians should keep in mind the ethnicity of their clients when setting up treatment plans, as people from different cultures will respond differently to treatment (Huey & Polo, 2008). The treatment experience will be filtered through each client's cultural lens. Given the historical mistreatment of some U.S. people of color by White health professionals (Corbie-Smith, 1999), some racial or ethnic groups may have justifiable difficulty trusting mental health clinicians. Research suggests that some people of color are more likely than Whites to distrust mental health professionals (Brown et al., 2010), seeking resources from emergency clinics and religious leaders instead (Ayalon & Young, 2005). Some from minoritized populations may have concerns about their child's diagnoses, afraid they may be stigmatized by the diagnosis which would add to the societal discrimination they already face (Breland-Noble, Bell, Burriss, & AAKOMA Project Adult Advisory Board, 2011). Clinicians must work hard to engender parents' trust in them. When clinicians educate parents about their child's mental health issues and engage them as partners in treatment, parents may be more open to and supportive of their child's treatment.

Therapists also should be aware of their own ethno-cultural biases and attitudes, considering how their biases and attitudes could impact adolescents and their parents. Clinicians need to be mindful of the differences between the cultures in which they were raised and the families with whom they work (Hsieh & Bean, 2014). Some research suggests that class differences between behavioral health specialists and their clients may cultivate misunderstandings and impede a sense of trust between them (Krupnick & Melnikoff, 2012), so clinicians should give careful consideration to socioeconomic differences between themselves and their clients.

Research suggests that, in some ethnic groups within the United States, adolescents may feel caught between their depressive symptoms and aspects of their families' traditional culture (Hsieh & Bean, 2014), due in part to stigma around depression (Fogel & Ford, 2005). Families from some cultures might find it hard to accept a depression diagnosis for their child, interpreting the depressive symptoms instead as laziness or selfishness. Culturally specific characteristics of some families, such as the importance of "saving face" or protecting the reputation of the family, may be a further obstacle to treatment (Hsieh & Bean, 2014). Some family members may expect clinicians to be the "expert," quickly resolving their child's depression (Chen & Davenport, 2005).

Be mindful that people from cultures different from yours may act differently than you expect. Be mindful of your client and family's culture: assess what they are expecting from you. How do they understand the diagnosis you have given their child? What are their expectations of that diagnosis or its treatment? What do they need from you in order to feel like partners in the treatment you provide? Providing culturally responsive treatment for adolescent depression means monitoring your own biases, assessing each family's culture, and adjusting your treatment to each family's cultural context.

Conclusion

This chapter addressed the risk factors for adolescent depression, how to assess adolescents for depression, and how to treat them. Depression manifests differently in different adolescent clients, so you must customize treatment for each adolescent's specific symptoms, wishes for treatment, needs, environment, cultural identities, family environment, and other factors. Using the available research presented here, make the best decisions you can for each individual client.

References

Agerup, T., Lydersen, S., Wallander, J., & Sund, A. M. (2014). Longitudinal course of diagnosed depression from ages 15 to 20 in a community sample: Patterns and parental risk factors. *Child Psychiatry & Human Development, 45,* 753–764. doi:https://doi.org/10.1007/s10578-014-0444-8

Angold, A., Costello, E. J., & Messer, S. C. (1995). Development of a short questionnaire for use in epidemiological studies of depression in children and adolescents. *International Journal of Methods in Psychiatric Research, 5,* 237–249.

Apter, A., Kronenburg, S., & Brent, D. (2005). Turning darkness into light: A new landmark study on the treatment of adolescent depression. Comments on the TADS study. *European Child and Adolescent Psychiatry, 14,* 113–116. doi:10.1007/s00787-005-0474-7

Asarnow, J. R., Scott, C. V., & Mintz, J. (2002). A combined cognitive–behavioral family education intervention for depression in children: A treatment development study. *Cognitive Therapy and Research, 26,* 221–229.

Auerbach, R. P., Stewart, J. G., & Johnson, S. L. (2017). Impulsivity and suicidality in adolescent inpatients. *Journal of Abnormal Child Psychology, 45,* 91–103. doi:https://doi.org/10.1016/j.jad.2015.08.034

Avenevoli, S., Swendsen, J., He, J. P., Burstein, M., & Merikangas, K. R. (2015). Major depression in the National Comorbidity Survey–Adolescent Supplement: Prevalence, correlates, and treatment. *Journal of the American Academy of Child & Adolescent Psychiatry, 54,* 37–44. doi:https://doi.org/10.1016/j.jaac.2014.10.010

Ayalon, L., & Young, M. A. (2005). Racial group differences in help-seeking behaviors. *The Journal of Social Psychology, 145,* 391–404. doi:https://doi.org/10.3200/SOCP.145.4.391-404

Bekker, M. J., Griffiths, K. M., & Barrett, P. M. (2016). Improving accessibility of cognitive behavioural therapy for children and adolescents: Review of evidence and future directions. *Clinical Psychologist, 21,* 157–164. doi:https://doi.org/10.1111/cp.12099

Borschuk, A. P., Jones, H. A., Parker, K. M., & Crewe, S. (2015). Delivery of behavioral health services in a pediatric primary care setting: A case illustration with adolescent depression. *Clinical Practice in Pediatric Psychology, 3,* 142. doi:http://dx.doi.org/10.1037/cpp0000087

Breland-Noble, A. M., Bell, C. C., Burriss, A., & AAKOMA Project Adult Advisory Board. (2011). "Mama just won't accept this": Adult perspectives on engaging depressed African American teens in clinical research and treatment. *Journal of Clinical Psychology in Medical Settings, 18,* 225–234.

Brent, D., Emslie, G., Clarke, G., Wagner, K. D., Asarnow, J. R., Keller, M., . . . Zelazny, J. (2008). Switching to another SSRI or to venlafaxine with or without Cognitive Behavioral Therapy for adolescents with SSRI-resistant depression: The TORDIA randomized controlled trial. *Journal of the American Medical Association, 299,* 901–913. doi:10.1001/jama.299.8.901

Brown, C., Conner, K. O., Copeland, V. C., Grote, N., Beach, S., . . . Reynolds, C. F., III. (2010). Depression, stigma, race, and treatment seeking behavior and attitudes. *Journal of Community Psychology, 38,* 350–368. doi:http://dx.doi.org/10.1002/jcop.20368

Brunstein-Klomek, A., Kopelman-Rubin, D., Apter, A., Argintaru, H., & Mufson, L. (2017). A pilot feasibility study of interpersonal psychotherapy in adolescents diagnosed with specific learning disorders, attention deficit hyperactive disorder, or both with depression and/or anxiety symptoms (IPT-ALD). *Journal of Psychotherapy Integration, 27,* 526–539. doi:http://dx.doi.org/10.1037/int0000036

Bühren, K., Schwarte, R., Fluck, F., Timmesfeld, N., Krei, M., Egberts, K., . . . Herpertz-Dahlmann, B. (2014). Comorbid psychiatric disorders in female adolescents with first-onset anorexia nervosa. *European Eating Disorders Review, 22,* 39–44. doi:10.1002/erv.2254

Burns, B. J., Phillips, S. D., Wagner, H. R., Barth, R. P., Kolko, D. J., Campbell, Y., & Landsverk, J. (2004). Mental health need and access to mental health services by youths involved with child welfare: A national survey. *Journal of the American Academy of Child & Adolescent Psychiatry, 43*, 960–970. doi:https://doi.org/10.1097/01.chi.0000127590.95585.65

Center for Behavioral Health Statistics and Quality. (2016). *Key substance use and mental health indicators in the United States: Results from the 2015 National Survey on Drug Use and Health* (HHS Publication No. SMA 16-4984, NSDUH Series H-51).

Center for Disease Control. (2016). *Ten leading causes of death by age group, United States—2016.* Retrieved from https://www.cdc.gov/injury/images/lc-charts/leading_causes_of_death_age_group_2016_1056w814h.gif on 5/22/2018

Chen, S. W. H., & Davenport, D. S. (2005). Cognitive-Behavioral therapy with Chinese American clients: Cautions and modifications. *Psychotherapy: Theory, Research, Practice, Training, 42*, 101–110.

Chuang, J. Y., Hagan, C. C., Murray, G. K., Graham, J. M., Ooi, C., Tait, R., . . . Lennox, B. R. (2017). Adolescent major depressive disorder: Neuroimaging evidence of sex difference during an affective go/no-go task. *Frontiers in Psychiatry, 8*, 119. doi:10.3389/fpsyt.2017.00119.

Clarke, G. N., Lewinsohn, P. M., & Hops, H. (1990). *Leader's manual for adolescent groups: Adolescent Coping with Depression Course.* Eugene, Oregon: Castalia Publishing.

Corbie-Smith, G. (1999). The continuing legacy of the Tuskegee Syphilis Study: Considerations for clinical investigation. *American Journal of the Medical Sciences, 317*, 5–8.

Costigan, S. A., Barnett, L., Plotnikoff, R. C., & Lubans, D. R. (2013). The health indicators associated with screen-based sedentary behavior among adolescent girls: A systematic review. *Journal of Adolescent Health, 52*, 382–392. doi:https://doi.org/10.1016/j.jadohealth.2012.07.018

Cruz-Fuentes, C. S., Benjet, C., Martínez-Levy, G. A., Pérez-Molina, A., Briones-Velasco, M., & Suárez-González, J. (2014). BDNF Met66 modulates the cumulative effect of psychosocial childhood adversities on major depression in adolescents. *Brain and Behavior, 4*(2), 290–297. doi:https://doi.org/10.1002/brb3.220

Curry, J., Rohde, P., Simmons, A., Silva, S., Vitiello, B., Kratochvil, C., . . . March, J. (2006). Predictors and moderators of acute outcome in the Treatment for Adolescents with Depression Study (TADS). *Journal of the American Academy of Child & Adolescent Psychiatry, 45*, 1427–1439. doi:https://doi.org/10.1097/01.chi.0000240838.78984.e2

Curry, J., Silva, S., Rohde, P., Ginsburg, G., Kratochvil, C., Simons, A., . . . Feeny, N. (2011). Recovery and recurrence following treatment for adolescent major depression. *Archives of General Psychiatry, 68*, 263–269. doi:10.1001/archgenpsychiatry.2010.150

Daryanani, I., Hamilton, J. L., McArthur, B. A., Steinberg, L., Abramson, L. Y., & Alloy, L. B. (2017). Cognitive vulnerabilities to depression for adolescents in single-mother and two-parent families. *Journal of Youth Adolescence, 46*, 213–227. doi:10.1007/s10964-016-0607-y

David-Ferdon, C., & Kaslow, N. (2008). Evidence-based psychosocial treatments for child and adolescent depression. *Journal of Child and Adolescent Psychology, 37*, 62–104. doi:10.1080/15374410701817865

Daviss, W. B. (2010). A review of co-morbid depression in pediatric ADHD: Etiologies, phenomenology, and treatment. *Journal of Child and Adolescent Psychology, 18,* 565–571. doi:http://doi.org/10.1089/cap.2008.032

Deas, D., & Brown, E. S. (2006). Adolescent substance abuse and psychiatric comorbidities. *Journal of Clinical Psychiatry, 67,* 18–23.

Derdikman-Eiron, R., Indredavik, M. S., Bakken I. J., Bratberg, G. H., Hjemdal, O., & Colton, M. (2012). Gender differences in psychosocial functioning of adolescents with symptoms of anxiety and depression: Longitudinal findings from the Nord-Trøndelag Health Study. *Social Psychiatry and Psychiatric Epidemiology, 47,* 1855–1863. doi:10.1007/s00127-012-0492-y

Dietz, L. J., Marshal, M. P., Burton, C. M., Bridge, J. A., Birmaher, B., Kolko, D., . . . Brent, D. A. (2014). Social problem solving among depressed adolescents is enhanced by structured psychotherapies. *Journal of Consulting and Clinical Psychology, 82,* 202–211. doi:10.1037/a0035718

Dubicka, B., & Brent, D. (2017). Pharmacotherapy and adolescent depression—an important treatment option. *Child and Adolescent Mental Health, 22,* 59–60. doi:10.1111/camh.12223

Eberhart, N. K., & Hammen, C. L. (2006). Interpersonal predictors of onset of depression during the transition to adulthood. *Personal Relationships, 13,* 195–206. doi:10.1111/j.1475-6811.2006.00113.x

Edlund, M. J., Forman-Hoffman, V. L., Winder, C. R., Heller, D. C., Kroutil, L. A., Lipari, R. N., & Colpi, L. J. (2015). Opioid abuse and depression in adolescents: Results from the National Survey on Drug Use and Health. *Drug & Alcohol Dependence, 152,* 131–138. https://doi.org/10.1016/j.drugalcdep.2015.04.010

Eley, T. C., Sugden, K., Corsico, A., Gregory, A. M., Sham, P., Mcguffin, P., . . . Craig, I. W. (2004). Gene-environment interaction analysis of serotonin system markers with adolescent depression. *Molecular Psychiatry, 9,* 908. doi:http://dx.doi.org.ezproxy.lib.utah.edu/10.1038/sj.mp.4001546

Emslie, G. J., Kennard, B. D., Mayes, T. L., Nakonezny, P. A., Moore, J., Jones, J. M., . . . King, J. (2015). Continued effectiveness of relapse prevention cognitive-behavioral therapy following fluoxetine treatment in youth with major depressive disorder. *Journal of the American Academy of Child and Adolescent Psychiatry, 54,* 991–998. doi:https://doi.org/10.1016/j.jaac.2015.09.014

Emslie, G. J., Mayes T., Porta, G., Vitiello, B., Clarke, G., Wagner, K. D., . . . & Brent, D. (2009). Treatment of Resistant Depression in Adolescents (TORDIA): Week 24 outcomes. *The American Journal of Psychiatry, 7,* 782–791. doi:https://doi.org/10.1176/appi.ajp.2010.09040552

Fogel, J., & Ford, D. E. (2005). Stigma beliefs of Asian Americans with depression in an internet sample. *The Canadian Journal of Psychiatry, 50,* 470–478.

Food and Drug Administration. (2004, October 15). *Suicidality in children and adolescents being treated with antidepressant medications. FDA public health advisory.* Wayback Machine. Retrieved from https://web.archive.org/web/20041118053951/http://www.fda.gov/cder/drug/antidepressants/SSRIPHA200410.htm

Garber, J., & Weersing, V. R. (2010). Comorbidity of anxiety and depression in youth: Implications for treatment and prevention. *Clinical Psychology: Science and Practice, 17,* 293–306. doi:10.1111/j.1468-2850.2010.01221.x

Glowinski, A. L., Madden, P. A., Bucholz, K. K., Lynskey, M. T., & Heath, A. C. (2003). Genetic epidemiology of self-reported lifetime DSM-IV major depressive disorder in a population-based twin sample of female adolescents. *Journal of Child Psychology and Psychiatry, 44,* 988–996. doi:10.1111/1469-7610.00183

Goodyer, I., Dubicka, B., Wilkinson, P., Kelvin, R., Roberts, C., Byford, S., . . . Harrington, R. (2007). Selective serotonin reuptake inhibitors (SSRIs) and routine specialist care with and without cognitive behaviour therapy in adolescents with major depression: Randomised controlled trial. *BMJ, 335,* 142. doi:10.1136/bmj.39224. 494340.55

Goodyer, I., Dubicka, B., Wilkinson, P., Kelvin, R., Roberts, C., Byford, S., . . . Rothwell, J. (2008). A randomised controlled trial of cognitive behaviour therapy in adolescents with major depression treated by selective serotonin reuptake inhibitors. The ADAPT trial. *Health Technology Assessment, 12,* 1–80.

Goodyer, I. M., Reynolds, S., Barrett, B., Byford, S., Dubicka, B., Hill, J., . . . Fonagy, P. (2017). Cognitive behavioural therapy and short-term psychoanalytical psychotherapy versus a brief psychosocial intervention in adolescents with unipolar major depressive disorder (IMPACT): A multicentre, pragmatic, observer-blind, randomised controlled superiority trial. *Lancet Psychiatry. 4,* 109–119. doi:https://doi.org/10.1016/S2215-0366(16)30378-9

Guerry, J. D., & Hastings, P. D. (2011). In search of HPA axis dysregulation in child and adolescent depression. *Clinical Child & Family Psychology Review, 14,* 135–160 doihttps://doi.org/10.1007/s10567-011-0084-5

Gunlicks-Stoessel, M., & Mufson, L. (2016). Innovations in practice: A pilot study of interpersonal psychotherapy for depressed adolescents and their parents. *Child and Adolescent Mental Health, 21,* 225–230. doi:10.1111/camh.12167

Gunlicks-Stoessel, M., Mufson, L., Jekal, A., & Turner, J. B. (2011). The impact of perceived interpersonal functioning on treatment for adolescent depression: IPT-A versus treatment as usual in school-based health clinics. *Journal of Consulting and Clinical Psychology, 78,* 260–267. doi:10.1037/a0018935

Hall, E. B., & Mufson, L. (2009). Interpersonal Psychotherapy for Depressed Adolescents (IPT-A): A case illustration. *Journal of Child and Adolescent Psychiatry, 38,* 582–593. doi:10.1080/15374410902976338

Hetrick, S. E., Cox, G. R., Witt, K. G., Bir, J. J., & Merry, S. N. (2016). Cognitive behavioural therapy (CBT), third-wave CBT and interpersonal therapy (IPT) based interventions for preventing depression in children and adolescents. *Cochrane Database of Systematic Reviews, 8,* 1465–1858. doi:10.1002/14651858.CD003380.pub4.

Hsieh, A. L., & Bean, R. A. (2014). Understanding familial/cultural factors in adolescent depression: A culturally competent treatment for working with Chinese American families. *The American Journal of Family Therapy, 42,* 398–412.

Huey, S. J., Jr., & Polo, A. J. (2008). Evidence-based psychosocial treatments for ethnic minority youth. *Journal of Clinical Child and Adolescent Psychology, 37,* 262–301. doi:https://doi.org/10.1080/15374410701820174

Jacobson, C. M., & Mufson, L. (2012). Interpersonal psychotherapy for depressed adolescents adapted for self-injury (IPT-ASI): Rationale, overview, and case summary. *American Journal of Psychotherapy, 66,* 349–374.

Keller, G. A., & Gottlieb, D. T. (2012). Reducing major depression in children at high risk: Opportunities for prevention. *The International Journal of Psychiatry in Medicine, 44,* 271–290.

Kelly, P. A., Viding, E., Wallace, G. L., Schaer, M., De Brito, S. A., Robustelli, B., & McCrory, E. J. (2013). Cortical thickness, surface area, and gyrification abnormalities in children exposed to maltreatment: Neural markers of vulnerability? *Biological Psychiatry, 74*, 845–852. doi:https://doi.org/10.1016/j.biopsych.2013.06.020

Kennard, B., Clarke, G., Weersing, V., Asarnow, J., Shamseddeen, W., Porta G., . . . Brent, D. (2009) Effective components of TORDIA cognitive–behavioral therapy for adolescent depression: Preliminary findings. *Journal of Consulting and Clinical Psychology. 77*, 1033–1041 doi:10.1037/a0017411.

Kessler, R. C., Berglund, P., Demler, O., Jin, R., Merikangas, K. R., & Walters, E. E. (2005). Lifetime prevalence and age-of-onset distributions of DSM-IV disorders in the National Comorbidity Survey Replication. *Archives of General Psychiatry, 62*, 593–602. doi:10.1001/archpsyc.62.6.593

Kilpatrick, D. G., Ruggiero, K. J., Acierno, R., Saunders, B. E., Resnick, H. S., & Best, C. L. (2003). Violence and risk of PTSD, major depression, substance abuse/dependence, and comorbidity: Results from the National Survey of Adolescents. *Journal of Consulting and Clinical Psychology, 71*, 692–700. http://dx.doi.org/10.1037/0022-006X.71.4.692

Kim-Cohen, J., Caspi, A., Moffitt, T. E., Harrington, H., Milne, B. J., & Poulton, R. (2003). Prior juvenile diagnoses in adults with mental disorder: Developmental follow-back of a prospective-longitudinal cohort. *Archives of General Psychiatry, 60*, 709–717. doi:10.1001/archpsyc.60.7.709

Kratochvil, C. J., & Vitiello, B. (2008). Recent NIMH clinical trials and implications for practice. *Journal of the American Academy of Child & Adolescent Psychiatry, 47*, 1369–1374. doi:https://doi.org/10.1097/CHI.0b013e31818960a7

Kremer, P., Elshaug, C., Leslie, E., Toumbourou, J. W., Patton, G. C., & Williams, J. (2014). Physical activity, leisure-time screen use and depression among children and young adolescents. *Journal of Science and Medicine in Sport, 17*, 183–187.

Krupnick, J. L., & Melnikoff, E. (2012). Psychotherapy with low-income patients: Lessons learned from treatment studies. *Journal of Contemporary Psychotherapy, 42*, 7–15. doi:http://dx.doi.org/10.1007/s10879-011-9182-4

Lanzi, R. G., Bert, S. C., Jacobs, B. K., & Centers for the Prevention of Child Neglect. (2009). Depression among a sample of first-time adolescent and adult mothers. *Journal of Child and Adolescent Psychiatric Nursing, 22*(4), 194–202. doi:https://doi.org/10.1111/j.1744-6171.2009.00199.x

Laughren, T. P. (2006, November 16). *Overview for December 13 meeting of Psychopharmacologic Drugs Advisory Committee (PDAC).* Wayback Machine. Retrieved from https://wayback.archive-it.org/7993/20170405070114/https://www.fda.gov/ohrms/dockets/ac/06/briefing/2006-4272b1-01-FDA.pdf

Liu, M., Wu, L., & Yao, S. (2015). Dose-response association of screen time-based sedentary behaviour in children and adolescents and depression: A meta-analysis of observational studies. *British Journal of Sports Medicine.* doi:10.1136/bjsports-2015-095084

March, J. S., Silva, S., Petrycki, S., Curry, J., Wells, K., Fairbank, J., . . . Rochon, J. (2007). The treatment for adolescents with depression study (TADS): Long-term effectiveness and safety outcomes. *Archives of General Psychiatry, 64*, 1132–1143. doi:10.1001/archpsyc.64.10.1132

March, J. S., Silva, S., & Vitiello, B. (2006). The treatment of adolescents with depression study (TADS): Methods and message at 12 weeks. *Journal of the American Academy of Child and Adolescent Psychiatry, 45*, 1393–1403. doi:https://doi.org/10.1097/01.chi.0000237709.35637.c0

Markowitz, J. C., & Weissman, M. M. (2004). Interpersonal psychotherapy: Principles and applications. *World Psychiatry, 3*, 136–139.

Marmorstein, N. R., Iacono, W. G., & McGue, M. (2012). Associations between substance use disorders and major depression in parents and late adolescent–emerging adult offspring: An adoption study. *Addiction, 107*, 1965–1973 doi:10.1111/j.1360-0443.2012.03934.x

Matthews, T., Danese, A., Wertz, J., Odgers, C. L., Ambler, A., Moffitt, T. E., & Arseneault, L. (2016). Social isolation, loneliness and depression in young adulthood: A behavioural genetic analysis. *Social Psychiatry & Psychiatric Epidemiology, 51*, 339–348. https://doi.org/10.1007/s00127-016-1178-7

McCarty, C. A. (2008). Adolescent school failure predicts depression among girls. *The Journal of Adolescent Health : Official Publication of the Society for Adolescent Medicine, 43*, 180–187. http://doi.org/10.1016/j.jadohealth.2008.01.023

McCarty, C. A., & Weisz, J. R. (2007). Effects of psychotherapy for depression in children and adolescents: What we can (and can't) learn from meta-analysis and component profiling. *Journal of the American Academy of Child and Adolescent Psychiatry, 46*, 879–886. doi:10.1097/chi.0b013e31805467b3

McLeod, J. D., Uemura, R., & Rohrman, S. (2012). Adolescent mental health, behavior problems, and academic achievement. *Journal of Health and Social Behavior, 53*, 482–497. doi:10.1177/0022146512462888

Mellin, E. A., & Beamish, P. M. (2002). Interpersonal theory and adolescents with depression: Clinical update. *Journal of Mental Health Counseling, 24*, 110–125.

Mojtabai, R., Olfson, M., & Han, B. (2016). National trends in the prevalence and treatment of depression in adolescents and young adults. *Pediatrics, 138*, [e20161878]. doi:10.1542/peds.2016-1878

Monroe, S. M., & Harkness, K. L. (2005). Life stress, the "kindling" hypothesis, and the recurrence of depression: Considerations from a life stress perspective. *Psychological Review, 112*, 417–445. doi:10.1037/0033-295X.112.2.417

Moses, T. (2009). Stigma and self-concept among adolescents receiving mental health treatment. *American Journal of Orthopsychiatry, 79*, 261–274. doi:http://dx.doi.org/10.1037/a0015696

Mufson, L., Dorta, K. P., Wickramaratne, P., Nomura, Y., Olfson, M., & Weissman, M. M. (2004). A randomized effectiveness trial of interpersonal psychotherapy for depressed adolescents. *Archives of General Psychiatry, 61*, 577–584. http://dx.doi.org/10.1001/archpsyc.61.6.577.

Mufson, L., Gallagher, T., Dorta, K. P., & Young, J. F. (2004). A group adaptation of interpersonal psychotherapy for depressed adolescents. *American Journal of Psychotherapy, 58*, 220–237.

Mufson, L., & Sills, R. (2006). Interpersonal psychotherapy for depressed adolescents (IPT-A): An overview. *Nordic Journal of Psychiatry, 60*, 431–437. doi:10.1080/08039480601022397

Mufson, L., Weissman, M. M., Moreau, D., & Garfinkel, R. (1999). Efficacy of interpersonal psychotherapy for depressed adolescents. *Archives of General Psychiatry, 56*, 573–579. http://dx.doi.org/10.1001/archpsyc.56.6.573

Mychailyszyn, M. P., & Elson, D. M. (2018). Working through the blues: A meta-analysis on interpersonal psychotherapy for depressed adolescents (IPT-A). *Children and Youth Services Review, 87*, 123–129. doi:https://doi.org/10.1016/j.childyouth.2018.02.011

Newman, T. (2004). A black-box warning for antidepressants in children? *New England Journal of Medicine, 351*, 1595–1598. doi:10.1056/NEJMp048279

Nock, M. K., Green, J. G., Hwang, I., McLaughlin, K. A., Sampson, N. A., Zaslavsky, A. M., & Kessler, R. C. (2013). Prevalence, correlates, and treatment of lifetime suicidal behavior among adolescents: Results from the National Comorbidity Survey Replication Adolescent Supplement. *JAMA Psychiatry, 70*, 300–310. http://doi.org/10.1001/2013.jamapsychiatry.55

Oar, E. L., Johnco, C., and Ollendick, T. H. (2017). Cognitive behavioral therapy for anxiety and depression in children and adolescents. *Psychiatric Clinics of North America, 40*, 661–674. doi:10.1016/j.psc.2017.08.002

Orth, U., Robins, R. W., Meier, L. L., & Conger, R. D. (2016). Refining the vulnerability model of low self-esteem and depression: Disentangling the effects of genuine self-esteem and narcissism. *Journal of Personality & Social Psychology, 110*, 133–149. http://dx.doi.org/10.1037/pspp0000038

O'Shea, G., Spence, H., and Donovan, C. (2014). Interpersonal factors associated with depression in adolescents: Are these consistent with theories underpinning interpersonal psychotherapy? *Clinical Psychology and Psychotherapy. 21*, 548–558. doi:10.1002/cpp.1849

Perloe, A., Esposito-Smythers, C., Curby, T. W., & Renshaw, K. D. (2014). Concurrent trajectories of change in adolescent and maternal depressive symptoms in the TORDIA study. *Journal of Youth and Adolescence, 43*, 612–628. doi:10.1007/s10964-013-9999-0

Pescosolido, B. A., Fettes, D. L., Martin, J. K., Monahan, J., & McLeod, J. D. (2007). Perceived dangerousness of children with mental health problems and support for coerced treatment. *Psychiatric Services, 58*, 619–625. doi:http://dx.doi.org/10.1176/appi.ps.58.5.619

Peters, A., Jacobs, R., Feldhaus, C., Henry, D, Albano, A., Langenecker, S., . . . Curry, J. (2016). Trajectories of functioning into emerging adulthood following treatment for adolescent depression. *Journal of Adolescent Health, 58*, 253–259. https://doi.org/10.1016/j.jadohealth.2015.09.022

Pino, E. C., Damus, K., Jack, B., Henderson, D., Milanovic, S., & Kalesan, B. (2018). Adolescent socioeconomic status and depressive symptoms in later life: Evidence from structural equation models. *Journal of Affective Disorders, 225*, 702–708. doi:https://doi.org/10.1016/j.jad.2017.09.005

Pinquart, M., & Shen, Y. (2011). Depressive symptoms in children and adolescents with chronic physical illness: An updated meta-analysis. *Journal of Pediatric Psychology, 36*, 375–384. doi:https://doi.org/10.1093/jpepsy/jsq104

Prinstein, M. J., Cheah, C. S., & Guyer, A. E. (2005). Peer victimization, cue interpretation, and internalizing symptoms: Preliminary concurrent and longitudinal findings for children and adolescents. *Journal of Clinical Child and Adolescent Psychology, 34*, 11–24. doi:https://doi.org/10.1207/s15374424jccp3401_2

Reeb, B. T., Conger, K. J., & Wu, Y. (2010). Paternal depressive symptoms and adolescent functioning: The moderating effect of gender and father hostility. *Fathering, 8*, 131–142. doi:10.3149/fth.0801.131

Rice, F. (2010). Genetics of childhood and adolescent depression: Insights into etiological heterogeneity and challenges for future genomic research. *Genome Medicine, 2*, 68. https://doi.org/10.1186/gm189

Richards, R., McGee, R., Williams, S. M., Welch, D., & Hancox, R. J. (2010). Adolescent screen time and attachment to parents and peers. *Archives of Pediatrics & Adolescent Medicine, 164*, 258–262.

Richardson, L., McCauley, E., & Katon, W. (2009). Collaborative care for adolescent depression: A pilot study. *General Hospital Psychiatry, 31,* 36–45. doi:http://dx.doi.org/10.1016/j.genhosppsych.2008.09.019

Rohde, P. (2017). Cognitive-behavioral treatment for adolescent depression. In J. R. Weisz & A. E. Kazdin (Eds.), *Evidence-based psychotherapies for children and adolescents* (pp. 49–65). New York, NY: Guilford Press.

Rohde, P., Silva, S., Tonev, S., Kennard, B., Vitiello, B., Kratochvil, M., . . . March, J. (2008). Achievement and maintenance of sustained response during TADS continuation and maintenance therapy. *Archives of General Psychiatry. 65,* 447–455. doi:10.1001/archpsyc.65.4.447

Rohde, P., Waldron, H. B., Turner, C. W., Brody, J., Jorgensen J. (2015). Sequenced versus coordinated treatment for adolescents with comorbid depressive and substance use disorders. *Journal of Consulting and Clinical Psychology, 82,* 342–348. doi:10.1037/a0035808

Rudolph, K. D., Troop-Gordon, W., Modi, H. H., & Granger, D. A. (2018). An exploratory analysis of the joint contribution of HPA axis activation and motivation to early adolescent depressive symptoms. *Developmental Psychobiology, 60,* 303–316. https://doi.org/10.1002/dev.21600

Sallis, H., Evans, J., Wootton, R., Krapohl, E., Oldehinkel, A. J., Davey Smith, G., & Paternoster, L. (2017). Genetics of depressive symptoms in adolescence. *BMC Psychiatry, 17,* 321. http://doi.org/10.1186/s12888-017-1484-y

Sburlati, E. S., Lyneham, H. J., Mufson, L. H., & Schniering, C. A. (2012). A model of therapist competencies for the empirically supported interpersonal psychotherapy for adolescent depression. *Clinical Child and Family Psychology Review,* 15, 93–112. doi:10.1007/s10567-012-0111-1.

Schmaal, L., Yücel, M., Ellis, R., Vijayakumar, N., Simmons, J. G., Allen, N. B., & Whittle, S. (2017). Brain structural signatures of adolescent depressive symptom trajectories: A longitudinal magnetic resonance imaging study. *Journal of the American Academy of Child & Adolescent Psychiatry,* 56, 593–601. doi:10.1016/j.jaac.2017.05.008

Schriber, R. A., Anbari, Z., Robins, R. W., Conger, R. D., Hastings, P. D., & Guyer, A. E. (2017). Hippocampal volume as an amplifier of the effect of social context on adolescent depression. *Clinical Psychological Science,* 5, 632–649. https://doi.org/10.1177/2167702617699277

Sheridan, D. C., Lin, A., & Zane Horowitz, B. (2017). Suicidal bupropion ingestions in adolescents: Increased morbidity compared with other antidepressants. *Clinical Toxicology,* 56, 1–5. https://doi.org/10.1080/15563650.2017.1377839

Silk, J. S., Steinberg, L., & Morris, A. S. (2003). Adolescents' emotion regulation in daily life: Links to depressive symptoms and problem behavior. *Child Development,* 74, 1869–1880. doi:10.1046/j.1467-8624.2003.00643.x

Suliman, S., Mkabile, S. G., Fincham, D. S., Ahmed, R., Stein, D. J., & Seedat, S. (2009). Cumulative effect of multiple trauma on symptoms of posttraumatic stress disorder, anxiety, and depression in adolescents. *Comprehensive Psychiatry,* 50, 121–127. doi:https://doi.org/10.1016/j.comppsych.2008.06.006

Tracy, M., Zimmerman, F. J., Galea, S., McCauley, E., & Vander Stoep, A. (2008). What explains the relation between family poverty and childhood depressive symptoms?. *Journal of Psychiatric Research,* 42, 1163–1175. https://doi.org/10.1016/j.jpsychires.2008.01.011

Tully, E. C., Iacono, W. G, & McGue, M. (2008). An adoption study of parental depression as an environmental liability for adolescent depression and childhood disruptive disorders. *American Journal of Psychiatry, 165,* 1148–1154 https://doi.org/10.1176/appi.ajp.2008.07091438

Twenge, J. M., Gentile, B., DeWall, C. N., Ma, D., Lacefield, K., & Schurtz, D. R. (2010). Birth cohort increases in psychopathology among young Americans, 1938–2007: A cross-temporal meta-analysis of the MMPI. *Clinical Psychology Review, 30,* 145–154. https://doi.org/10.1016/j.cpr.2009.10.005

Usala, T., Clavenna, A., Zuddas, A., & Bonati, M. (2008). Randomised controlled trials of selective serotonin reuptake inhibitors in treating depression in children and adolescents: A systematic review and meta-analysis. *European Neuropsychopharmacology, 18,* 62–73.

Vitiello, B. (2009). Combined cognitive-behavioural therapy and pharmacotherapy for adolescent depression: Does it improve outcomes compared with monotherapy? *CNS Drugs 23,* 271–280.

Wagner, S., Müller, C., Helmreich, I., Huss, M., & Tadić, A. (2015). A meta-analysis of cognitive functions in children and adolescents with major depressive disorder. *European Child & Adolescent Psychiatry, 24,* 5–19. https://doi.org/10.1007/s00787-014-0559-2

Wilkinson, P., Kelvin, R., Roberts, C., Dubicka, B., & Goodyer, I. (2011). Clinical and psychosocial predictors of suicide attempts and nonsuicidal self-injury in the adolescent depression antidepressants and psychotherapy trial (ADAPT). *The American Journal of Psychiatry, 168,* 495–501. doi:https://doi.org/10.1176/appi.ajp.2010.10050718

Williams, J. S., Cunich, M., & Byles, J. (2013). The impact of socioeconomic status on changes in the general and mental health of women over time: Evidence from a longitudinal study of Australian women. *International Journal for Equity in Health, 12,* 142–153. doi:http://dx.doi.org/10.1186/1475-9276-12-25

Wolff, J. C., Jandasek, B., Michel, B. D., Becker, S. J., & Spirito, A. (2017). Concurrent treatment of depression in parents and adolescents: A case example. *Cognitive and Behavioral Practice, 24,* 14–25. doi:https://doi.org/10.1016/j.cbpra.2016.02.001

Wolff, J. C., & Ollendick, T. H. (2006). The comorbidity of conduct problems and depression in childhood and adolescence. *Clinical Child & Family Psychology Review, 9,* 201–220. https://doi.org/10.1007/s10567-006-0011-3

Wu, P., Katic, B. J., Liu, X., Fan, B., & Fuller, C. J. (2010). Mental health service use among suicidal adolescents: Findings from a U.S. national community survey. *Psychiatric Services, 61,* 17–24.

Xia, L., & Yao, S. (2015). The involvement of genes in adolescent depression: A systematic review. *Frontiers in Behavioral Neuroscience, 9,* 329. doi:10.3389/fnbeh.2015.00329

Young, J. F., Kranzler, A., Gallop, R., & Mufson, L. (2012). Interpersonal psychotherapy-adolescent skills training: Effects on school and social functioning. *School Mental Health, 4,* 254–264. doi:https://doi.org/10.1007/s12310-012-9078-9

Yuan, S., Zhou, X., Zhang, Y., Shang, H., Juncai, P., Lining, Y., . . . Peng, X. (2018). Comparative efficacy and acceptability of bibliotherapy for depression and anxiety disorders in children and adolescents: A meta-analysis of randomized clinical trials. *Neuropsychiatric Disease and Treatment, 14,* 353–365. doi:10.2147/NDT.S152747

Zhou, H., Hao, N., Du, Y., Liu, Y., Sui, Y., Wang, Y., . . . Kutcher, S. (2016). Reliability and validity of the eleven item Kutcher Adolescent Depression Scale, Chinese version (KADS-11CV). *Journal of Child and Adolescent Behavior, 4.* doi:10.4172/2375-4494.1000308

8

Evidence-Based Interventions for Adolescents With Disruptive Behavior Disorders

Joanna E. Bettmann and Taylor Berhow

Tom was a 15-year-old boy who presented to outpatient treatment with severe oppositional behavior. He described himself as a reluctant participant in treatment, explaining that he was only coming to therapy because his school was about to expel him. He described a long history of problems at school, including mouthing off to teachers, defying school rules about where he was allowed to be and when, and getting into frequent verbal fights with teachers and peers on school grounds. He described that he had poor grades because "all my teachers hate me" and "no one believes in me." He also described troubled relationships at home: a mother who "loves my younger brother more than me," a stepfather who "never wanted me anyway," and three brothers with model grades. He said that he was "a bad kid" who "deserved nothing from nobody." Tom said that he wanted to be a fighter pilot someday, but had no idea about how to achieve that. Tom's experience of the world was colored by his extreme oppositionality: his resistance to accepting direction from the authority figures in his life and his difficulty with rule following. His oppositionality could also be a product of a difficult relational environment: his experience was that adults neither loved him or wanted him. Tom met criteria for oppositional defiant disorder, a type of disruptive behavior disorder.

Disruptive behavior disorders (DBDs) manifest as adolescent behaviors that cause personal and familial dysfunction. The DBDs discussed in this chapter include conduct disorder (CD), oppositional defiant disorder (ODD), and attention-deficit/hyperactivity disorder (ADHD). These disorders share behavioral commonalities and often present comorbidly. Adolescents with DBDs generate significant strain on societal resources because a small number of DBD-diagnosed teenagers access a disproportionate amount of adolescent mental health resources (Steiner & Remsing, 2007). Only 10% of school-aged children and adolescents meet criteria for a DBD (Gresham, 2015), but adolescents with DBDs constitute nearly half of all adolescent outpatient referrals and more than half of all adolescent psychiatric inpatient referrals (Oruche et al., 2015; Fonagy et al., 2002). Additionally, adolescents diagnosed with DBDs are vulnerable to developing chronic mental health issues, including personality disorders, which can persist through adulthood (Helgeland, Kjelsberg, & Torgersen, 2005).

Notably, 30% of all arrests occur with children and adolescents under the age of 18; research suggests that number is rising (Fonagy et al., 2002). Adolescents who commit crimes often have a disruptive behavior disorder (Aebi et al., 2016; Colins, Vermeiren, Schuyten, & Broekaert, 2009; Gresham, 2015). Untreated DBDs contribute to delinquency and affect juvenile justice, school, and healthcare systems (Farrington & Welsh, 2009; Fonagy, Target, Cottrell, Phillips, & Kurtz, 2002).

Diagnostic comorbidity is common among teenagers with DBDs (Fonagy et al., 2002; Hogue, Evans, & Levin, 2017; Oruche et al., 2015). The presence of more than one DBD significantly increases the likelihood of antisocial personality disorder in adulthood and increases the presence of destructive social behaviors, such as criminal behaviors (Gresham, Lane, & Lambros, 2000).

DBDs are often comorbid with substance abuse (Disney, Elkins, McGue, & Iacono, 1999; Erskine et al., 2014; Schutter, van Bokhoven, Vanderschuren, Lochman, & Matthys, 2011). Adolescents diagnosed with a substance use disorder are 4 times more likely to be diagnosed with a DBD as well (Ryan, Stranger, Thostenson, Whitmore, & Budney, 2013). This comorbidity may be because substance use disorders and DBDs share many common risk factors, such as parenting practices (Ryan et al., 2013). For example, low levels of parental involvement links to the development of both DBDs and substance use disorders (Ryan et al., 2013).

The economic costs of DBDs manifest as victim costs and justice costs (including police, court systems, and prison systems), as well as a loss of productivity if the adolescent becomes incarcerated (Cohen & Piquero, 2009). Given the destructive and disruptive behaviors associated with DBDs, effective treatment of DBDs generates significant positive societal impacts: keeping one 14-year-old high-risk adolescent out of the juvenile justice system can save society as much as $2.3 million over that adolescent's lifespan (Cohen & Piquero, 2009).

Risk Factors for DBDs

Early-Life Risk Factors

Some early-life factors appear to contribute to later development of DBDs. Maternal smoking during pregnancy, drug and alcohol abuse during pregnancy, maternal medical illness during pregnancy, maternal anxiety during pregnancy, and postpartum depression are risk factors for development of adolescent DBDs (Latimer et al., 2012; Muratori et al., 2014; Waller, Gardner, & Hyde, 2013). Additionally, stress and resource deprivation during infancy, as well as adoption within the first year of life, appear to increase DBD risk (Latimer et al., 2012).

Childhood Risk Factors

During childhood, poor parental supervision, coercive parent-child interactions, and low positive parent-child engagement all link to childhood behavioral issues (Muratori et al., 2014; Waller, Gardner, & Hyde, 2013). Research suggests that DBD symptoms tend to present early in an adolescent's lifespan (Gresham, 2015) and that adolescents who develop disruptive behaviors at a young age are at greater risk for increased difficulties into adolescence (Qi & Kaiser, 2003). For example, Qi and Kaiser (2003) found that preschoolers who had behavior problems were more likely to develop serious social skill deficits, academic difficulties, and disruptive behaviors in adolescence. In the case of Tom at the beginning of this chapter, we saw an adolescent who appeared to experience difficult parent-child interactions, as well as low positive parent-child engagement. Tom's experience was that no adults loved him or believed in him. His familial relational experiences clearly impacted his oppositionality with authority figures at school and other adults.

Biological Risk Factors

DBDs also appear to have significant biological risk factors. These include genetic predisposition toward mental illness, poor biological responsiveness to medication, and genetic propensity to poor physical health (McKinney

& Morse, 2012). Notably, both biological and environmental factors appear to impact adolescents who develop disruptive behaviors in early childhood, while environmental symptoms alone appear more impactful to those who develop symptoms in adolescence (McKinney & Morse, 2012). This is important for clinicians to know as they develop treatment interventions. For example, if a parent reports that their child's DBD symptoms began in early childhood, it is likely that biological risk factors may need addressing in treatment.

Environmental Risk Factors

Environmental risk factors for DBDs include low quality of personal/familial relationships, low socioeconomic status, inadequate access to medical treatment, and inadequate access to essential social resources like adequate childcare (McKinney & Morse, 2012). One environmental risk factor involves the adolescent's caregivers and their ability to build a positive relationship with strong boundaries, loving and effective discipline, and warmth (Latimer et al., 2012). For example, parents who exhibit poor supervision or who pay little attention to their children are more likely to have children with callous-unemotional traits, a conduct disorder specifier (American Psychiatric Association, 2013; Waller, Gardner, & Hyde, 2013).

There appears to be a link between parenting techniques and the development of DBDs. When caregivers utilize warmth and empathy in disciplining, their children are more likely to develop prosocial behaviors, advocate for themselves, and solve problems in appropriate ways (Waller, Gardner, & Hyde). Children are typically more compliant when their parents use "positive" or "neutral" discipline techniques (Kremer, Smith, & Lawrence, 2010, p. 254). Kremer et al. describe positive techniques as being "encouraging or comforting" and neutral techniques as "not speaking/ignoring" (Kremer et al., 2010, p. 254). Positive and neutral techniques stand in contrast to negative discipline techniques which include "threatening" or using physically abusive punishment (Kremer et al., 2010, p. 254). Research suggests that harsh, aggressive forms of parental punishment, including physical punishment, link to undesirable outcomes, including children's heightened aggression and antisocial behavior (Kremer, Smith, & Lawrence, 2010). Severe physical discipline and inconsistent parental discipline also link to adolescent disruptive behaviors (Muratori et al., 2014; Waller, Gardner, & Hyde, 2013).

Parents with mental health problems, such as depression and anxiety, often exhibit inconsistent boundaries and discipline, establish inconsistent communication and support, and are less emotionally available for relationships with their children (Duncombe, Havighurst, Holland, & Frankling, 2012). Research shows links between maternal depression and aggressive behavior in childhood, which can later develop into adolescent DBD symptoms (Latimer et al., 2012; Muratori et al., 2014).

For Assessment

Clinicians should evaluate the mental health of all adolescents' caregivers. Make sure to include a focus on the mother's emotional experiences, ask questions about her experiences during pregnancy, and explore whether she considers her mental and physical states to be stable and healthy (McKinney & Morse, 2012).

DBD risk factors present with increased frequency in low-income homes and communities (Fonagy et al., 2002; Qi & Kaiser, 2003). Notably, adolescent disruptive behavior problems in the general population average 3–6% while up to 30% of adolescents from low-income households present with disruptive behavior patterns (Qi & Kaiser, 2003). Low socioeconomic status is associated with increased financial and emotional stress for families, low social support for families, and general familial instability (Qi & Kaiser, 2003). All of these are risk factors for the development of DBDs (Åslund et al., 2013; Fonagy et al., 2002; Qi & Kaiser, 2003). Adolescents from low-income households are more likely to develop behavioral aggression and DBD symptoms (Åslund et al., 2013) and less likely to receive adequate treatment (Hodgkinson, Godoy, Beers, & Lewin, 2017). Impoverished families have less access to financial, scholastic, and therapeutic resources, often experience compounding trauma, and thus may have less resilience against environmental stressors (Kaltman, de Mendoza, Serrano, & Gonzales, 2016; Klasen & Crombag, 2013; Taylor & Distelberg, 2016).

Importantly, research suggests that mental health therapy is often less efficacious in families who experience financial strain (Grimes & McElwain, 2008). This problem may be because there are increased barriers in receiving for families living below the poverty line, like unreliable communication devices (important for making contact), limited financial resources for therapeutic services, and less discretionary time to attend therapy and implement suggested interventions and coping skills, like exercising or meditation (Grimes & McElwain, 2008).

Gender Risk Factors

Boys tend to develop disruptive behaviors earlier than girls, often before puberty (Kroneman, Loeber, Hipwell, & Koot, 2009). Boys also exhibit more violent, aggressive DBD behaviors aimed at physically harming others than girls do (McKinney & Morse, 2012). While girls are treated for disruptive behaviors less often than boys, research suggests that DBDs may be increasing among adolescent girls (Kroneman et al., 2009). Girls often direct their aggression in more socially damaging ways, such as gossiping, threatening, and spreading rumors (McKinney & Morse, 2012).

Assessing DBDs

Differentiating between normally disruptive childhood behaviors and disruptive behaviors of clinical concern can be difficult (McKinney & Morse, 2012). For example, most preschool-aged children exhibit overt anger, opposition, and defiance, but the vast majority learn to regulate these behaviors as they grow, developing socially appropriate ways of solving problems (Tremblay, 2010). Disruptive behaviors manifest throughout all phases of childhood development and are often normative in childhood and adolescence (McKinney & Morse, 2012). But behavioral problems that manifest in adolescents who have environmental risk factors (such as those referenced above) are more likely manifest in DBDs (Latimer et al., 2012).

There are several measures that can assist you in assessing disruptive behavior (Fonagy et al., 2002; McKinney & Morse, 2012). Your assessment should gather information from multiple sources, including your adolescent client, their caregivers, and other involved parties such as teachers, coaches, and so forth (Fonagy, Allison, & Ryan, 2017; Fonagy et al., 2002). Gathering information from multiple sources helps to account for the fact that adolescent behavior varies in different environments and relationships (Fonagy et al., 2002).

For Assessment
  Make sure that you collect data from:
  • Your adolescent client
  • Your client's caregivers
  • Your client's teachers
  • Any other key adults involved in the client's life (e.g., coach, religious leader, family therapist, etc.)

Involving teachers, parents, and other important caregivers in the assessment process also paves the way for later intervention with both environmental and biological risk factors (Fonagy, Allison, & Ryan, 2017; van der Pol et al., 2017). Your assessment should include an analysis of risk factors, providing a detailed picture of the client's environment which allows you to implement interventions that target not just troubling behaviors, but also the context in which those behaviors occur (Liddle, 2010).

Because of the influence caregivers have on adolescents in the development of disruptive behaviors, caregiver reports are particularly helpful when assessing for DBD behavior (Reedtz et al., 2007). Collecting data from caregivers promotes discussion between clinicians and parents; it is an easy way to discuss difficult topics related to parent-child relationship challenges, address relevant risk factors, and explore ways parents are managing the disruptive behaviors (Reedtz et al., 2007). Clinicians should assess caregiver functioning, mental health, and stress because of the risk factors discussed earlier (Liddle, 2010). Teacher-reported data is also important to DBD assessment. Teachers often report disruptive behaviors more frequently than parents, perhaps because of their significant face-to-face time with students and the opportunities they have to observe interactions with peers (Kroneman et al., 2009).

Clinicians should considering using an assessment inventory that gathers information from all of these sources. One option is the Behavior Assessment System for Children (BASC-3). It is a questionnaire that takes approximately 40 minutes to administer and gathers information from the parent via a Parent Rating Scale and Structured Developmental History, and from the teacher via its Teacher Rating Scale and its Student Observation System (Pearson Clinical, 2017). Additionally, the Parenting Relationship Questionnaire section of this assessment gathers information about how the parent and adolescent interact with each other which is significant in terms of DBDs (Pearson Clinical, 2017). The BASC-3 also asks the clients to complete a Self-Report of Personality scale. The BASC-3's SRP (Parent and Self-Report) has an adolescent-specific version (Pearson Clinical, 2017). However, a qualification process is required before a clinician can order the assessment from Pearson Clinical (Pearson Clinical, 2017). Additionally, the cost and training required to use this measure is a potential barrier to use. The BASC-3 is available for purchase via the Pearson Clinical website; costs start at $122.70 for the most basic testing kit, and can be as high as $932.90 for a comprehensive package which includes a year of online support and materials in English and Spanish. Training to use the BASC-3 requires the viewing of a 47-minute presentation, available on the Pearson Clinical website, as well as the use of a manual available for purchase (Pearson Clinical, 2017).

Another option, which requires less training and is free to use, is the Strengths and Difficulties Questionnaire (SDQ: Goodman, Ford, Simmons, Gatward, & Meltzer, 2003). Teachers, parents, or clinicians can use this 25-question tool to screen for various mental health symptoms and behavioral problems (McKinney & Morse, 2012). The tool also assesses for peer interaction concerns and prosocial behaviors (McKinney, 2013). The assessment is designed for use with youth up to 16 years and is available in over 60 languages (McKinney & Morse, 2012). The SDQ is accessible free of charge at www.sdqinfo.com. Information on administering and scoring the questionnaire is also available on that website.

Practice Techniques

With parents: Caregivers who use mindful parenting techniques in child interaction, relationship building, and disciplining appear more effective in decreasing their own stress and maladaptive discipline practices (Friedmutter, 2016). Research indicates that caregivers who are taught mindful parenting practices report improved parent-child relationships and lower levels of stress and depression (Cohen & Semple, 2010). Consider teaching caregivers the mindfulness technique of nonjudgmental acceptance. Explain how using mindfully aware practices can help caregivers identify parenting practices which result in disconnection with their children (Cohen & Semple, 2010; Friedmutter, 2016). For example, using mindful awareness techniques can help caregivers identify when they are engaging in anger projection or emotional withdrawing when adolescents make a decisions with which the caregivers do not agree.

> *With adolescents*: It can be challenging to build rapport with adolescents who exhibit DBD behaviors. Directly asking teenagers developmentally appropriate questions about parental relationships and discipline is a good way to gather more information about these relationships and to build rapport with DBD teenagers who can be difficult to connect with (Latimer et al., 2012). Also, give your adolescent clients choices: Do you want to talk about this first or that? Should we sit here in my office or over there? Giving your clients choices engages them more fully in the treatment process.

Treatment of Oppositional Defiant Disorder and Conduct Disorder

Since parent-child relationship factors appear to impact adolescents' disruptive behaviors (Henderson, Rowe, Dakof, Hawes, & Liddle, 2009), involving adolescents' caregivers in the treatment process for DBDs is essential. DBD treatments that target an adolescent's environment are more successful at managing and altering negative behaviors than treatments which intervene with the behaviors alone (Kersten et al., 2016). Research also suggests that treatments which employ both individual and parent-focused interventions for DBDs are most likely to be effective (Baruch, Vrouva, & Wells, 2011; Calin, Muscalu, & Macovei, 2014; Honeycutt, Khavjou, Jones, Cuellar, & Forehand, 2015; Kersten et al., 2016; Liddle, 2016; van der Pol et al., 2017).

I (JEB) have found that DBD treatment involving family can be quite powerful. One adolescent that I worked with some time ago exemplifies this. Annie was a 15-year-old white adolescent whose family brought her to outpatient treatment following several years of misbehavior at home and school. Annie grew up in a middle class home in a suburban neighborhood in the U.S. Midwest. Her parents were perplexed by her occasional running away, her apparent drug use, and potential involvement in a local gang. After an uneventful elementary education, Annie's arrival in middle school prompted a precipitous drop in her grades. She changed peer groups, from girls that her parents knew to friends she was unwilling to bring home. Unknown to her parents, Annie had joined a gang at age 12, engaging in the criminal behaviors of that group and serving critical roles in their drug selling and distribution business.

When I met her, Annie would tell me only vague details of her life in the gang. She described frequent and heavy drug use, using whatever drugs were available. She talked about her gang peers, but was unwilling to state even their first names or other personal details. She referenced their "bad [i.e., criminal] behavior," but refused to provide details. Annie shared how she relished getting suspended from school for mouthing off or swearing at teachers, explaining how school suspensions meant she could spend more time with her friends in the gang. She described alienation in her relationships with her mother and longtime stepfather, stating that she never told them anything about her life. She described little interest in her two younger sisters. She said that she often spent nights away from home with friends without telling her parents where she was or when she was coming home.

When Annie began treatment with me, I found her a likeable person. She readily engaged with me in individual therapy, but stated that she didn't want to share concrete details about her life. Our therapeutic relationship developed over a period of several months as we met for individual sessions weekly. I encouraged her to share details about her life that she hadn't previously shared with other adults. First, I assigned her to write down a list of 10 things or events she hadn't ever told the adults in her life. She took several weeks to accomplish this task, utilizing lots of stalling tactics. Eventually, she brought the list to our individual session, but she didn't show it to me. Instead, we focused on how it felt for her to write these things down. I encouraged her to share with me the feelings that emerged for her when she did so. After much encouragement, she shared that she felt massive amounts of shame looking at that list. For the first time in our months of sessions, she cried, sharing how ashamed she felt of things she had done.

After several more months of weekly meetings, Annie finally felt ready to share one of the items on her list of 10. I was horrified by the story she shared because of its violence and criminality but was encouraged by how badly she felt about the incident. While she certainly met criteria for conduct disorder, she didn't appear callous or unemotional. I was hopeful that she felt bad about the violent and criminal behavior she had displayed towards others.

After several months more of individual outpatient treatment, Annie's mother and stepfather came to agency for a family therapy session. Annie and I had discussed and planned for months that Annie would begin to share some of the items on her list with her parents. During my family session with them, Annie began to share some small details from incidents on her list. Her parents' response was initially shock and horror, and then anger and blame directed at Annie. I began to understand why Annie had chosen to share so little with her family in the past. Her resistance to familial relationships, her seeking gang relationships for important relational connections, now made more sense. Annie's disruptive behaviors made sense to me when viewed in the context of her environment. Annie's resistance to her home life perhaps grew from the judgment and blame she experienced from her caregivers.

The task for me then was to support Annie's parents in developing skills to connect with Annie. Both her mother and stepfather had a difficult time recognizing how their own behaviors contributed to Annie's feelings of alienation at home and how her alienation may have impacted her decision to seek important relationships within a gang. I coached Annie's parents extensively, trying to build their insight into Annie's DBD, helping them to see the emotional needs behind her oppositional and aggressive behaviors. I encouraged them to recognize how their own emotional needs impacted their responses to Annie. Slowly, Annie's mother and stepfather began to identify how important it was to them to look like a "good family" to their neighbors, how their responses to Annie were colored by the judgments they expected to receive from community members when they learned about Annie's disruptive behaviors. Over many more months of treatment, Annie's parents grew in their capacity for insight into their daughter's behavior. As their insight grew, they began to feel more comfortable showing their vulnerabilities as parents to Annie. These disclosures engendered trust between Annie and her parents, which helped to rebuild their relationships. This process was not instant, but occurred over time. This relational rebuilding process also continued in the months and years after Annie ended treatment.

This case study provides one example of how an adolescent's DBD symptoms can make sense in the context of their home and school environments. The case study illuminates too how family treatment is often critical to improving an adolescent's DBD. I have often told adolescents' parents: "You may not be part of the problem here in terms of your child's behaviors, but you *must* be part of the solution." Engaging families in modifying their own behaviors and relationships can be key in treating adolescent DBDs.

Multisystemic Therapy

Research suggests there are several evidence-based approaches to DBD treatment that involve adolescent clients and their families. One such multipronged approach is multisystemic therapy (MST). MST was developed at the University of South Carolina and bases its theory of change on the idea that adolescents' delinquent behaviors are directly related to multisystem risk factors in their environment (Henggeler et al., 2009; MST Services, LLC., 2017). MST holds that poor adolescent behavior is often associated with poor parental disciplining principles, association with delinquent or drug-abusing peers, and academic challenges among other things (Henggeler et al., 2009). Thus, MST's approach uses family and peer interventions to change family systems and peer relationships (Henggeler, Schoenwald, Borduin, Rowland, & Cunningham, 2009).

Clinicians using MST first assess adolescent clients for initial referral behaviors, then determine the behavior outcomes desired by family members (Henggeler et al., 2009). MST-trained clinicians help both the adolescent and family develop behavioral goals and then assess for and intervene with barriers to goal completion (Henggeler et al., 2009). The clinician assesses the adolescent and each family member for strengths and weaknesses, as well as desired outcomes (Henggeler et al., 2009). MST is a goal-based model: weekly goal assessments and realignments, for both individuals and families, are a large part of the treatment intervention (Henggeler et al., 2009). Clinicians can get trained in MST with a 5-day orientation training, followed up with supervision by an onsite MST supervisor and an offsite MST consultant (Henggeler et al., 2009). More information about the required training can be found at both mstservices.com and msti.org (MST Institute, 2017; MST Services, LLC, 2017). Some research demonstrates MST's effectiveness with violent and disruptive adolescent populations (Henggeler, Melton, Brondino, Scherer, & 1997).

Multidimensional Family Therapy

Multidimensional family therapy (MDFT) is another family-based treatment approach which appears to be effective in treating severe DBDs, including when the adolescent is engaged in comorbid substance abuse (Fonagy, Allison, & Ryan, 2017; Liddle, 2016; van der Pol et al., 2017). MDFT is a manualized treatment which appears to improve adolescent delinquent behavior, substance abuse, and family relationships (Drake, 2012; French et al., 2003; Henderson et al., 2009; Zavala et al., 2005).

MDFT was developed in the early 1990s by Howard Liddle, a counseling psychologist and family therapist from the University of Miami

School of Medicine (MDFT, 2017). The model utilizes a comprehensive assessment of all involved systems and considers both risk and protective factors when developing treatment intervention (Liddle, 2010). MDFT administered in an outpatient setting may cost families less than other nonintegrated family treatments, while providing strong results (French et al., 2003; Liddle, 2016; Zavala et al., 2005). Additionally, MDFT, when compared to intensive adolescent residential treatment, provided superior results (Liddle, 2016).

MDFT is built on the idea that evaluating adolescents' environmental contexts helps clinicians to identify and intervene with meaningful risk factors in order to decrease problematic behaviors (Liddle, 2010). MDFT begins with a comprehensive assessment which includes an investigation of four areas: the adolescent, the parents, the family, and the community (MDFT, 2017). Clinicians explore each of these areas in detail, assessing for strengths and weaknesses in each area (MDFT, 2017). Additionally, MDFT therapists consider assessment to be an ongoing process, revising treatment plans as new information emerges (Liddle, 2010).

The adolescent portion of the assessment includes questions about the adolescent's life story (MDFT, 2017). Therapists question the adolescent about inappropriate behaviors, including drug use, peer and workplace relationships, and legal problems (Liddle, 2010). Assessment includes inquiry into the adolescent's experiences with school, dating and sex, and employment (Liddle, 2010).

The assessment process includes a meeting with the entire family so that therapists have the opportunity to observe family interactions and gather information from each family member (Liddle, 2010). In the MDFT model, clinicians also meet separately with parents, analyzing marriage/partnership functionality, parenting strengths and weaknesses, and parents' emotional connection to and investment in their child (Liddle, 2010). Additionally, clinicians evaluate parents' mental health and substance use, as these can be obstacles to adolescent treatment (Liddle, 2010). MDFT clinicians also inquire about general parenting styles, parental knowledge and competence, and parents' experience with their own families of origin (Liddle, 2010). MDFT clinicians focus on generating optimism and confidence with parents and addressing them with compassion, as parents of adolescents with DBDs often express hopelessness around their child's situation (MDFT, 2011). Generating hope here is important: caregivers who treat their children with impatience and negativity can contribute to a destructive cycle that encourages problematic behaviors and limits the chances of successful intervention (Liddle, 2010; Gresham, 2015).

In the family assessment, clinicians give special consideration to how each family member contributes to the adolescent's environment, questioning each family member about their experience with the adolescent's behavior and their own contributions to it (Liddle, 2010). If necessary, clinicians use assessment time to speak with each individual separately in order to develop a comprehensive picture of the adolescent's family environment. MDFT clinicians aim to develop a comprehensive understanding of anything which contributes to the disruptive behaviors (MDFT, 2017).

MDFT also requires a detailed assessment of relevant social systems, such as educational systems, juvenile justice and court systems, and employers (Liddle, 2010; van der Pol et al., 2017). Therapists should gather information about these social systems from parents and family members, teachers, administrators, probation officers, and employers by visiting settings outside clinical offices (Liddle, 2010; MDFT, 2017). An assessment of relevant social systems allows a clinician to understand an adolescent's external functioning and to develop interventions that improve adolescent functioning and prosocial behaviors (Liddle, 2010).

MDFT interventions aim to impact the adolescent, the parents and family, and relevant social systems (Liddle, 2010). Treatment is divided into three main phases; all three phases together span approximately 4 months (MDFT, 2011). In the first phase, the therapist establishes treatment goals with the adolescent and their family. These goals address unhealthy coping mechanisms and identify emotional needs expressed by the adolescent (MDFT, 2011). Often, these identified needs center on feeling unloved, unconfident, or confused about one's own identity (Liddle, 2010). In this first phase, therapists help adolescents identify healthier ways of coping with family or school-related stressors (MDFT, 2011). Adolescents sometime use disruptive behaviors in lieu of knowing how to properly express needs or emotions (Fonagy et al., 2002). After these needs/emotion are identified, therapists can model healthy ways of labeling and expressing emotions (MDFT, 2011).

During the second phase, therapists work to eliminate specific barriers to treatment. This is done by carefully assessing for these barriers, and then implementing appropriate measures to remove them. For example, clinicians may notice that certain parenting and discipline styles are ineffective. First noting these styles and then teaching more effective approaches is part of the MDFT process. Clinicians help both adolescents and family members implement change. These second-phase therapeutic sessions may involve meetings with teachers, administrators, probation officers, and so forth. To accommodate the needs of all involved parties, some therapy sessions should be conducted outside the clinical office at schools, workplaces, or other clinics (MDFT, 2011).

In this second phase, individual sessions with the adolescent explore identity development and healthy relationship expression with peers and family members. Therapists can use a mixture of their preferred approaches to explore these issues. Clinicians also continue to focus on improving adolescent coping skills, focusing on productive emotional expression. This second phase also involves connecting the adolescent with other resources, such as tutors and employment coaches/resources as needed. MDFT clinicians sometimes visit their clients in the classroom or in the home in order to more effectively employ these interventions, as well as teach coping skills and educate about emotional awareness (MDFT, 2011).

MDFT clinicians work with parents during this second phase, leading family sessions and individual parent sessions. The aim of these sessions is to deliver psychoeducational material, helping parents identify ineffective parenting techniques, differentiate between control and influence, and practice radical acceptance strategies (MDFT, 2011). In this context, radical acceptance refers to the idea that parents will not always agree with the decisions their children make. Therapists teach parents how to express concern appropriately and lovingly, as well as communicate devotion to their adolescent child, while still maintaining boundaries (Liddle, 2010). In the family sessions, therapists encourage direct communication between family members, encouraging healthy communication and family interaction. Finally, therapists in these family sessions introduce external resources that may be helpful for families, like 12-step groups (MDFT, 2011).

Phase three of MDFT aims to solidify the interventions and changes made by the adolescent and family. This process includes preparing a transition plan that sets clients up for future success and progress. Success in MDFT is measured by reductions in disruptive behavior, improvement in interpersonal relationships, and decreased substance abuse (MDFT, 2011). MDFT therapists are trained to provide comprehensive support to both the adolescent and family through the conclusion of the treatment process, a process which involves reviewing goals, following up with tools and coping skills discussed throughout phase two, and encouraging feelings of hope about the prospect of moving forward (Liddle, 2010; MDFT, 2011).

Research shows MDFT's effectiveness with adolescents who exhibit severe delinquent behaviors and substance abuse problems (Henderson et al., 2010; van der Pol et al., 2017). Several meta-analyses show MDFT's efficacy in adolescent populations with DBDs and substance abuse (Liddle, 2016; van der Pol et al., 2017). However, MDFT's efficacy with adolescent populations whose DBD behaviors and drug abuse are less severe appears to be similar to outpatient cognitive behavioral therapy. For example, one study randomly assigned 224 adolescents with conduct disorder and substance abuse issues to weekly treatment groups which administered either MDFT or CBT. This study administered these modalities in an office-based setting once a week and therefore did not utilize the outreach components that full MDFT-implementation recommends. Despite this, study results showed MDFT was more effective than CBT with adolescents with severe DBD behavior. However, for adolescents with only moderate DBD symptomology and drug use, CBT and MDFT were equally effective (Henderson et al., 2010).

Additionally, while MDFT appears effective in treating adolescents who have comorbid DBDs and substance use disorders (Henderson et al., 2010; Liddle, 2016; van der Pol et al., 2017), there is little available research showing MDFT's efficacy with adolescents who exhibit DBDs without substance problems. However, MDFT's thorough assessment model, multidimensional and multisystems approach to intervention, and comprehensive follow-up process make it a strong choice for treating DBDs and intervening with systemic factors that contribute to adolescent disruptive behaviors.

In order to deliver MDFT, clinicians must be trained in the model. MDFT International, a nonprofit organization, delivers this clinical training for both individuals and agencies (MDFT, 2017). Clinicians can participate in trainings at three different levels of intensity. The first is a one-time, 2.5 day training session for individual therapists and agencies who want basic training in MDFT principles and therapeutic techniques (MDFT, 2017). This initial training is followed up with consultations over subsequent months. The second training level, offered over a 6-month period, is accessed by individual clinicians who want to implement MDFT into their clinical practices (MDFT, 2017). Both training levels contain multiple training components, including a treatment manual, experiential workshops, consultation and review of real cases, and supervision (MDFT, 2017). Training in the modality is expensive. The first level of basic training costs agencies $6,000 for 30 people (MDFT, 2018). Subsequent training levels are even more expensive (MDFT,

2018). Those wanting to get certified in MDFT can find information on this website: mdft.org or MDFT's Youtube channel (MDFT, 2017).

Treatment of Attention-Deficit/ Hyperactivity Disorder

Attention-deficit/hyperactivity disorder (ADHD) is one of the most common disorders in childhood, but nearly half of children with an ADHD diagnosis carry that diagnosis into adolescence (Evans, Axelrod, & Langberg, 2004). Approximately 5% of adolescents meet criteria for ADHD (Rhode et al., 1999). ADHD's impulsivity coupled with possible social rejection can create social and academic problems for adolescents (Fonagy et al., 2002). Additionally, adolescents with ADHD often present with comorbid mental health conditions, including conduct disorder, oppositional defiant disorder, depression, anxiety, and learning disorders (Fonagy et al., 2002). Unlike other DBDs, ADHD is often treated effectively with pharmacological interventions (Fonagy et al., 2002). Research suggests that pharmacological treatments for ADHD combined with behavior therapy are generally more effective than behavior therapy alone (MTA Cooperative Group, 1999).

There is a rich body of research that supports the combination of pharmacological and behavioral interventions for ADHD (Fonagy et al., 2002; The MTA Cooperative Group, 1999). Research suggests behavioral interventions are generally less effective when used without medication, but are effective in the assistance of prosocial behavior development (Fonagy et al., 2002). Other available literature suggests variants of CBT which teach problem-solving and socialization and intervene with interpersonal problems are effective for adolescent ADHD (Fonagy et al., 2002).

Some research suggests that behavioral training programs that target systems, like school and home environments, are important in treating adolescent ADHD (Young & Amarasinghe, 2010). These training programs can include instruction on note-taking skills, instruction on basic organizational skills, and instruction on problem-solving measures (Evans, Axelrod, & Langberg, 2004). One study of early adolescents receiving this intervention three times a week in individual, group, and family therapy showed improved grades and measureable improvement in social interactions (Evans, Axelrod, & Langberg, 2004).

Some behavioral training approaches for adolescent ADHD focus on parents or teachers (Jones, Daley, Hutchings, Bywater, Eames, 2007). Behavioral training for teachers includes educating teachers on effective goal setting, management, and disciplining techniques (Young & Amarasinghe, 2010). Behavioral training for parents includes instruction on effective discipline, such as when to remove specific privileges or when to offer specific rewards (Barkley, Edwards, Laneri, Fletcher, & Metevia, 2001; Young & Amarasinghe, 2010).

A case study may illuminate the presentation and treatment of ADHD. Jonas was a 16-year-old boy whose ADHD symptoms severely impacted his school and home environments. The first time I (JEB) met with him in my office at a community mental health clinic, Jonas was unable to sit still. He bounced in his chair the entire 50-minute session. He fidgeted with whatever was closest to his chair, he chewed on a pen, and his legs moved up and down rhythmically. The stimuli in my office with the door closed was relatively low, but Jonas still seemed interested in every small noise he heard outside my office door. He was willing, even eager, to talk with me. But he recounted a long history of difficult school experiences and home conflicts.

Jonas described that, ever since he could remember, he had a difficult time keeping his attention on whatever he was doing. It didn't matter if he was interested or excited by the task he was working on or if he was unexcited and interested: regardless, he seemed to be distracted by everything else happening around him. If his dog walked by while he was doing his homework, he followed the dog to play with him. If Jonas could hear that his brother started watching television while Jonas himself was reading, Jonas left what he was doing to join his brother. Whatever the distraction, it was compelling to Jonas. Further, he often failed to complete tasks he was supposed to be doing: emptying the dishwasher at home, setting the table for dinner, completing a timed test at school, or filling the paint bottles at school for the art teacher. If he got distracted while completing the task, he left what he was doing and generally didn't return to it unless directed by a parent or teacher. This got him into a lot of trouble—both at school and at home. He often felt that adults thought he was stupid for not following clear directions that his peers seemed to follow without difficulty. His report cards had always been poor. While he thought he understood his schoolwork, he typically had trouble completing it. Jonas also struggled with his peer relationships. He often interrupted others when they were speaking, in his eagerness to share, and often had difficulty waiting his turn in games he played with peers.

In working with Jonas, I immediately understood that individual therapy alone was likely to have only limited effectiveness in terms of addressing Jonas' severe ADHD symptomology. Thus, I started by engaging Jonas' caregivers in that planning sessions which also included Jonas. We established goals for treatment which included behavior changes at home and at school. To accomplish these, I met regularly with Jonas and his caregivers together to set up behavioral plans that would support him in addressing his ADHD symptoms at home. For example, I explained to Jonas' caregivers that they should give him only one task at a time to complete, to provide supervision while he completed the task, to provide supports for completing each task (like providing quiet and uninterrupted places for Jonas to work), and to establish behavioral incentives for task completion. I also worked with Jonas' school to establish an Individualized Educational Plan (IEP) for Jonas that included supports for his symptomology at school. Additionally, I recommended that Jonas meet with a psychiatrist for medication evaluation. I also referred him to a social skills support group for adolescents with ADHD to assist him in tackling some of the social skills issues which accompanied Jonas' ADHD symptomology.

The case of Jonas illustrates how significant ADHD symptomology can manifest in adolescents and what comprehensive treatment planning might look like. Jonas needed assistance not just at home or at school, but also with peers. A multipronged approach for Jonas' ADHD included supportive individual therapy, family therapy, advocacy at his school for his IEP, pharmacological intervention, and group therapy focused on building social skills.

The comprehensive approach described above in the case of Jonas is supported by existing research summarized in this chapter. Treatment for adolescent ADHD and other DBDs should address the creation of supports in all the adolescent's contexts: home, school, youth group, church group, hobby group, and so forth. Further, treatment for all DBDs should be thorough, including individual as well as family intervention, comprehensive assessment, thorough treatment planning, and delivery of evidence-based interventions as detailed in this chapter.

References

Aebi, M., Barra, S., Bessler, C., Steinhausen, H., Walitza, S., & Plattner, B. (2016). Oppositional defiant disorder dimensions and subtypes among detained male adolescent offenders. *Journal of Child Psychology and Psychiatry, 57*, 729–736. doi:10.1111/jcpp.12473

American Psychiatric Association. (2013). *Diagnostic and statistical manual of mental disorders: DSM-5*. Washington, DC: American Psychiatric Association

Åslund, C., Comasco, E., Nordquist, N., Leppert, J., Oreland, L., & Nilsson, K. W. (2013). Self-reported family socioeconomic status, the 5-HTTLPR genotype, and delinquent behavior in a community-based adolescent population. *Aggressive Behavior, 39*, 52–63. doi:10.1002/ab.21451

Barkley, R. A., Edwards, G., Laneri, M., Fletcher, K., & Metevia, L. (2001). The efficacy of problem-solving communication training alone, behaviour management training alone, and their combination for parent–adolescent conflict in teenagers with ADHD and ODD. *Journal of Consulting & Clinical Psychology, 69*, 926.

Baruch, G., Vrouva, I., & Wells, C. (2011). Outcome findings from a parent training programme for young people with conduct problems. *Child and Adolescent Mental Health, 16*, 47–54. doi:10.1111/j.1475-3588.2010.00574.x

Calin, O. D., Muscalu, M., & Macovei, S. C. (2014). Perspectives in treatment of conduct disorder in children and adolescents. *Romanian Journal of Child and Adolescent Psychiatry, 2*, 10–14.

Cohen, M. A., & Piquero, A. R. (2009). New evidence on the monetary value of saving a high risk youth. *Journal of Quantitative Criminology, 25*, 25–49. doi:10.1007/s10940-008-9057-3

Colins, O., Vermeiren, R., Schuyten, G., & Broekaert, E. (2009). Psychiatric disorders in property, violent, and versatile offending detained male adolescents. *American Journal of Orthopsychiatry, 79*, 31–38. doi:10.1037/a0015337

Cunningham, N. R., Wolff, J. C., & Jarrett, M. A. (2013). Assessment of disruptive behavior disorders in anxiety. In D. McKay & E. A. Storch, (Eds.), *Handbook of Assessing Variants and Complications in Anxiety Disorders* (pp 231-241). New York, NY: Springer. doi:10.1007/978-1-4614-6452-5_15

Disney, E. R., Elkins, I. J., McGue, M., & Iacono, W. G. (1999). Effects of ADHD, conduct disorder, and gender on substance use and abuse in adolescence. *American Journal of Psychiatry, 156*, 1515–1521. doi:10.1176/ajp.156.10.1515

Drake, E. K. (2012, December). *Chemical dependency treatment for offenders: A review of the evidence and benefit-cost findings*. Retrieved from http://www.wsipp.wa.gov/Reports/331

Duncombe, M. E., Havighurst, S. S., Holland, K. A., & Frankling, E. J. (2012). The contribution of parenting practices and parent emotion factors in children at risk for disruptive behavior disorders. *Child Psychiatry & Human Development, 43*, 715–733. doi:10.1007/s10578-012-0290-5

Erskine, H. E., Ferrari, A. J., Polanczyk, G. V., Moffitt, T. E., Murray, C. J., Vos, T., . . . Scott, J. G. (2014). The global epidemiology and burden of attention-deficit/hyperactivity disorder and conduct disorder. *The Journal of Child Psychology and Psychiatry, 55*, 328–336. doi:10.1111/jcpp.12186

Evans, S. W., Axelrod, J. L., & Langberg, J. M. (2004). Efficacy of a school-based treatment program for middle school youth with ADHD: Pilot data. *Behavior Modification, 28*, 528–547.

Farrington, D. P., & Welsh, B. (2009). *Saving children from a life of crime: Early risk factors and effective interventions*. New York, NY: Oxford University Press.

Fonagy, P., Allison, L., & Ryan, A. (2017). Therapy outcomes: What works for whom? In N. Midgley, J. Hayes, & M. Cooper (Eds.), *Essential research findings in child and adolescent counseling and psychotherapy* (pp. 79–118). London: SAGE Publications.

Fonagy, P., Target, M., Cottrell, D., Phillips, J., & Kurtz, Z. (2002). *What works for whom?: A critical review of treatments for children and adolescents.* New York, NY: Guilford Press.

French, M. T., Roebuck, M. C., Dennis, M., Godley, S., Liddle, H. A., & Tims, F. (2003). Outpatient marijuana treatment for adolescents: Economic evaluation of a multisite field experiment. *Evaluation Review, 27,* 421–459.

Friedmutter, R. (2015). *The effectiveness of mindful parenting interventions: A meta-analysis* (Doctoral dissertation). Retrieved from ProQuest (3663064).

Goodman, R., Ford, T., Simmons, H., Gatward, R., & Meltzer, H. (2003). Using the Strengths and Difficulties Questionnaire (SDQ) to screen for child psychiatric disorders in a community sample. *International Review of Psychiatry, 15,* 166–172.

Gresham, F. M. (2015). *Disruptive behavior disorders: Evidence-based practice for assessment and intervention.* New York, NY: Guilford Press.

Gresham, F. M., Lane, K. L., & Lambros, K. M. (2000). Comorbidity of conduct problems and ADHD: Identification of 'fledging psychopaths.' *Journal of Emotional and Behavioral Disorders, 8,* 83–93. doi:10.1177/106342660000800204

Grimes, M. E., & McElwain, A. D. (2008). Marriage and family therapy with low-income clients: Professional, ethical, and clinical issues. *Contemporary Family Therapy, 30,* 220–232. doi:10.1007/s10591-008-9071-5

Helgeland, M. I., Kjelsberg, E., & Torgersen, S. (2005). Continuities between emotional and disruptive behavior disorders in adolescence and personality disorders in adulthood. *American Journal of Psychiatry, 162,* 1941–1947. doi:10.1176/appi.ajp.162.10.1941

Henderson, C. E., Dakof, G. A., Greenbaum, P. E., & Liddle, H. A. (2010). Supplemental material for effectiveness of multidimensional family therapy with higher severity substance-abusing adolescents: Report from two randomized controlled trials. *Journal of Consulting and Clinical Psychology, 78,* 885–897. doi:10.1037/a0020620.supp

Henderson, C. E., Rowe, C. L., Dakof, G. A., Hawes, S. W., & Liddle, H. A. (2009). Parenting practices as mediators of treatment effects in an early-intervention trial of multidimensional family therapy. *The American Journal of Drug and Alcohol Abuse, 35,* 220–226.

Henggeler, S. W., Melton, G. B., Brondino, M. J., Scherer, D. G., & Hanley, J. H. (1997). Multisystemic therapy with violent and chronic juvenile offenders and their families: The role of treatment fidelity in successful dissemination. *Journal of Consulting and Clinical Psychology, 65,* 821–833. doi:10.1037/0022-006x.65.5.821

Henggeler, S. W., Schoenwald, S. K., Borduin, C. M., Rowland, M. D., & Cunningham, P. B. (2009). *Multisystemic therapy for antisocial behavior in children and adolescents.* New York, NY: Guilford Press.

Hodgkinson, S., Godoy, L., Beers, L. S., & Lewin, A. (2017). Improving mental health access for low-income children and families in the primary care setting. *Pediatrics, 139,* 1–9. doi:10.1542/peds.2015-1175

Hogue, A., Evans, S. W., & Levin, F. R. (2017). A clinicians' guide to co-occurring ADHD among adolescent substance users: Comorbidity, neurodevelopmental risk, and evidence-based treatment options. *Journal of Child & Adolescent Substance Abuse, 26,* 277–292. doi:10.1080/1067828x.2017.1305930

Honeycutt, A. A., Khavjou, O. A., Jones, D. J., Cuellar, J., & Forehand, R. L. (2015). Helping the noncompliant child: An assessment of program costs and cost-effectiveness. *Journal of Child & Family Studies, 24,* 499–504. doi:10.1007/s10826-013-9862-7

Implement an MDFT Program. (n.d.). Retrieved from http://www.mdft.org/MDFT-Program/How-it-Works

Jones, K., Daley, D., Hutchings, J., Bywater, T., & Eames, C. (2007). Efficacy of the incredible years basic parent training programme as an early intervention for children with conduct problems and ADHD. *Child: Care, Health and Development, 33,* 749–756. doi:10.1111/j.1365-2214.2007.00747.x

Kaltman, S., Mendoza, A. H., Serrano, A., & Gonzales, F. A. (2016). A mental health intervention strategy for low-income, trauma-exposed Latina immigrants in primary care: A preliminary study. *American Journal of Orthopsychiatry,86,* 345–354. doi:10.1037/ort0000157

Kersten, L., Prätzlich, M., Mannstadt, S., Ackermann, K., Kohls, G., Oldenhof, H., . . . Stadler, C. (2016). START NOW—A comprehensive skills training programme for female adolescents with oppositional defiant and conduct disorders: Study protocol for a cluster-randomised controlled trial. *Trials, 18,* 1–16. doi:10.1186/s13063-017-1817-7

Klasen, H., & Crombag, A. (2013). What works where? A systematic review of child and adolescent mental health interventions for low and middle-income countries. *Social Psychiatry and Psychiatric Epidemiology, 48,* 595–611. doi:10.1007/s00127-012-0566-x

Kremer, M., Smith, A. B., & Lawrence, J. A. (2010). Family discipline incidents: An analysis of parental diaries. *Journal of Family Studies, 16,* 251–263. doi:10.5172/jfs.16.3.251

Kroneman, L. M., Loeber, R., Hipwell, A. E., & Koot, H. M. (2009). Girls' disruptive behavior and its relationship to family functioning: A review. *Journal of Child and Family Studies, 18,* 259–273. doi:10.1007/s10826-008-9226-x

Latimer, K., Wilson, P., Kemp, J., Thompson, L., Sim, F., Gillberg, C., . . . Minnis, H. (2012). Disruptive behaviour disorders: A systematic review of environmental antenatal and early years risk factors. *Child: Care, Health and Development, 38,* 611–628. doi:10.1111/j.1365-2214.2012.01366.x

Liddle, H. A. (2010). Multidimensional family therapy: A science-based treatment system. *The Australian and New Zealand Journal of Family Therapy, 31,* 133–148-354.

Liddle, H. A. (2016). Multidimensional family therapy: Evidence base for transdiagnostic treatment outcomes, change mechanisms, and implementation in community settings. *Family Process, 55,* 558–576. doi:10.1111/famp.12243

McKinney, C., & Morse, M. (2012). Assessment of disruptive behavior disorders: Tools and recommendations. *Professional Psychology: Research and Practice, 43,* 641–649.

MDFT. (n.d.-a). *Crime and delinquency.* Retrieved from MDFT website: http://mdft.org/Effectiveness/Criminal-and-delinquent-behavior

MDFT. (n.d.-b). *How MDFT works.* Retrieved from MDFT website: http://mdft.org/MDFT-Program/How-it-Works

MDFT. (n.d.-c). *Three levels of training.* Retrieved from MDFT website: http://mdft.org/Training-Program/3-Levels-of-Training

MDFT. (n.d.-d). *What is MDFT?* Retrieved from MDFT website: http://mdft.org/MDFT-Program/What-is-MDFT

MDFT. (n.d.-e). *Why choose MDFT?* Retrieved from MDFT website: http://mdft.org/MDFT-Program/Why-choose-MDFT

MDFT. (2011, February 25-a). *Adolescent drug abuse—MDFT case presentation (part 1 of 2)* [Video file]. Retrieved from https://www.youtube.com/watch?v=oQS5g-iKhpM

MDFT. (2011, February 25-b). *Adolescent drug abuse—MDFT case presentation (part 2 of 2)* [Video file]. Retrieved from https://www.youtube.com/watch?v=00uPtkyt5qU

MDFT. (2011, February 25-c). *Multidimensional family therapy, an introduction (1 of 2)* [Video file]. Retrieved from https://www.youtube.com/watch?v=FiOiOERc82o

MDFT. (2011, February 25-d). *Multidimensional family therapy (2 of 2)* [Video file]. Retrieved from https://www.youtube.com/watch?v=YzjGqlPIU-g&t=12s

MDFT. (2011, March 22-a). *Adolescent treatment* [Video file]. Retrieved from https://www.youtube.com/watch?v=gZBWAVDMUVs

MDFT. (2011, March 22-b). *Risk and protective factors* [Video file]. Retrieved from https://www.youtube.com/watch?v=7MnalNpbQrg&t=188s

MST Services. (n.d.-a). *Resources and training.* Retrieved from http://www.mstservices.com/resources-training

MST Institute (n.d.-b). *Welcome to the MST institute website.* Retrieved from https://www.msti.org/mstinstitute/index.html

MTA Cooperative Group. (1999). A 14-month randomized clinical trial of treatment Strategies for attention-deficit/hyperactivity disorder. *Archives of General Psychiatry, 56,* 1073–1086. doi:10.1001/archpsyc.56.12.1073

Muratori, P., Milone, A., Nocentini, A., Manfredi, A., Polidori, L., Ruglioni, L., ... Lochman, J. E. (2014). Maternal depression and parenting practices predict treatment outcome in Italian children with disruptive behavior disorder. *Journal of Child & Family Studies, 24,* 2805–2816. doi:10.1007/s10826-014-0085-3

Oruche, U. M., Draucker, C. B., Al-Khattab, H., Cravens, H. A., Lowry, B., & Lindsey, L. M. (2015). The challenges for primary caregivers of adolescents with disruptive behavior disorders. *Journal of Family Nursing, 21,* 149–167. doi:10.1177/1074840714562027

Oruche, U. M., Draucker, C., Al-Khattab, H., Knopf, A., & Mazurcyk, J. (2014). Interventions for family members of adolescents with disruptive behavior disorders. *Journal of Child and Adolescent Psychiatric Nursing, 27,* 99–108. doi:10.1111/jcap.12078

Pearson Clinical. (n.d.). Behavior Assessment System for Children: Third Edition (BASC-3). (2018). Retrieved from *SpringerReference.* doi:10.1007/springerreference_179758

Pearson Clinical. (n.d.). PreK-16 education and special needs. (2018). Retrieved from https://www.pearsonclinical.com/education/landing/basc-3.html

Qi, C. H., & Kaiser, A. P. (2003). Behavior problems of preschool children from low-income families: Review of the literature. *Topics in Early Childhood Special Education, 23,* 188–216. doi:https://doi.org/10.1177/02711214030230040201

Reedtz, C., Bertelsen, B., Lurie, J., Handegård, B. H., Clifford, G., & Mørch, W. (2007). Eyberg Child Behavior Inventory (ECBI): Norwegian norms to identify conduct problems in children. *Scandinavian Journal of Psychology, 49,* 31–38. doi:10.1111/j.1467-9450.2007.00621.x

Rhode, L. A., Biederman, J., Busnello, E. A., Zimmerman, H., Schmitz, M., & Martins, S. (2000). ADHD in a school sample of Brazilian adolescents. *Journal of The American Academy of Child y Adolescent Psychiatry, 38,* 716–722.

Ryan, S. R., Stanger, C., Thostenson, J., Whitmore, J. J., & Budney, A. J. (2013). The impact of disruptive behavior disorder on substance use treatment outcome in adolescents. *Journal of Substance Abuse Treatment, 44,* 506–514. doi:10.1016/j.jsat.2012.11.003

Cohen, J. A. S., & Semple, R. J. (2010). Mindful parenting: A call for research. *Journal of Child and Family Studies, 19,* 145–151. doi:https://doi.org/10.1007/s10826-009-9285-7

Schutter, D. J., van Bokhoven, I., Vanderschuren, L. J., Lochman, J. E., & Matthys, W. (2011). Risky decision making in substance dependent adolescents with a disruptive behavior disorder. *Journal of Abnormal Child Psychology, 39*, 333–339. doi:10.1007/s10802-010-9475-1

Spencer, T., Biederman, J., Wilens, T., Harding, M., O'Donnell, D., & Griffin, S. (1996). Pharmacotherapy of attention-deficit hyperactivity disorder across the life cycle. *Journal of the American Academy of Child and Adolescent Psychiatry, 35*, 409–432.

Steiner, H., & Remsing, L. (2007). Practice parameter for the assessment and treatment of children and adolescents with oppositional defiant disorder. *Journal of the American Academy of Child & Adolescent Psychiatry, 46*, 126–141. doi:10.1097/01.chi.0000246060.62706.af

Taylor, S. D., & Distelberg, B. (2016). Predicting behavioral health outcomes among low-income families: Testing a socioecological model of family resilience determinants. *Journal of Child and Family Studies, 25*, 2797–2807. doi:10.1007/s10826-016-0440-7

Tremblay, R. E. (2010). Developmental origins of disruptive behaviour problems: The 'original sin' hypothesis, epigenetics and their consequences for prevention. *Journal of Child Psychology & Psychiatry, 51*, 341–367. doi:10.1111/j.1469-7610.2010.02211.x

van der Pol, T. M., Hoeve, M., Noom, M. J., Stams, G. J., Doreleijers, T. A., Domburgh, L. V., & Vermeiren, R. R. (2017). Research review: The effectiveness of multidimensional family therapy in treating adolescents with multiple behavior problems—A meta-analysis. *Journal of Child Psychology and Psychiatry, 58*, 532–545. doi:10.1111/jcpp.12685

Waller, R., Gardner, F., & Hyde, L. W. (2013). What are the associations between parenting, callous–unemotional traits, and antisocial behavior in youth? A systematic review of evidence. *Clinical Psychology Review, 33*, 593–608. doi:10.1016/j.cpr.2013.03.001

Young, S., & Amarasinghe, J. M. (2010). Practitioner review: Non-pharmacological treatments for ADHD: A lifespan approach. *Journal of Child Psychology and Psychiatry, 51*, 116–133. doi:10.1111/j.1469-7610.2009.02191.x

Youth in Mind. (n.d.). *Information for researchers and professionals about the strengths & difficulties questionnaires.* Retrieved from http://www.sdqinfo.com/

Zavala, S. K., French, M. T., Henderson, C. E., Alberga, L., Rowe, C., & Liddle, H. A. (2005). Guidelines and challenges for estimating the economic costs and benefits of adolescent substance abuse treatments. *Journal of Substance Abuse Treatment, 29*, 191–205. doi:10.1016/j.jsat.2005.06.004

9

Evidence-Based Interventions
for Traumatized Adolescents

Joanna E. Bettmann, Katherine V. Ovrom, and Tracie Peñúñuri

In this chapter, we introduce types of trauma that adolescents experience, describe groups who are at higher risk for certain traumas, and detail the impact of trauma on adolescent development and behavior. We also explore the landmark Adverse Childhood Experiences (ACEs) study and provide information on how to use the ACE screening tool as part of a clinical assessment. In this chapter, we also describe trauma that occurs during adolescence, as well as how trauma in childhood can put adolescents at increased risk for poor outcomes. Finally, we review several evidence-based interventions for traumatized adolescents and provide a lengthy case example of treatment with one traumatized adolescent.

Definition of Trauma

The DSM-5 states that an event is considered traumatic if the event resulted in death or threatened death, actual or threatened physical injury, or actual or threatened sexual violation (American Psychiatric Association, 2013). While older versions of the DSM included *an intense emotional response to the event* as a critical component of the event qualifying as traumatic, research shows that an individual's emotional response at the time of the traumatic event is not predictive of later mental health problems (Ruglass & Kendall-Tackett, 2014). Clinicians need to understand this because a client may be exhibiting signs of acute stress disorder, post-traumatic stress disorder, or other trauma-related symptomology but may not be able to link their symptoms to the precipitating event if they did not have an intense emotional reaction at the time of the event. Alternatively, a person who has an extreme emotional response to a traumatic event in the moment may not have any sequelae from the trauma.

Mental health issues arising from trauma can result whether an individual experiences a single traumatic event or multiple, compounding events. Examples of single-event traumas include witnessing a violent death, experiencing a physical assault, surviving a rape, and so forth. Unfortunately, many children and adolescents experience multiple severe traumas which can lead to symptoms beyond those encompassed within the diagnosis of PTSD (Wamser-Nanney & Vandenberg, 2013). Research links traumas of an interpersonal nature, those that occur within one's relational system such as child abuse or domestic violence, to more severe and complex symptoms than non-interpersonal traumas (Ford, Stockton, Kaltman, & Green, 2006). The term "complex trauma" was developed to describe the problem of repeated exposure to traumatic events as well as the symptoms that can follow severe and repeated interpersonal traumas (Cook, Blaustein, Spinazzola, & van der Kolk, 2003). "Complex trauma" most commonly refers to simultaneous or sequential occurrences of childhood maltreatment which are chronic and begin early in life, such as experiencing abuse or neglect or witnessing domestic violence (Cook et al., 2003).

Screening for Adverse Childhood Experiences

How should we screen our adolescent clients for their trauma histories? One useful tool for clinicians is the Adverse Childhood Experiences Questionnaire (ACEs). In the ACEs questionnaire (available free on the Centers for Disease Control website: www.cdc.gov), ACEs are categorized into three main groups: abuse, neglect, and family/household challenges (Centers for Disease Control and Prevention [CDC], 2016). The ACEs questions inquire about physical, sexual, and emotional abuse, physical or emotional neglect, and household challenges such as witnessing domestic violence, household-member substance abuse, household mental illness, parental separation or divorce, and criminal household member (CDC, 2016). Utilizing the ACEs questionnaire with adolescent clients will inform the clinician as to clients' risk for health and mental health disorders and may clarify other presenting disorders such as substance use that may be rooted in childhood traumatization.

The original ACEs study was conducted from 1995 to 1997 with a sample size of more than 17,000 participants (Felitti et al., 1998). Study participants filled out a questionnaire that asked them to indicate if they had experienced specific traumatic events in childhood, where childhood was defined as ages 0–18. The findings of the ACE study established a correlation between traumatic events in childhood and poor psychosocial, medical, and mental health outcomes in adulthood (Felitti et al., 1998). We can think about the ACE study as a flow chart with adverse childhood experiences leading to disrupted neurodevelopment, followed by social, emotional, and cognitive impairment, the adoption of health-risk behaviors which lead to disease, disability, and, finally, earlier death (CDC, 2016).

The ACEs study clearly showed the compounding effect of traumatic childhood experiences. ACEs survey respondents who were exposed to one ACE category were 86.5% more likely to be exposed to at least one other ACE category (Dube et al., 2003). Further, as the number of ACEs increased, so did the risk for poor health outcomes, risky behaviors such as substance abuse, and lower high school graduation rates (Felitti et al., 1998).

Impact of ACEs Across the Life Span

The body of work examining the impact of ACEs on lifetime outcomes is substantial. To illustrate the compounding effect of ACEs, one study used the ACEs questionnaire to create a cumulative adversity score that ranged from 0–6 based on how many ACEs an individual experienced. The researchers found that each unit increase in the cumulative adversity score was significantly associated with younger ages at first psychiatric hospitalization, first arrest, and onset of aggressive behavior (Stinson, Quinn, & Levenson, 2016). Some studies link the number of ACEs an individual experiences with increased risk for PTSD, depression, substance abuse, and suicide attempts later in life (Brockie, Dana-Sacco, Wallen, Wilcox, & Campbell, 2015). Some research links ACEs to higher incarceration rates and younger age at first arrest (Stinson et al., 2016). This literature collectively tells us that adolescents who were traumatized in childhood are at significant risk and need targeted treatment plans which address these root issues.

Trauma in childhood and adolescence is also associated with higher risk for mental and substance use disorders in adolescence (Huang et al., 2011; Sumner et al., 2015). Youth who experience physical abuse are 54%

more likely to develop a depressive disorder and 92% more likely to use substances (Sumner et al., 2015). Childhood emotional abuse or neglect links to even higher rates of psychological disorders. Childhood emotional abuse increases the likelihood of a depressive disorder later in life by more than 300%, while neglect raises the odds to over 200% in comparison to children who did not experience abuse (Sumner et al., 2015). Notably, childhood PTSD is associated with the onset of several other mental health disorders, the most common being oppositional defiant disorder, separation anxiety disorder, attention-deficit/hyperactivity disorder, and major depressive disorder (Simonelli, 2013).

Childhood traumas, especially those that are interpersonal, intentional, and chronic such as those measured by the ACEs Questionnaire, link to increased levels of depression, PTSD, suicidality, and substance abuse (De Bellis & Zisk, 2014). Childhood sexual abuse links to higher levels of psychotic, affective, anxiety, and personality disorders in adulthood (Matulis, Resick, Rosner, & Steil, 2014). A recent study found that for each additional adverse event, reported emotional problems rose by 32% even after controlling for gender, race, and age among adolescents (Balistreri & Alvira-Hammond, 2016). Troublingly, Dube et al. (2001) found that ACEs increase the risk of attempted suicide 2–5 fold.

For adolescents, experiencing chronic or repeated traumas links to greater trauma symptomology than single-event trauma or later-life trauma (Wamser-Nanney & Vandenberg, 2013). Further, complex trauma links to difficulties in self-regulation, affect, behavior, impulse control, attention, and identity issues (Cook et al., 2003). Complex trauma in childhood or adolescence may play a role in the development of antisocial behavior, defined as behavior that violates the rights of others, societal norms, or rules (Podgurski, Lyons, Kisiel, & Griffen, 2014). The multitude of mental and physical disorders associated with childhood trauma prompts experts to argue that childhood trauma should be regarded as an environmentally induced complex developmental disorder (De Bellis & Zisk, 2014; Ford, 2011).

Prevalence of ACEs and Trauma in Adolescence

More than half of U.S. adolescents have experienced at least one ACE and 17% have experienced three or more (Balistreri & Alvira-Hammond, 2016). Since ACE categories include traumas of an interpersonal nature, those 17%

who experienced three or more ACEs meet criteria for complex trauma, defined as multiple, severe, and/or repeated interpersonal traumas (Wamser-Nanney & Vandenberg, 2013). Even adolescents who don't experience ACEs sometimes experience trauma in the form of severe bullying, sexual assault, or physical assault, rates of which all increase in adolescence (CDC, 2011; Haller & Chassin, 2012). We will highlight here several types of trauma that are unfortunately common and harmful to adolescent development: sexual assault, bullying, and family violence.

Sexual Assault

In a 2011 CDC survey, 8% of U.S. high school students reported they had been physically forced to have sexual intercourse against their will. These reports were higher among female (11.8%) than male (4.5%) students (CDC, 2011). Troublingly, this report is consistent with data the CDC has collected since 2001. The risk of rape appears to be a consistent threat for adolescents.

For some adolescents, sexual assault is not a single event trauma, but an ongoing trauma that began in childhood at the hands of an adult caregiver. Meta-analytic research suggests that approximately 20% of women and 8% of men experience some form of sexual abuse in childhood (Pereda, Guilera, Forns, & Gómez-Benito, 2009). Notably, childhood sexual abuse in both boys and girls links to significant risk for severe mental health disorders, especially PTSD (Matulis et al., 2014).

Childhood sexual trauma and physical abuse can also impact adolescent sexual development and behavior. Childhood sexual and nonsexual violence are associated with earlier age at first sexual intercourse, multiple partners, failure to use condoms, and other sexual behaviors that increase the risk of sexually transmitted infections. Youth under 18 who experience physical abuse are 78% more likely to contract a sexually transmitted infection or to engage in risky sexual behavior (Sumner et al., 2015).

Bullying and Victimization

Another common trauma for adolescents is bullying or victimization. A national study found that 20.1% of high schoolers were bullied on school property while 16.2% were bullied electronically (CDC, 2011). Bullying can include verbal and physical assaults. Research suggests bullying is a threat to the mental health of adolescents (Bannink, Broeren, van de Looij, De Waart, & Raat, 2014). Bullying links to many of the same risk behaviors and mental health disorders associated with other traumas including substance abuse, depression, anxiety, and suicide (Turner, Exum, Brame, & Holt, 2013). Some argue that victimization from bullying should be categorized as an adverse childhood experience based on the multitude of negative outcomes that increase in conjunction with exposure to bullying and compound as adolescents' experience bullying across multiple settings (Hertz, Jones, Barrios, David-Ferdon, & Holt, 2015).

Family Violence

Family violence refers to intimate partner violence or child abuse (Hultmann & Broberg, 2016). Studies of the U.S. population place the lifetime prevalence of childhood physical abuse at 8.9% (Finkelhor, Vanderminden, Turner, Hamby, & Shattuck, 2014). Nearly 14% of U.S. children experience some form of abuse (physical, sexual, psychological, neglect) from a caregiver (Sumner et al., 2015). Unfortunately, family violence is generationally interconnected: a survivor of caregiver sexual abuse may perpetrate abuse later in life. Exposure to violence as a child is a strong predictor of future violence exposure in adolescence and adulthood (Sumner et al., 2015).

Population-Specific Traumas

Gender and Trauma

Females are more likely than males to experience both adverse childhood experiences and other kinds of trauma (Stinson et al., 2016). Further, both child and adult females are at higher risk of developing PTSD following trauma than males (Cicero, Nooner, & Silva, 2011). Adolescent females are almost 3 times as likely to experience rape as their male counterparts (CDC, 2011).

Dating violence is another common experience for female adolescents. Approximately 10% of U.S. adolescent girls experienced physical victimization, 7% experienced sexual victimization, and 29% reported psychological victimization from a dating partner (Eaton, Davis, Barrios, Brener, & Noonan, 2007). This is particularly alarming since dating violence in adolescence is predictive of dating victimization in young adulthood (Vézina et al., 2015). Of note, a history of family violence puts females at greater risk for being victimized psychologically, physically, and/or sexually in a dating relationship; males do not experience the same risk (Vézina et al., 2015).

In the context of bullying, females experience a greater negative impact on their mental health from exposure to cyber-bullying than males (Bannink et al., 2014). Cyber-bullying has become a significant issue since the advent of smart phones and peaks during adolescence when teens often become deeply engaged with social media (Bannink et al., 2014). Clinicians should always assess adolescent clients' experiences of cyber-bullying, since such behaviors often go unnoticed by or are hidden from adults.

Forensic Population

Traumatization links to criminal behaviors, aggression, and consequent incarceration (Stinson et al., 2016). Forensic clients are more likely to have experienced ACEs than community samples (Stinson et al., 2016). This reinforces the need for treatment, rather than punishment, for traumatized adolescents in the juvenile justice system.

Impact of Trauma on Development

Chronic stress caused by childhood trauma can alter brain structure and neurological development, impacting adolescent functioning. For example, stress in childhood leads to overactivity in the amygdala. The amygdala serves as a key component of humans' socio-emotional system that responds to fear and elevated levels of cortisol, both of which contribute to difficulties regulating fear and anxiety (Shonkoff et al., 2012). Additionally, chronic stress can lead to loss of neurons and neuronal connections in the prefrontal cortex, which is responsible for regulating impulses, planning, and performing other executive functions (Shonkoff et al., 2012). These impacts to the brain can lead to impairments in learning and memory and predispose children and adolescents to increased fear and anxiety (Shonkoff et al., 2012).

The National Child Traumatic Stress Network identified seven domains impacted by complex trauma: attachment, biology, affect regulation, dissociation, behavioral control, cognition, and self-concept (Cook et al., 2003). The biological domain includes problems with coordination and balance, somatization, and sensorimotor developmental problems (Cook et al., 2003). Cognitive deficits associated with complex trauma include problems with processing information, problems with focus and task completion, learning difficulties, problems with language development, difficulties in attention regulation, and problems with orientation in time and space (Cook et al., 2003). Toxic stress exposure due to ACEs may also negatively impact immune response and hormone activity, which could help explain the well-established link between ACEs and poorer lifetime physical health outcomes (Balistreri & Alvira-Hammond, 2016). Complex trauma thus impacts multiple domains of adolescent development, including physical, cognitive, and emotional domains.

Working With Trauma: Practice Considerations

Working with traumatized adolescents can be overwhelming and exhausting. I (JEB) can remember shaking for about 20 minutes after leaving a session with an adolescent who described horrific physical and emotional abuse from his mother. I can remember sobbing by myself after leaving a session with an adolescent girl who described multiple episodes of childhood sexual abuse as well as promiscuous sexual behavior in adolescence and mistreatment by her current sexual partners. Clinicians working with traumatized adolescents need to be mindful of their own countertransference, seek support and supervision regularly, and avoid burnout by engaging in healthy coping skills.

Many new clinicians will push clients to expose their full trauma histories and the related details in treatment. This is not a therapeutic approach. Clients have developed strong defenses for dealing with their traumas over time. These defenses can include denial, avoidance, isolation of affect (describing traumatic events without any emotion attached to it), repression of aspects of the trauma, dissociation, or withdrawal. Clinicians should think of such defenses as walls within our clients' brains, walls which prevent overwhelming anxiety and emotional dysregulation. These walls should be respected, not pushed aside by the therapist. Think of these walls as helping to protect your client's psyche. When you create a safe enough space in therapy, the client over time will want to take those walls down, brick by brick, slowly. You should not push your clients to speak about their traumas or to detail them. Work on creating a space safe enough in therapy and your clients will begin to share what is painful with you. They will share at a pace that they can handle, exactly the right pace for them. You should not push clients to share or expose trauma histories at a pace that *you* think is right.

You should be aware that sometimes adolescent clients lie about the traumas they experienced. They might exaggerate what they have been through or state that a traumatic experience happened to them when it did not. You might feel angry at your clients when you discover that they lied to you. But please consider this: your clients will generally represent to you what feels true to them. Maybe your female client feels violated, but worries that no one will understand this or believe it. So instead she says that she has been raped. Perhaps your adolescent male client feels victimized by his brothers, so instead represents to you that he has been stalked or bullied by his peers at school. Clients often share with us aspects of their experience, what feels emotionally true rather than factually accurate. Again, if you create a safe enough space in therapy by being empathic, warm, and accepting, your clients will want to share all of their experiences with you and will be as honest with you as they can.

Evidence-Based Interventions for Traumatized Adolescents

There are a variety of treatment options available to clinicians working with adolescents exhibiting trauma symptomology or disorders. Two evidence-based interventions are trauma-focused cognitive behavioral therapy (TF-CBT; Cohen, Mannarino, & Deblinger, 2012) and eye movement desensitization and reprocessing (EMDR; Diehle, Opmeer, Boer, Mannarina, & Lindauer, 2015).

TF-CBT

TF-CBT may be the most extensively researched therapy for youth with PTSD (Diehle et al., 2015). TF-CBT was developed by Anthony

Mannarino, Judith Cohen, and Esther Deblinger to address the impact of trauma on children or adolescents who had experienced severe childhood abuse or other complex trauma (Cohen et al., 2012). They began the first studies that would lead to the creation of TF-CBT in the mid-1980s (Cohen et al., 2012). In its current form, TF-CBT consists of three treatment phases or modules. The first phase centers on skills-building components meant to enhance the adolescents' emotional and behavioral regulation skills as well as parenting interventions to enhance parents' coping, behavior management, and child support skills (Cohen et al., 2012). During the second phase, the adolescent describes and cognitively processes their trauma experiences (Cohen et al., 2012). The third phase includes family sessions and safety planning to prepare for treatment termination (Cohen et al., 2012).

Research finds that TF-CBT leads to greater reductions of PTSD symptomology than control conditions (de Arellano et al., 2014). These reductions hold true for samples of children exposed to multiple types of trauma, complex traumas, and those who experienced a single event such as a motor vehicle accident (Cohen, Mannarino, Kliethermes, & Murray, 2012; Diehle et al., 2015). TF-CBT is a useful model for clinicians working with traumatized adolescents because it is a short-term, standardized treatment. Protocol for TF-CBT delivery includes twelve sessions with components of psychoeducation, relaxation, affective expression and regulation, cognitive coping, gradual exposure by creating a trauma narrative, parent management skills, at least one parent-child session, and focus on enhancing future safety and development (Diehle et al., 2015).

The TF-CBT model assumes that troubling emotional, cognitive, and behavioral reactions to trauma originate from learning that occurred at the time of the traumatic event and immediately after (Pollio, McLean, Behl, & Deblinger, 2014). Youth may react with intense fear to nonthreatening stimuli that remind them of a traumatic experience to such a degree that it interferes with their learning, memory formation, and daily living. If such youth are successful in reducing their anxiety by avoiding stimuli that are associated with a previous trauma, their avoidant behavior is reinforced and becomes problematic as they avoid people, places, and stimuli that could be beneficial or are innocuous (Pollio et al., 2014). TF-CBT proposes that fear and subsequent avoidance generated by trauma interfere with children and adolescents' ability to learn and psychosocial development (Pollio et al., 2014). Some youth imitate negative behaviors they are exposed to during traumatic events, rather than avoiding such stimuli (Pollio et al., 2014). A sexually abused child may behave inappropriately around other children, while a physically abused adolescent may act out aggressively against classmates and peers.

Further, TF-CBT proposes that many traumatized youth internalize stigma and guilt around the trauma that leads to a negative self-concept or the belief that there is something wrong with them (Pollio et al., 2014). Since children learn through modeling, some may observe their parents' negative reactions to trauma and interpret those reactions to mean that they are damaged (Pollio et al., 2014). Such internalization can lead to depression or behavioral problems (Pollio et al., 2014).

TF-CBT thus seeks to revisit and reprocess the learned thoughts, associations, beliefs, and behaviors that occurred during or shortly after traumatic experiences. A clinician delivering TF-CBT will first help the client to establish healthy coping skills to utilize in moments of anxiety and fear. Then clinicians may gradually work with clients to revisit traumatic memories, a type of exposure therapy, so that clients learn that the memories cannot hurt them and that they do not need to be afraid of memories or trauma cues (Pollio et al., 2014). This component may help break the avoidance cycle that can be so disruptive to daily living.

Next, clinician and client work together to develop a narrative about the trauma that discusses the client's experience, feelings, physical reactions, and beliefs associated with the trauma (Pollio et al., 2014). This narrative is a powerful tool for identifying negative cognitions, such as the belief that one is wrong or damaged, that can be challenged and possibly changed over the course of treatment (Pollio et al., 2014). TF-CBT embraces family work, believing that a youth's strong support system can better support their recovery. Coaching on parenting skills, utilizing family interventions regarding the stories and behaviors associated with trauma, and role playing new types of behaviors are all tools that clinicians use in TF-CBT to build families' confidence and support (Pollio et al., 2014).

For clinicians interested in practicing TF-CBT, there are trainings available both online and in-person with certified trainers. The TF-CBT National Therapist Certification Program requires that clinicians are enrolled in or have completed a masters program and as well as a 10-hour webinar training, before registering for a 2-day in-person workshop facilitated by certified trainers ("Trauma-focused cognitive behavioral therapy national therapist certification program," n.d.).

To become a certified TF-CBT therapist, a clinician must complete several other tasks after the in-person training, including supervision from a designated trainer and completion of at least three treatment cases with children or adolescents. Consult the website for details: https://tfcbt.org/tf-cbt-certification-criteria/.

TF-CBT in Practice: The Case of Angelo

The TF-CBT model may be made more clear by seeing a description of the treatment with a traumatized client. Angelo was a 15-year-old Latino male who was referred to a hospital-based agency for mental health services after experiencing extensive sexual, emotional, and physical abuse. He was the first child born to a 15-year-old mother and 24-year-old father. Angelo was born in Mexico, and his parents were married shortly before his birth. Prior to his first birthday, his father decided to bring the family to the United States in search of employment. When Angelo was 3 years old, his father left the family and severed all contact. At that point, Angelo's mother was 19 years old in a foreign country where she did not speak the language and did not have access to many resources. She was eventually able to rent a room from an aunt and obtained work as a housekeeper. Angelo was often left with whoever was in the home at the time, as his mother tried to provide a steady income for the family's needs. He reported that he often felt alone then and worried that his mother would not return.

When Angelo was 7, his mother moved them to the home of José, a man she had been dating and eventually married. By that time, Angelo had two younger siblings, and he provided a significant amount of their care while the adults worked. Angelo's stepfather was known in his social circle for being a mid-level drug distributor. Angelo reported that, by the age of 10, he was expected to contribute to the family income by working in his stepfather's drug business. He reported that he had to make deliveries to drug customers and witnessed gang and other illegal activities as a result. At the age of 13, Angelo was introduced to his stepfather's boss, a high-level drug distributor who recognized what he saw as "promise" in Angelo. Within a month, Angelo reported that he was making deliveries to drug dealers instead of to customers, and he became even more entrenched in the drug community.

During this time at home, Angelo became more distant with his family. He avoided interaction and often stayed in his room. His academic performance suffered, and he began to have fights with students who called him "druggie." Suspensions from school and fighting at home became more frequent. His relationship with his stepfather deteriorated as Angelo expressed anger and resistance at being involved in the drug business.

As Angelo approached his 14th birthday, his drug boss called him into the office. He praised Angelo's work and told him that he was one of the best delivery workers of the group. He then took Angelo to the makeshift bedroom in the back of the office and sodomized him as a "reward" for his "good work." For the next 8 months, Angelo was forced to watch pornography videos and engage in sex acts with his boss. His boss threatened him daily with the risk of deportation of himself and his family. The abuse intensified over the months to include oral sex, object rape, severe physical assault, and forced drug use to decrease Angelo's ability to resist or fight.

Shortly after the sexual abuse began, Angelo realized that other boys were also being abused by the boss. As he became more aware of what was happening to him and other children, he became suicidal and considered ways that he could end his life in an effort to stop the abuse. His mother confronted him about the anger and distance she observed, and it was then that he disclosed. His mother immediately contacted police. They interviewed Angelo and subsequently arrested his boss. Despite the arrest, Angelo continued to live in fear of retaliation from other drug dealers who were part of his boss's team. The police investigation ultimately led to a large group of arrests; Angelo was one of only a few adolescents who were willing to testify in the case.

As he became more overwhelmed with the legal proceedings, Angelo's trauma symptoms became more pronounced and included intrusive thoughts, nightmares, shame, increased anger, withdrawal from his family, and engaging in risky behaviors. Angelo's mother encouraged him to seek out mental health treatment to cope with his experience. When his mother called to schedule the intake appointment, I (TP) gathered basic assessment information to determine the appropriateness of a referral for our community-based trauma therapy center. Based on Angelo's reported symptoms, trauma history, and legal involvement, the intake staffing team approved the case as appropriate for treatment with TF-CBT therapy at our center.

I initiated the first phase of the TF-CBT modality, psychoeducation, while on the phone with Angelo's mother. I briefly explained TF-CBT along with specific ways it had been used to treat some of the symptoms she identified from her son's experiences. I asked Angelo's mother, Anita, about her thoughts and expectations for treatment. This was an important part of the process because it allowed Anita to feel empowered about and committed to the therapy process. Engaging Anita right away was also especially important because she reported that seeking out therapy was seen as a sign of weakness in her culture, and she expressed hesitation about it. However, she also expressed a strong desire to help her son.

When Angelo was brought into the clinic by his mother, he expressed nervousness about participating in therapy. This disclosure provided me an opportunity for exploration of his concerns and expectations. At the time, he lived with several younger siblings, his biological mother, and his stepfather. Though his mother actively supported seeking out services to help Angelo with his trauma, she reported that Angelo's stepfather was more reluctant. His stepfather's reluctance contributed to some of Angelo's hesitation about therapy. At the time, he was attending high school intermittently, and he struggled in the areas of social functioning, academic performance, and emotional regulation.

Angelo, though reluctant, was engaged and cooperative during the intake interview. He shared his struggles with hyperarousal, nightmares, somatic symptoms including headaches and stomachaches, increased irritability with his parents and siblings, risk-taking behaviors like drug use and driving under the influence, truancy, sadness, increased anger, self-blame, fear of retribution from his abuser, and shame. Cultural influences may have impacted his closed communication style and difficulty expressing emotion; he reported that he was taught to view vulnerable emotion as weakness.

As Angelo demonstrated an increased level of comfort in the initial three psychotherapy sessions, we were able to focus more on the psychoeducation phase of TF-CBT. A main emphasis of the psychotherapy was to help Angelo and his mother understand the format and planned focus of future sessions. One of those elements of TF-CBT was the heavy reliance on a conjoint session format, so I discussed this aspect of treatment with Angelo and his mother right away. I encouraged Angelo to give feedback on the format of psychotherapy sessions he would prefer: meeting initially with both his mother and me *or* meeting individually with me and then bringing his mom in at the end of the session for review. Because it was difficult for Angelo to see his mother crying or upset, Angelo chose the latter option of working on trauma and skills building first, then bringing his mother into the session at the end. Angelo and I began to develop a therapeutic rapport as he had more input into therapy decisions. That rapport continued to grow as he was included in treatment planning and was able to understand more of what to expect from the experience.

I explained the other components of TF-CBT and basic treatment outcomes as part of psychoeducation. Angelo became more talkative and at ease as he learned that treatment had a start and end. His mother became engaged in the therapeutic process as she learned that she would be involved in treatment and that her son would be learning specific skills to cope with the trauma he experienced. Psychoeducation also included a discussion of the types of abuse Angelo experienced, typical responses to normalize his symptoms, and an exploration of the court process as Angelo would be involved in a legal case. Angelo gradually became less guarded and demonstrated surprise at the frequency and similarities of others who experienced abuse. As I listed various common trauma responses, he was able to confirm those that he experienced, providing valuable assessment information. He also reported feeling more hopeful, that if others were able to "deal with it," maybe he could too.

As we further discussed areas of concern, increased tensions at home came up as a primary issue. This provided the opportunity to introduce the parenting component of TF-CBT. I addressed parenting in session by working on specific targets like helping Angelo's mother set clear expectations regarding limits and compliance. Anita, like many other parents of traumatized teens, expressed concern that setting rules would not be a compassionate way to help Angelo. We were able to then discuss the importance of predictability and security in dealing with trauma. This discussion seemed to give Anita more validation in her parenting efforts. Anita was able to share more about her feelings when interacting with Angelo— she described she often felt attacked, ignored, and unappreciated. These types of confrontations were happening on an almost daily basis, and Angelo expressed feelings of guilt because it was important to him to treat his mother in a respectful way. He struggled to understand why he felt so "out of control" of his emotions, and this discussion provided more opportunity for exploration of typical trauma responses. Angelo learned about anger as a secondary emotion, and he was able to connect the underlying emotions to his experiences. The focus then turned to how Angelo and his mother would like to feel in interactions. I encouraged them to identify new communication parameters including (a) talking to each other respectfully by not calling names or swearing, (b) waiting for the other person to finish talking before responding, and (c) repeating back what was understood to clarify. They also agreed on the rule that physical violence could not continue in the home, as Angelo would hit his younger siblings at times when he became angry. Setting these expectations in session not only provided Anita with additional support, but it provided a source of accountability for both Anita and Angelo to commit to and practice the new skills knowing that they would be reporting on progress in future sessions.

Assistance with limit setting, increasing positive parenting strategies, and clearly identifying Angelo's emotional needs helped his mother feel more confident in her ability to support her child. Meeting alone with Angelo's mother also provided the opportunity for her to share the overwhelming sadness and guilt she was feeling about failing to protect her son. I encouraged her to seek out her own individual therapy and shared information about the importance of getting appropriate emotional support so that she could be fully emotionally present when her son needed support.

The treatment goals in Angelo's case had five purposes: (a) reducing symptoms; (b) increasing future safety through identification of warning signs, strengthening personal boundaries, and involving his support network; (c) improving coping skills through mindfulness, cognitive coping, and other relaxation strategies; (d) promoting healthy sexuality, including exploring issues of consent, healthy relationships, and sex education; and (e) processing thoughts and feelings about the trauma through the sharing of a trauma narrative. After we developed the treatment goals together, I focused with Angelo on symptom reduction and coping through the use of relaxation skills. This focus aimed to relieve distress, as well as increase his hope for and engagement in therapy. Teaching relaxation skills early in the treatment process, before exploring his trauma in detail, would also enable Angelo to have more tools to manage discomfort in session.

I used psychoeducation to help Angelo learn basic body responses to trauma and trauma reminders. He reported feeling "my heart beat really fast" and "feeling dizzy with fast breathing" in response to trauma-related triggers, like going near the house where he was abused or seeing someone that reminded him of his abuser. First, I encouraged him to identify a variety of physical ways that his body responded when triggered. We moved into the relaxation component of TF-CBT by discussing different skills that could help with each of his symptoms. I started by teaching Angelo how to control the speed and depth of his breathing. He practiced the skill in session several times. Once he was able to do it appropriately, I introduced him to the concept of external monitoring. I asked Angelo to think about a moderately upsetting memory or thought, like getting in a disagreement at school or with his stepfather. I then placed a pulse oximeter monitor (purchased at any major retailer for home use) on his finger. We noted his heart rate. Then I asked him to utilize the breathing skills we had practiced earlier in session. As he applied the relaxation technique, he could watch his heart rate decrease as well as feel the calming change in his body. I then showed him how he could monitor his pulse and breathing rate at home.

Another relaxation skill that I introduced was progressive muscle relaxation. Though some adolescents struggle with this activity, progressive muscle relaxation can help adolescents connect to their bodies, a connection they sometimes feel less due to sexual abuse. I practiced the skill alongside Angelo in session and explained that it is quite normal to feel uncomfortable or strange the first few times as one learns the skill. He stated that he was willing to try progressive muscle relaxation outside of session and report on his progress.

Many adolescents respond to multisensory experiences, which electronic applications can provide. So, in Angelo's session after a brief practice of muscle relaxation, we used the "Calm" application on my phone to enhance the experience. This app provides verbal prompts for progressive muscle relaxation. Angelo and I both participated in this relaxation exercise. Then we discussed how his body felt. Angelo stated that he thought he could use this skill to help him with physical sensations like increased heart rate, rapid breathing, and headaches. We also discussed ways it could help ease emotional symptoms including feelings of fear, anxiousness, and sadness. He downloaded the application to his phone while in session and committed to use it once per day at a minimum as practice. Angelo also reported that he would practice progressive muscle relaxation at home nightly prior to bed to help with sleep.

I invited his mother to join our session at the end, and Angelo taught the technique to her. She committed to practice the skill with Angelo as a way for them to connect. Over two subsequent sessions, I shared new skills, including mindfulness and guided imagery, to increase his options for self-soothing. Angelo practiced these skills at home using the "Calm" application as well.

After Angelo demonstrated a mastery of basic calming skills, he noticed the impact of those skills in his improved sleep and decreased anxiety symptoms. At that point, I turned treatment focus to the next component of TF-CBT, affect modulation. During this phase, I focused on helping Angelo understand his feelings and how those feelings impacted his functioning. Angelo readily expressed, "I'm so angry. I hate him for what he did. I hate feeling mad all the time, and I don't know how to stop feeling so pissed all the time." I first validated his feelings as a normal and understandable response to the abuse he endured. We explored how his feelings were connected to the trauma. In sessions, he recognized his own feelings of guilt, sadness, worry, shame, betrayal, and so forth. I invited him to express these feelings in session without fear of judgment or consequence.

This was a particularly difficult part of the process for me. I felt strong countertransference: I wanted to stop his suffering and confirm that everything would work out. However, one of my most important roles in TF-CBT is as a guide who can sit with emotion and its intensity. I needed to lead him through the process of incorporating his emotions as part of his experience.

One of the ways we worked on recognizing his emotions as parts of the entire trauma experience was through the feelings circle activity, an activity created by the third author. During this activity, Angelo selected feeling cards from a deck. Each card had one feeling word printed on it. Angelo chose those that represented feelings he had about his trauma. He then sat on the floor, placing the cards around him in a circle. I then gave him a bag of dry beans and instructed him to place the number of beans on each card that he thought indicated the intensity of that feeling for him. After he completed that task, we discussed each feeling and the number of beans assigned to it. I made comments like, "I noticed that the feeling *anger* has the most beans. Can you tell me about that?" and "What about the sexual abuse made you feel guilt?" Through this process, Angelo shared more details about his trauma, and he was more able to express emotion in session. He cried openly and yelled in anger. I reminded him that each emotion was a part of him and his experience, and that judgment about the emotions was not necessary. Each feeling played a role in his experience. The feelings circle exercise also provided him with in vivo exposure to the traumatic events, improving his ability to talk about the events more openly and in more detail. This talking was important because it prepared him for the writing of the trauma narrative. I assigned Angelo some homework: (a) to notice any emotions he felt during the week as he thought about the trauma, and (b) to journal about what triggered the emotions and how intense they felt. I also encouraged him to continue using his relaxation strategies when he wanted to increase feelings of calm.

As Angelo's awareness of his emotions and their impact in his life became more apparent, I focused the next stage of therapy on another component of TF-CBT, cognitive coping. During cognitive coping, I focused treatment on increasing Angelo's ability to understand the connection between his thoughts, feelings, and actions. The treatment aimed to help Angelo to acquire new cognitive processing skills through activities that helped him identify and change unhelpful thoughts that could contribute to trauma-related symptoms.

One activity consisted of different scenarios that were listed on strips of paper and placed in a bowl. Angelo chose a paper from the bowl, and he identified the thought, feeling, and action from each scenario. He then practiced sharing other alternate thoughts that could lead to more healthy or helpful feelings and actions. I utilized in vivo exposure during this step as well, by exploring actual experiences that Angelo shared and helping him identify the different components in each personal experience. This helped Angelo understand the trauma's impact on his thinking patterns and choices. This activity allowed him to integrate his previously learned skills and information into the process of changing thoughts and regulating emotion.

Once Angelo demonstrated an understanding of and ability to use relaxation, affective modulation, and cognitive coping, he was ready to begin the trauma narrative. I introduced this aspect of treatment at the beginning of treatment and referenced it numerous times after in an effort to decrease client resistance and anxiety about the experience. I used phrases like "we will talk more about that in your trauma story" and "that might be something important to include in your trauma narrative" strategically to help him prepare for that component. These statements gave Angelo opportunities to express reservations, ask questions, and explore the discomfort he felt using healthy coping skills. I taught him about the role of the narrative in his recovery and described it as "just another part" of what needed to be done for healing.

I also gave Angelo choices in this part of our treatment. I told him that he could express his trauma narrative through art, write it on the computer, communicate it through song or rap, or dictate it to me. Angelo chose to write his story and chose a title for the narrative: "Angelo's Song of Life." Then I encouraged him to create a table of contents for the trauma narrative. His table of contents included sections on life prior to the trauma, his interests and goals, when the trauma started, how it stopped, what the court or legal process was like, being involved in therapy, what was learned from the trauma experience, and what Angelo would share with someone else experiencing trauma.

Though we use the table of contents as a guideline for the story, we can increase adolescents' engagement when we invite them to choose a starting point for sharing the narrative. The starting point does not have to be at the beginning, though it may be easier for some adolescents to start by sharing about their life and interests prior to the trauma. This kind of beginning point can help them adjust to the role of storyteller. Therapists can also use open-ended questions to encourage additional information and details: "What else would you like to include about that time in your life?" As Angelo shared his trauma narrative, he began connecting his thoughts and feelings to the trauma. In this way, the narrative became a tool for emotional processing, correcting cognitive errors, and increasing future safety through identification of potential risks and supports in his life.

One additional consideration for the clinician when approaching the trauma narrative is to decide how to process it. Two main options are to process cognitions and affect as it is shared, or to process after the client shares the entire narrative. In Angelo's case, we processed throughout the narrative. I did this because Angelo exhibited strong feelings of guilt and self-blame for the trauma he experienced. Processing during the narrative allowed treatment to focus on correcting some of the cognitions that were feeding his emotions and increasing trauma responses.

Angelo was initially reluctant to share details about the abuse. I utilized empathic responses, open-ended questions, and agreements to work on trauma specifics in time-limited segments. As Angelo became more attuned to his emotional responses, he requested distractions like playing a game or discussing a favorite topic for a few minutes as a break. We also used that "break" time for him to explore what he was thinking and feeling, increasing his insight and empowerment over the difficult process of sharing his story.

Angelo's story was vague at first. This is common because it is uncomfortable to discuss details of abuse. But the therapeutic alliance we created in earlier sessions provided a safe environment for disclosure to occur. I encouraged Angelo to speak and asked for additional detail at times. Angelo eventually described how he met his abuser, how the relationship progressed, and what he thought and felt in various situations. He described details such as the first time the abuse occurred, the worst time, and how the abuse stopped. Each of those scenarios gave us the opportunity to process his feelings and thoughts about the situation, about his abuser, and about himself. For example, Angelo stated, "if I wouldn't have gone into the back room with him, he wouldn't have abused me." That belief contributed to feelings of self-blame which resulted in Angelo withdrawing from others to punish himself. Through the treatment process, we evaluated how true and helpful the thought was. I also asked Angelo to consider if he would think the same if someone he cared about went through the same experience and thought the same about themselves. He replied, "I would know it wasn't their fault and that he was going to find a way to abuse them if that's what he wanted because he was a bad man." We then practiced applying that thought to his situation until it felt truer for him. We repeated this process for each cognitive distortion in his narrative.

As Angelo included more details in his narrative, he cried, expressed anger, and began to place blame where it belonged, on the abuser. Increasingly, Angelo identified unhealthy thoughts related to the abuse and created new, more helpful beliefs that he wanted to incorporate. We created a list to help him remember and incorporate those beliefs. This process took place over the course of four to six sessions. During these sessions, we explored themes of responsibility, regret, grief, safety, and change. The sessions began with a check-in on symptoms and progress, then Angelo read aloud what he had written during previous sessions. This reading activity provided opportunities for in vivo exposure and practice for the conjoint session sharing of the narrative.

As Angelo's ability to reread his narrative without significant trauma responses increased, he reported less self-blame, improved school attendance and academic performance, and fewer intrusive thoughts. He also expressed interest in sharing the narrative with his mother, leading into the next phase of TF-CBT: conjoint sessions. We structured conjoint sessions so that the first 20–30 minutes included a meeting between the clinician and Angelo's mother. We dedicated the remaining time to a review of progress and an exploration of any issues of concern, until Angelo was ready to share his narrative. Prior to the conjoint sessions, I provided an opportunity for Angelo's mother to practice hearing Angelo's trauma narrative. We role-played the experience to allow her to share emotions and thoughts, as well as respond to the details of the narrative without worrying about Angelo's concern about her emotional state. Over the course of several sessions, Angelo's mother became more calm when hearing the narrative, and she practiced supportive statements expressing her concern for his pain and pride in her son's strength, all while maintaining emotional composure. Once she reached that stage, it was time to facilitate Angelo's sharing of the narrative with his mother.

During the capstone conjoint session, Angelo read the narrative to his mother. I had previously instructed his mother to allow him to read it through completely before sharing her thoughts. After he read, she shared supportive statements regarding her son's bravery and strength which we had previously practiced. She encouraged him to talk about his trauma in the future whenever he felt the need to do so. Angelo shared his goals for the future with his mother, and she committed to support him in those goals.

After sharing the narrative and reviewing the coping, processing, and regulation skills learned throughout the TF-CBT process, I introduced the final component of TF-CBT. Though safety planning occurs throughout therapy as needed, TF-CBT has its final focus on enhancing future safety, allowing for a more thorough discussion of safety issues. In Angelo's case, I provided psychoeducation about healthy sexuality and specific safety rules related to sexual abuse, texting and driving, substance use, and other age-appropriate safety situations. Angelo readily identified ways that he could remain safe. He also shared how he would handle any uncomfortable or dangerous situations in the future by involving his mother or other trusted adults. We also explored the potential for future symptoms and how to address them.

Finally, we reviewed Angelo's accomplishments in treatment. Angelo and his mother reported his significant improvement in coping, family interactions, compliance with rules, and overall functioning. We reviewed skills he learned in the various components of TF-CBT, and discussed termination. I provided Angelo and his mother referral support information available in the community. I terminated the therapy by encouraging the family to contact the agency with any concerns or for additional assistance in the future.

Angelo returned for a brief period about 8 months after completing TF-CBT treatment. He reported that he found out his abuser was killed by another inmate in prison, and he struggled with conflicted feelings of happiness and sadness over the news. We explored the thoughts and feelings he had about his abuser. Through this process, he applied cognitive coping skills to understand why he was conflicted. He reported that he had returned to school and a part-time job, and that his social relationships were strong. He has not sought additional treatment since that time.

Analysis of Angelo's Case

The case above highlights critical components of the TF-CBT approach: the initial focus around skills building, the second-phase focus on the trauma narrative, and the third-phase focus on family sessions and safety planning. TF-CBT can be a useful approach with adolescents and their families, but requires specialized training for its practitioners. This case study provides an example of how the modality can be applied to reduce symptoms, improve healthy coping, increase future safety, and strengthen family interactions.

Other Treatment Approaches for Trauma

Eye Movement Desensitization and Reprocessing

Eye movement desensitization and reprocessing (EMDR) is an integrated therapeutic approach based on the adaptive information processing model which attributes the physical, cognitive, and emotional disturbances related to trauma to unprocessed dysfunctional memories (Wizansky, 2011). To date, more than two dozen randomized controlled studies have verified the effectiveness of EMDR as an intervention for both single-event and complex trauma (Shapiro, 2014). The first single-case study of EMDR was conducted by EMDR founder Francine Shapiro in 1989 (Shapiro, 1999). EMDR utilizes a series of rapid eye movements and mindfulness exercises to reprocess traumatic memories so they are less disturbing or disappear from conscious memory (EMDR International Association [EMDRIA], 2012).

EMDR utilizes a series of eight stages to work through previous trauma (EMDRIA, 2012). The first phase consists of taking client history and treatment planning. Clients must have a base of coping skills and social support to sustain exposure to distressing memories, so clinicians sometimes utilize psych-education and stabilization first before initiating EMDR treatment (EMDRIA, 2012). For those with unstable self-concept or a total lack of social support, EMDR may never be suitable.

The second phase involves preparation, when the clinician introduces the client to EMDR procedures and explains the rationale so the client can give informed consent (EMDRIA, 2012). This stage can take some time as it is important to prepare the client for possible disturbances between sessions and strengthen coping skills to maintain stability in the face of potential disturbances (EMDRIA, 2012). Importantly, clients need to have skills to self-regulate, so clinicians may teach relaxation techniques in session before beginning the next phase of treatment (EMDRIA, 2012).

Next, client and clinician embark on the assessment phase (EMDRIA, 2012). They work together to identify target issues or memories the client would like to address with EMDR. The purpose here is to establish the client's baseline response to the identified memory or issue (EMDRIA, 2012). Then, the clinician asks the client to identify a negative belief that is associated with that memory/issue and a positive belief that could potentially replace the negative (EMDRIA, 2012). The final component of this phase is to identify the locations of physical sensations which are stimulated when focusing on the memory/issue (EMDRIA, 2012).

At this point, the fourth phase of desensitization begins. During this fourth phase, the client identifies one traumatic memory and an associated negative cognition to reprocess during a single session (EMDRIA, 2012). Clients are also asked to come up with an alternative, kinder cognition that could re-place the current negative belief. The clinician then asks the client to follow the clinician's finger with their eyes to generate rapid eye movements while they hold the traumatic memory and associated feelings in mind (EMDRIA, 2012). As clients are doing the eye movements, the therapist continually checks in to see how they are feeling. Client and clinician continue to pro-cess the traumatic memory and arising feelings until the clients' anxiety or distress lowers significantly (EMDRIA, 2012). Each target memory usually takes a few sessions to overcome fully.

Once the target memory has been addressed, client and clinician work together in the fifth phase, installation, to install the positive replacement cognition to reprocess the thoughts and feelings associated with previous trauma (EMDRIA, 2012). After installation, the clinician begins the sixth stage, which consists of a body scan (EMDRIA, 2012). Specifically, the cli-nician ask the client to focus on the target memory *and* the positive belief while they mentally scan their body to identify any positive or negative sensations. If any negative sensations are present, the clinician returns to the bilateral stimulation, or finger movements, until the client reports only neutral or positive sensations (EMDRIA, 2012). Phase seven is the closure phase, which is used at the end of every session whether or not the target has been fully reprocessed. Closure consists of techniques meant to ground the client in the present moment, to stabilize them emotionally, and to create a plan to maintain stability between sessions (EMDRIA, 2012). The final and eighth phase is that of reevaluation. Here, the clinician assesses the effects of the reprocessing by working with the client to look for any new memories or issues that have arisen, to find any potential challenges to maintained stability, and to determine which memories should be targeted next by repeating phases three through eight (EMDRIA, 2012). This cycle can be used to work through multiple traumas with the use of self-soothing and regulation techniques between sessions (EMDRIA, 2012).

Substantial literature supports the efficacy of EMDR as a trauma treatment (Diehle et al., 2015; Shapiro, 2014). A review of 24 studies evaluating the effectiveness of EMDR concluded that EMDR is an effective treatment for trauma victims (Shapiro, 2014). While EMDR and TF-CBT are equally recommended for PTSD treatment in adolescents, (Diehle et al., 2015; Shapiro, 2014), EMDR does not require detailed descriptions of the traumatic event, direct challenging of beliefs, extended exposure, or homework (Shapiro, 2014). Shapiro (2014) suggests that these differences render EMDR more efficient and less confrontational than TF-CBT.

To practice EMDR as a clinician requires a significant amount of training after receiving a graduate degree in a mental health field. EMDR certification is offered by EMDR International Association (EMDRIA), a non-profit organization. Individuals seeking EMDR certification must be fully licensed and have a minimum of 2 years of experience in their field. The training process involves two separate in-person trainings followed by 50 sessions of EMDR practice, 20 hours of consultation with an approved consultant, letters of recommendations, and continuing education requirements every 2 years (EMDRIA, n.d.). Portions of the EMDR training such as the in-person sessions can be completed prior to receiving full mental health licensure to expedite the process. For more information on trainings and certification requirements, visit emdria.org.

Current literature supports both TF-CBT and EMDR as efficacious interventions to address trauma-related mental issues (de Arellano et al., 2014; Shapiro, 2014). However, several other approaches have gained traction recently as trauma treatment alternatives for adolescents.

Cognitive Processing Therapy

Cognitive processing therapy (CPT) is a well-researched and efficacious treatment for adult PTSD (Voelkel, Pukay-Martin, Walter, & Chard, 2015).

Developed in the early 1990s to focus on PTSD symptoms in victims of sexual violence (Matulis et al., 2014), CPT consists of 12 weekly sessions delivered in a manualized, sequential form. It is a form of cognitive therapy that uses few elements of exposure, hypothesizing that PTSD is a result of negative beliefs or cognitions, such as negative self-talk, that render individuals unable to move forward with the natural recovery process (Matulis et al., 2014). The goal of CPT is to identify these stuck points or problematic cognitions and to change them through dialogue and worksheets (Matulis et al., 2014).

Little research has evaluated CPT for adolescents. One study examining the impact of CPT for incarcerated adolescents with self-reported symptoms of trauma including anxiety, depression, intrusion, avoidance, and numbing, found significant declines in those symptoms after treatment completion while those in a wait-list control group exhibited no improvement (Ahrens & Rexford, 2002). A modified version of CPT, which increased the number of sessions to 16 and shortened treatment length to 4 weeks, showed efficacy in treating PTSD and secondary symptoms of depression and dissociation for adolescent survivors of childhood physical/sexual abuse (Matulis et al., 2014). Thus, while CPT appears promising for the treatment of adolescents, more studies with diverse adolescent populations are needed to verify its efficacy.

Other Interventions

Numerous other approaches show significant promise. For example, mindfulness-based interventions, including yoga, show great potential both for building coping mechanisms to improve emotional regulation and contributing to physical and emotional wellbeing (Racco & Vis, 2015). The breathing practices taught in yoga may stabilize the autonomic nervous system leading to a lower heart rate and blood pressure and relieving many of the anxiety-based symptoms associated with trauma disorders (Racco & Vis, 2015; van der Kolk, 2006). Further, the emphasis on body awareness in yoga can benefit those struggling with dissociation or a lack of mind-body connection (Racco & Vis, 2015; van der Kolk, 2006). These benefits lead some trauma experts to recommend yoga as a complementary approach to psychotherapy (Racco & Vis, 2015). A few studies supports yoga as beneficial for adolescents with trauma histories (Racco & Vis, 2015; Spinazzola, Rhodes, Emerson, Earle, & Monroe, 2011).

Trauma Responses and Resiliency

While trauma is linked to a host of negative outcomes, trauma does not always lead to pathology. In fact, pathology is the exception rather than the rule (Burton, Cooper, Feeny, & Zoellner, 2015; Feeny & Zoellner, 2014). In recent years, the study of trauma has expanded to incorporate all the responses to trauma rather than focusing only on psychopathology. One model identifies seven different potential responses to trauma: (a) stress resistance, which refers to stable functioning before and after a trauma, (b) resilience, which describes a decrease in functioning after a trauma followed by a recovery, (c) protracted recovery which indicates more acute symptoms of trauma and a slower recovery, (d) post-traumatic growth, in which individuals experience meaningful psychological or spiritual growth following a trauma, (e) severe persisting distress, defined as chronic pathology without recovery, (f) decline, characterized by a period of stability after trauma followed by decompensation, and (g) stable maladaptive functioning, which refers to persistently poor functioning before, during, and after a trauma (Burton et al., 2015; Layne et al., 2009).

This model attempts to account for the wide range of responses to trauma that are dependent on a range of biological, environmental, and social factors. For example, resilience and post-traumatic growth are more likely among populations with strong social and familial support, while severe persisting distress or maladaptive functioning are more likely for those who experience complex, interpersonal trauma in childhood (Burton et al., 2015). Healthy family functioning is especially impactful for adolescents as it moderates the negative impact of cumulative ACEs on adolescent well-being (Balistreri & Alvira-Hammond, 2016).

Resilience

Resilience is an important concept in trauma-focused research and practice. Broadly defined, resilience refers to the lack of psychopathology, or rapid recovery, following a traumatic event or series of events (Kalisch, Müller, & Tüscher, 2015). Resilience does not suggest a lack of reaction to a trauma, but rather allows for an appropriate response to the trauma followed by a pattern of recovery (Feeny & Zoellner, 2014). Conceptualized in this way, resilience is an outcome rather than an individual characteristic (Kalisch et al., 2015).

Thus, resilience-focused research seeks to understand what prevents a traumatic response rather than the mechanisms that lead to psychopathology (Kalisch et al., 2015).

One of the appeals of resiliency as a field of study and practice is that resiliency may have a protective effect against the physical and mental consequences associated with the overactivation of the stress response system after trauma (Kalisch et al., 2015). Empirical evidence for specific contributing factors to resiliency remains limited (Burton et al., 2015). However, some studies propose person-centered factors such as pragmatic coping strategies, positive emotions, optimism, cognitive flexibility, and emotion-regulation skills as correlates of resilience (Burton et al., 2015). Others assert that environmental factors that protect against PTSD may contribute to resilience. These factors include social support and parental mental health (Burton et al., 2015; Trickey, Siddaway, Meiser-Stedman, Serpell, & Field, 2012).

One way to incorporate the concept of resiliency when working with trauma survivors is to apply the lens of resilience as a principle of practice. For example, Feeny and Zoellner (2014) outline three domains that may underline natural resilience: *social support, reestablishing normalcy*, and *making meaning* of thoughts and memories. Clinicians can work with adolescent clients to enhance these three domains, setting treatment goals and interventions which support these components. Social support protects against the development of PTSD across populations (Burton et al., 2015), while reestablishing normalcy encourages individuals not to engage in avoidance behaviors after trauma, rather reclaiming their lives through regular daily routines and activities (Feeny & Zoellner, 2014). Finally, the meaning-making process encourages trauma survivors to integrate the traumatic memories and their thoughts about those memories so that they can process what happened and address any negative beliefs or self-talk that may arise in conjunction with their memories (Feeny & Zoellner, 2014). While this process may be very difficult, meaning-making creates the possibility for post-traumatic growth or a sense of peace and acceptance rather than avoidance or fear of trauma reminders (Feeny & Zoellner, 2014).

Implications for Treatment

Adolescents in treatment settings, especially those in inpatient, residential, and forensic settings, are more likely to have been traumatized than their nontreated peers (Stinson et al., 2016). Further, trauma, and especially complex trauma, predicts many of the maladaptive behaviors, mental disorders, and substance use disorders that prompt parents and educators to refer an adolescent to treatment (Sumner et al., 2015). Knowledge of the developmental impact of trauma empowers clinicians to dig deeper with adolescent clients. The substance-abusing 15-year-old may have turned to substances after a series of ACEs. The physically aggressive 17-year-old may have experienced physical, emotional, or sexual abuse that led to their own aggression.

Clinicians need to screen for early childhood trauma and traumatic events in adolescence given the association of trauma with mental disorders and substance use (Huang et al., 2011; Sumner et al., 2015). The ACEs questionnaire is one potential screening tool that allows clinicians to effectively screen for many types of traumatic experiences. Once trauma has been identified in an adolescent's history, evidence-based interventions such as TF-CBT, EMDR, and others can aid in the recovery from that trauma and the integration of that experience. Finally, the lens of resiliency reminds clinicians to work with adolescents and their families to improve social supports, to encourage return to normal behaviors and routines, and to engage with trauma memories and narratives to move toward acceptance, integration, and recovery.

References

Ahrens, J., & Rexford, L. (2002). Cognitive processing therapy for incarcerated adolescents with PTSD. *Journal of Aggression, Maltreatment, & Trauma, 6,* 201–216. doi:10.1300/J146v06n01_10

American Psychiatric Association. (2013). *Diagnostic and statistical manual of mental disorders* (5th ed.). Arlington, VA: American Psychiatric Association.

Balistreri, K. S., & Alvira-Hammond, M. (2016). Adverse childhood experiences, family functioning and adolescent health and emotional well-being. *Public Health, 132,* 72–78. doi:10.1016/j.puhe.2015.10.034

Bannink, R., Broeren, S., van de Looij-Jansen, P. M., de Waart, F. G., & Raat, H. (2014). Cyber and traditional bullying victimization as a risk factor for mental health problems and suicidal ideation in adolescents. *PLoS ONE, 9,* 1–8. doi:10.1371/journal.pone.0094026

Brockie, T., Dana-Sacco, G., Wallen, G., Wilcox, H., & Campbell, J. (2015). The relationship of adverse childhood experiences to PTSD, depression, poly-drug use, and suicide attempt in reservation-based Native American adolescents and young adults. *American Journal of Community Psychology, 55,* 411–421. doi:10.1007/s10464-015-9721-3.

Burton, M. S., Cooper. A. A., Feeny, N. C., & Zoellner, L. A. (2015). The enhancement of natural resilience in trauma interventions. *The Journal of Contemporary Psychotherapy, 45,* 193–204. doi:10.1007/s10879-015-9302-7

Centers for Disease Control and Prevention. (2011). Youth risk behavior surveillance—United States, 2011. *Morbidity and Mortality Weekly Report, 61,* 1–162.

Centers for Disease Control and Prevention. (2016). *About the CDC-Kaiser ACE study.* Retrieved from https://www.cdc.gov/violenceprevention/acestudy/about.html

Cicero, S. D., Nooner, K., & Silva, R. (2011). Vulnerability and resilience in childhood trauma and PTSD. In V. Ardino (Ed.), *Post-traumatic syndromes in childhood and adolescence: A handbook of research and practice* (pp. 43–60). West Sussex, UK: Wiley & Blackwell.

Cohen, J. A., Mannarino, A. P., & Deblinger, E. (2012). *Trauma-focused CBT for children and adolescents.* New York, NY: Guildford Press.

Cohen, J. A., Mannarino, A. P., Kliethermes, M., & Murray, L. A. (2012). Trauma-focused CBT for youth with complex trauma. *Child Abuse & Neglect, 36,* 528–541. doi:10.1016/j.chiabu.2012.03.007

Cook, A., Blaustein, M., Spinazzola, J., & van der Kolk, B. (2003). *Complex trauma in children and adolescents.* National Child Traumatic Stress Network. Retrieved from http://www.nctsnet.org

De Arellano, M. A. R., Lyman, R. D., Jobe-Shields, L., George, P., Dougherty, R. H., Daniels, A. S., . . . Delphin-Rittmon, M. E. (2014). Trauma-focused cognitive-behavioral therapy for children and adolescents: Assessing the evidence. *Psychiatric Services, 65,* 591–602. doi:10.1176/appi.ps.201300255

De Bellis, M. D., & Zisk, A. (2014). The biological effects of childhood trauma. *Child and Adolescent Psychiatric Clinics of North America, 23,* 185–222. doi:10.1016/j.chc.2014.01.002

Diehle, J., Opmeer, B. C., Boer, F., Mannarino, A. P., & Lindauer, R. J. L. (2015). Trauma-focused cognitive behavioral therapy or eye movement desensitization and reprocessing: What works in children with posttraumatic stress symptoms? A randomized controlled trial. *European Child & Adolescent Psychiatry, 24,* 227–236. doi:10.1007/s00787-014-0572-5

Dube, S. R., Anda, R. F., Felitti, V. J., Chapman, D. P., Williamson, D. F., & Giles, W. H. (2001). Childhood abuse, household dysfunction, and the risk of attempted suicide throughout the life span: Findings from the adverse childhood experiences study. *Journal of the American Medical Association, 286,* 3089–3096.

Dube, S. R., Felitti, V. J., Dong, M., Chaptman, D. P., Giles, W. H., & Anda, R. F. (2003). Childhood abuse, neglect, and household dysfunction and the risk of illicit drug use: The adverse childhood experiences study. *Pediatrics, 111,* 564–572.

Eaton, D. K., Davis, K. S., Barrios, L., Brener, N. D., & Noonan, R. K. (2007). Associations of dating violence victimization with lifetime participation, co-occurrence, and early initiation of risk behaviors among U.S. high school students. *Journal of Interpersonal Violence, 22,* 585–602.

Eye Movement Desensitization and Reprocessing International Association. (n.d.). *EMDRIA certification in EMDR.* Retrieved from the EMDRIA website: http://www.emdria.org/?page=21

Eye Movement Desensitization and Reprocessing International Association. (2012). EMDRIA's definition of EMDR (eye movement desensitization and reprocessing).

Retrieved   from   http://c.ymcdn.com/sites/www.emdria.org/resource/resmgr/imported/EMDRIA%20Definition%20of%20EMDR.pdf

Feeny, N. C., & Zoellner, L. A. (2014). Conclusion: Risk and resilience following trauma exposure. In L. A. Zoeller, & N. C. Feeny (Eds.), *Facilitating resilience and recovery following trauma* (pp. 325–334). New York, NY: Guilford Press.

Felitti, V. J, Anda, R. F., Nordenberg, D., Williamson, D. F., Spitz, A. M., Edwards, V., . . . Marks, J. S. (1998). Relationship of childhood abuse and household dysfunction to many of the leading causes of death in adults. *American Journal of Preventative Medicine, 14,* 245–258. doi:10.1016/S0749-3797(98)00017-8

Finkelhor, D., Vanderminden, J., Turner, H., Hamby, S., & Shattuck, A. (2014). Child maltreatment rates assessed in a national household survey of caregivers and youth. *Child Abuse & Neglect, 38,* 1421–1435. https://doi.org/10.1016/j.chiabu.2014.05.005

Ford, J. D. (2011). Future directions in conceptualizing complex post-traumatic stress syndromes in childhood and adolescence: Toward a developmental trauma disorder diagnosis. In V. Ardino (Ed.), *Post-traumatic syndromes in childhood and adolescence: A handbook of research and practice* (pp. 433–448). West Sussex, UK: Wiley-Blackwell.

Ford, J. D., Stockton, P., Kaltman, S., & Green, B. L. (2006). Disorders of extreme stress (DESNOS) symptoms are associated with type and severity of interpersonal trauma exposure in a sample of healthy young women. *Journal of Interpersonal Violence, 21,*1399–1416. doi:10.1177/0886260506292992

Haller, M. & Chassin, L. (2012). A test of adolescent internalizing and externalizing symptoms as prospective predictors of type of trauma exposure and posttraumatic stress disorder. *Journal of Traumatic Stress Disorder, 25,* 691–699. doi:10.1002/jts.21751.

Hertz, M. F., Jones, S. E., Barrios, L., David-Ferdon, C., & Holt, M. (2015). Association between bullying victimization and health risk behaviors among high school students in the United States. *Journal of School Health, 85,* 833–842. doi:10.1111/josh.12339

Huang, S., Trapido, E., Fleming, L, Arheart, K., Drandall, L, French, M., . . . Prado, G. (2011). The long-term effects of childhood maltreatment experiences on subsequent illicit drug use and drug-related problems in young adulthood. *Addictive Behaviors, 36,* 95–102. doi:10.1016/j.addbeh.2010.09.001

Hultmann, O., & Broberg, A. G. (2016). Family violence and other potentially traumatic interpersonal events among 9- to 17-year-old children attending an outpatient psychiatric clinic. *Journal of Interpersonal Violence, 31,* 2958–2986. https://doi.org/10.1177/0886260515584335

Kalisch, R., Müller, M., & Tüscher, O. (2015). A conceptual framework for the neurobiological study of resilience. *Behavioral and Brain Sciences,38,* E92. doi:10.1017/S0140525X1400082X

Layne, C. M., Beck, C. J., Rimmasch, H., Southwick, J. S., Moreno, M. A., & Hobfoll, S. E. (2009). Promoting 'resilient' posttraumatic adjustment in childhood and beyond: 'Unpacking' life events, adjustment trajectories, resources, and interventions. In D. Brom, R. Pat-Horenczyk, & J. D. Ford (Eds.), *Treating traumatized children: Risk, resilience, and recovery* (pp. 13–47). New York, NY: Routledge/Taylor & Francis.

Matulis, S., Resick, P. A., Rosner, R., & Steil, R. (2014). Developmentally adapted cognitive processing therapy for adolescents suffering from posttraumatic stress disorder after childhood sexual or physical abuse: A pilot study. *Clinical Child and Family Psychology Review, 17,* 173–90. doi:10.1007/s10567-013-0156-9

Pereda, N., Guilera, G., Forns, M., Gómez-Benito, J. (2009). Prevalence of child sexual abuse in community and student samples: A meta-analysis. *Clinical Psychology Review, 29*, 328–338. doi:10.1016/j.cpr.2009.02.007

Podgurski, I., Lyons, J. S., Kisiel, C. & Griffin, G. (2014). Understanding bad girls: The role of trauma in antisocial behavior among female youth. *Residential Treatment for Children & Youth, 31*, 80–88. doi:10.1080/0886571X.2014.880275

Pollio, E., McLean, M., Behl, L. E., & Deblinger E. (2014). Trauma-focused cognitive behavioral therapy. In R. Reece, R. F. Hanson, & J. Sargent (Eds.), *Treatment of child abuse: Common ground for mental health, medical, and legal practitioners* (2nd ed., pp. 31–38). Baltimore, MD: John Hopkins University Press.

Racco, A., & Vis, J. (2015). Evidence based trauma treatment for children and youth. *Child & Adolescent Social Work Journal, 32*, 121–129. doi:10.1007/s105600-014-0347-3

Ruglass, L., & Kendall-Tackett, K. (2014). *Psychology of trauma 101*. New York, NY: Springer.

Shapiro, F. (1999). Eye movement desensitization and reprocessing (EMDR) and the anxiety disorders: Clinical and research implications of an integrated psychotherapy treatment. *Journal of Anxiety Disorders, 13*, 35–67.

Shapiro, F. (2014). The role of eye movement desensitization and reprocessing (EMDR) therapy in medicine: Addressing the psychological and physical symptoms stemming from adverse life experiences. *The Permanente Journal, 18*, 71–77. doi:10.7812/TPP/13-098

Shonkoff, J. P., Garner, A. S., & the Committee on Psychosocial Aspects of Child and Family Health, Committee on Early Childhood, Adoption, and Dependent Care, and Section on Developmental and Behavioral Pediatrics (2012). Lifelong effects of early childhood adversity and chronic stress. *Pediatrics, 129*, e232–e246. doi:10.1542/peds.2011-2663

Simonelli, A. (2013). Posttraumatic stress disorder in early childhood: Classification and diagnostic issues. *European Journal of Psychotraumatology, 4*, 1–11. doi:10.3402/ejpt.v4i0.21357

Spinazzola, J., Rhodes, A. M., Emerson, D., Earle, E., & Monroe, K. (2011). Application of yoga in residential treatment of traumatized youth. *Journal of American Psychiatric Nurses Association, 17*, 431–444. doi:10.117/1078390311418359

Stinson, J. D., Quinn, M. A., & Levenson, J. S. (2016). The impact of trauma on the onset of mental health symptoms, aggression, and criminal behavior in an inpatient psychiatric sample. *Child Abuse & Neglect, 61*, 13–22. doi:10.1016/j.chiabu.2016.09.005

Sumner, S. A., Mercy, J. A., Dahlberg, L. L., Hillis, S. D., Klevens, J., & Houry, D. (2015). Violence in the United States: Status, challenges, and opportunities. *Journal of the American Medical Association, 314*, 478–488. doi:10.l001/jama.2015.8371

"Trauma-focused cognitive behavioral therapy national therapist certification program." (n.d.). Retrieved from https://tfcbt.org/

Trickey, D., Siddaway, A. P., Meiser-Stedman, R., Serpell, L., & Field, A. P. (2012). A meta-analysis of risk factors for post-traumatic stress disorder in children and adolescents. *Clinical Psychology Review, 32*, 122–138. doi:10.1016j.cpr.2011.12.001

Turner, M. G., Exum, M. L., Brame, R., & Holt, T. J. (2013). Bullying victimization and adolescent mental health: General and typological effects across sex. *Journal of Criminal Justice, 41*, 53–59. doi:10.1016/j.jcrimjust.2012.12.005

van der Kolk, B.A. (2006). Clinical implications of neuroscience research in PTSD. *Annals of the New York Academy of Sciences, 1071*, 277–293. doi:10.1196/annals.1364.022

Vézina, J., Hébert, M., Poulin, F., Lavoie, F., Vitaro, F., & Tremblay, R. E. (2015). History of family violence, childhood behavior problems, and adolescent high-risk behaviors as predictors of girls' repeated patterns of dating victimization in two developmental periods. *Violence Against Women, 21*, 435–459. doi:10.1177/1077801215570481

Voelkel, E., Pukay-Martin, N. D., Walter, K. H., & Chard, K. M. (2015). Effectiveness of cognitive processing therapy for male and female U.S. veterans with and without military sexual trauma. *Journal of Traumatic Stress, 28*, 174–182. doi:10.1002/jts.22006

Wamser-Nanney, R., & Vandenberg, B. R. (2013). Empirical support for the definition of a complex trauma event in children and adolescents. *Journal of Traumatic Stress, 26*, 671–678. doi:10.1002/jts.21857

Wizansky, B. (2011). EMDR and the challenge of treating childhood trauma: A theoretical and clinical discussion with case examples. In V. Ardino (Ed.), *Post-traumatic syndromes in childhood and adolescence: A handbook of research and practice* (pp. 297–321). West Sussex, UK: Wiley & Blackwell.

10

Evidence-Based Interventions for Substance-Abusing Adolescents

Joanna E. Bettmann, Katherine V. Ovrom, and Gretchen Anstadt

Nearly all individuals who use an addictive substance initiate their substance use before adulthood (Peiper, Ridenous, Hochwalt, & Coyne-Beasly, 2016; Poudel & Gautam, 2017). Substance use disorders (SUDs) most commonly begin in adolescence. Evidence suggests that the earlier an individual begins using substances, the greater the potential negative impact on physical health, peer relationships, work adjustment, and family systems (Poudel & Gautam, 2017). In this chapter, we present an introduction to adolescent substance use, its associated psychosocial consequences, frequent comorbid mental disorders, and tools for the assessment and treatment of adolescents with SUDs. To be clear, we use the definition of substance provided by Peiper et al. (2016): the term "substance" refers to any substance with addictive potential except food.

Adolescent Substance Use Prevalence

Studies by the U.S. Centers for Disease Control (CDC) found that 38.6% of adolescents have tried marijuana, 7.5% used it prior to age 13, and 21.7% were currently using as defined by use one or more times within the last 30 days (CDC, 2015). Furthermore, 6.4% reported using hallucinogenic drugs, 7.0% inhalants, 5.0% ecstasy, 2.1% heroin, and 16.8% a prescriptive drug without a doctor's prescription (CDC, 2015). Alcohol was the most widely used: 63.2% reported at least one drink in their lifetime, 17.2% reported consuming alcohol prior to age 13, 32.8% reported one or more drinks in the last month, and 17.7% reported recent binge drinking of five or more drinks within a couple hours (CDC, 2015). Similarly, the U.S. Substance Abuse and Mental Health Services Administration (SAMHSA, 2015) found that 1.3 million adolescents ages 12 to 17 had SUDs, representing 5% of U.S. adolescents. Older adolescents and young adults had higher rates, with 16.3% of young adults aged 18 to 25 meeting criteria for a SUD (SAMHSA, 2015). The numbers collectively draw a picture of U.S. adolescents as engaging in significant substance use.

Consequences of Substance Use

Drug use at younger ages links to higher risk for SUDs, conduct disorder, academic problems, and risky sexual behaviors (Poudel & Gautam, 2017). For example, adults who try marijuana at age 14 or younger are 6 times more likely to be diagnosed with illicit drug dependence than those who tried it at age 18 or older (SAMHSA, 2013). In some cases, substance use can serve as an indicator of risk rather than a predictor. For example, a population-based study designed to examine the relationship between cannabis and general mental health found that mental health problems, truancy, victimization, and others contributed to cannabis use (van Gastel et al., 2013). Alcohol use in adolescence consistently links to a host of poor adolescent outcomes including academic problems, high school drop-out, criminal behavior, and SUDs (Irons, Iacono, & McGue, 2015).

Neurological and Developmental Consequences

Substance abuse appears to have significant impact on adolescent brains. While much brain growth happens during the first 10 years of life, neurological development in terms of axonal growth, myelination, and synaptic pruning occur during adolescence (Johnson, Blum, & Giedd, 2009; Rosner, 2013). During adolescence, a decrease in gray brain matter and an increase in the brain's white matter takes place after the processes of pruning and myelination occur, allowing for a more efficient transmission of information and communication between different parts of the brain (Johnson et al., 2009).

Troublingly, brain development during adolescence appears significantly impacted by substance abuse. For example, adolescents who abuse alcohol evidence smaller hippocampal and frontal volumes, poorer memory, and altered white brain matter microstructures compared to their nonusing peers (Rosner, 2013). In one study, adolescents who drank heavily showed deficits in visuospatial skills, attention, memory, and executive function after as little as 1 to 2 years of drinking (Silveri, Dager, Cohen- Gilbert & Sneider, 2016; Squeglia, Jacobus, & Tapert, 2009). Another study using Magnetic Resonance Imaging technology examined the brains of young adults with alcohol dependence. That study found that the brains of young adults who reported heavy drinking during adolescence evidenced damage to the prefrontal cortex and hippocampus (Silveri et al., 2016). Brain maturation continues into young adulthood and the prefrontal cortex is especially vulnerable to alcohol's neurotoxic effect (Medina et al, 2008). Silveri et al.'s finding suggests that attention, memory, new learning, creativity, attitude, goal development, conceptual reasoning and planning, and other functions of the prefrontal cortex may be negatively affected after heavy drinking in adolescence (Siddiqui, Chatterjee, Kumar, Siddiqui, & Goyal, 2008).

Adolescent binge drinking appears linked to altered frontal, cerebellar, temporal, and parietal regions of the brain (Rosner, 2013). Damage associated to these brain areas can lead to problems such as apathy, depression, poor appetite, decreased sexual drive, diminished judgment, and reduced emotional control (Siddiqui et al., 2008). Changes in adolescents' important brain structures can affect the myelination process and quality of white matter and white matter maturation, leading to increased deficits in cognitive functioning such as poor attention, memory, concentration, and diminished ability to acquire new skills (Bava & Tapert, 2010; Squeglia et al., 2009). Tapert et al. (2002) found that starting at age 16, over a period of substance use and withdrawal for 8 years, heavy substance use leads to learning, memory, attention, and retention difficulties as well as poor concentration and worse psychomotor processing speed.

In another study, adolescents followed from ages 16 to 24 who started drinking earlier in adolescence and drank for longer periods of time throughout adolescence had smaller hippocampi compared to adolescents who drank less (DeBellis et al., 2000). Adolescents with alcohol use disorders evidence changes in the corpus callosum, as well as the frontal, cerebellar, temporal, and parietal regions of the brain (DeBellis et al., 2000; Medina et al., 2008; Squeglia et al., 2009). These brain changes suggest that adolescent drinking, especially binge drinking, can negatively impact adolescent brain structure and functions, causing less efficient transfer of information and slower brain maturation (Squeglia et al., 2009). Adolescents who drink heavily also evidence diminished frontal cortex activation during spatial working memory tasks, attention tests, memory retrieval tasks, and visuospatial functioning decreases (Casey & Jones; DeBellis et al., 2000; Rosner, 2013). The research reviewed above implicates substance use in significant damage to adolescent brains, suggesting the critical nature of assessing and remedying adolescent substance use.

Another study showed differences in prefrontal cortex size in the brains of female adolescents who drank compared to males who drank (Medina et al., 2008), suggesting gender differences in the impact of adolescent drinking on brain function. When alcohol-abusing male and female adolescents were compared to each other in another study, females showed poorer frontal response to spatial working memory and reduced gray matter than males with alcohol abuse (Bava & Tapert, 2010; Rosner, 2013; Squeglia et al., 2009). Thus, while both male and female adolescents showed negative effects from heavy alcohol consumption, females showed greater performance deficits than their male peers in attention, memory, spatial skills, and executive functioning. Specifically, female adolescents appeared more susceptible to compromises in brain structures especially with increased use and duration of alcohol use (Squeglia et al., 2009).

In fMRI studies, adolescents who use marijuana consistently display less efficient brain activation in terms of working memory, cognitive control tasks, and verbal learning (Tapert et al., 2008; Squeglia et al., 2009). Compared to nonsmokers, marijuana users show increased cerebellar volumes, which link to impaired synaptic pruning and myelination thus preventing smoother and more efficient communication between brain regions as well as slowed cognitive control (Medina, Nagel, & Tapert, 2010). This finding suggests that marijuana-using adolescents trying to complete a voluntary cognitive task requiring attention will evidence a slowed response when naming a color, for example (Medina, Nagel, & Tapert, 2010).

Alcohol and marijuana use among adolescents is frequently combined and can lead to many challenges related to brain development and structure. In a study exploring the impact of cannabis use and heavy drinking with adolescents aged 16 to 19, white matter reliability was diminished in fronto-parietal and fronto-temporal circuits (Bava et al. Tapert, 2009), which links increased risk for depression, poorer psychomotor speed, difficulty with complex attention, compromised verbal memory, and difficulty sequencing and planning even a month after adolescents discontinued use (Bava et al., 2009; Medina et al., 2007).

This research collectively suggests that adolescents who use substances, particularly alcohol and marijuana and especially when used at the same time and in large amounts, evidence negative outcomes. What does this research mean for the substance-abusing adolescent clients that you see? Research suggests that adolescents abusing substances evidence damage to the prefrontal cortex and hippocampus (Silveri et al., 2016). A client experiencing negative effects in these brain areas may report difficulty paying attention and concentrating at school, inability to remember new concepts, and/or dissatisfaction with school performance (Siddiqui et al., 2008; Squeglia et al., 2009). These client's brains may be slower to process information, so they might be slower while spelling, performing simple math problems, or interpreting abstract concepts. They might have difficulty establishing goals and future plans and may require additional support to develop those (Siddiqui et al., 2008; Squeglia et al., 2009). Parents may notice that their child is not keeping up with academics, engaging positively with nonsubstance using peers, setting future goals or planning, showing creativity, or evidencing good judgment (Squeglia et al., 2009). Substance-abusing adolescents might also show depressive symptoms such as changes in sleeping patterns, poor appetite, or apathy, potentially indicative of white matter decreases in the brain caused by damage due to substance use (Squeglia et al., 2009).

Comorbidity

Research suggests that as many as 75% of adolescents with SUDs could have co-occurring mental health disorders (Lichtenstein, Spirito, & Zimmermann, 2010). When adolescents' co-occurring disorders are unassessed or untreated, they experience increased risk of medical illnesses, incarceration, homelessness, suicide, and early death (SAMHSA, 2016).

Adolescents most commonly show comorbidities of SUDs with disruptive behavior disorders (Eme, 2016; Hawkins, 2009; Stone, Vander Stoep, & McCauly, 2016). Youth who abuse substances are also 4 times more likely to experience comorbid depression and 2 times more likely to have an anxiety disorder (Hawkins, 2009). But research also links adolescent substance use to PTSD and personality disorders (Eme, 2016; Stone et al., 2016). Some literature suggests that adolescents with mental health disorders may turn to substance use to self-medicate (Zullig, Divin, Weiler, Haddox, & Pealer, 2015). For example, trauma from adverse childhood experiences and other traumatic events link to increased rates of substance use (Carliner et al., 2016).

However, not all research suggests that the mental health disorder came first. For example, co-occurring depressive and conduct symptoms in early adolescence are associated with greater likelihood of substance use than depressive symptoms alone (Stone et al., 2016). Clinicians often wonder about their adolescent clients: which came first—the mental health difficulties or the substance use disorder? Researchers agree that various contributing factors such as family history, personality values, environmental factors, and traumatic events play a role in co-occurring disorders (Hawkins, 2009; Libby, Orton, Stover, & Riggs, 2005).

But mental health problems often occur before substance abuse in adolescents (Hawkins, 2009). The median age of onset for a mental disorder is 11, while SUDs typically develop 5 to 10 years later (Kessler, 2004). Furthermore, approximately 83% of those with lifetime co-occurring disorders reported the onset of a SUD after having at least one mental disorder. Notably, 13% of those reported a SUD occurring before a mental disorder, while only 4% reported onset of an SUD and mental health disorder in the same year (Hawkins, 2009). Thus, clinicians must carefully assess all adolescents for SUDs as well as other comorbid disorders.

Stages of Change

An integral component of substance abuse treatment involves assessing and encouraging adolescents' motivation to change their substance abuse. In the past, clinicians perceived believed that clients were either self-motivated or not, that motivation was beyond the control of the clinician (Kennedy & Gregoire, 2009). But when Prochaska (1979) introduced a transtheoretical model which included stages of change, clinicians began to understand client motivation as something they could measure and encourage with specific tasks and techniques (Prochaska & Norcross, 2014). Originally developed to understand clients' attempts to change nicotine addiction (Prochaska & DiClemente, 1983), the stages of change model is useful in thinking about substance use (Kennedy & Gregoire, 2009; Prochaska & Norcross, 2014). Each stage of change represents a collection of attitudes, intentions, and behaviors related to an individual's readiness to change (Prochaska & Norcross, 2014). Each stage also includes a period of time and set of tasks necessary to get to the next stage (Prochaska & Norcross, 2014). The six stages of change are *precontemplation, contemplation, preparation, action, maintenance,* and *termination.*

Precontemplation refers to a stage when an individual has no intention to change (Prochaska & Norcross, 2014). Individuals in precontemplation are generally unaware that they have a problem (Prochaska & Norcross, 2014). For example, an adolescent who believes her binge drinking has no consequences or who states that it is only her parents or caregivers who have a problem with her drinking may be in precontemplation. Precontemplative adolescents present to treatment often because an external force such as parents or the legal system forced them to engage in it. Adolescents in the precontemplation stage may comply with treatment and cease substance use due to pressure from external forces; but once the pressure is off, they are likely to resume the same behaviors (Prochaska & Norcross, 2014). To progress past the precontemplation stage, an adolescent must recognize that they have a problem and take ownership and accountability of their substance use.

In the *contemplation* stage, individuals are aware that they have a problem and are thinking about addressing it (Prochaska & Norcross, 2014). However, they lack the commitment to take action toward addressing the problem (Prochaska & Norcross, 2014). Clinicians who lack an understanding of *contemplation* may find adolescents in this stage frustrating because such clients understand what they need to do, but are not ready to do it. Individuals can become stuck in the contemplation stage (Prochaska & Norcross, 2014). The key to moving past contemplation stage is to not think too long about how to move forward, but instead make a firm decision to take action that involves concrete steps and goals (Prochaska & Norcross, 2014). Once an adolescent takes any form of action, even preparatory action, they begin transitioning toward the next stage.

The *preparation* stage describes individuals who intend to take action toward change and report some early behavioral changes (Prochaska & Norcross, 2014). For example, an adolescent who is preparing to reduce substance use may delay their next substance use, such as not using until the weekend or until a special occasion. While individuals in preparation stage have taken some action, they have not yet established a strong plan to execute and evaluate change (Prochaska & Norcross, 2014). At this stage, the primary task for clinicians is to help clients set goals and priorities that will empower them to move forward into full action (Prochaska & Norcross, 2014).

During the *action* stage, individuals change their behavior and environment to address their problems (Prochaska & Norcross, 2014). This stage tends to be the most visible and is often applauded by those around the individual (Prochaska & Norcross, 2014). Unlike earlier stages, the action stage carries a specific time requirement. Individuals are in the action stage if they have successfully changed their problem behaviors for at least 1 day and up to 6 months (Prochaska & Norcross, 2014). This time component is one of the keys to differentiating preparation from action. Cutting back on a behavior is considered preparation, while successful behavior change occurs during action. Individuals in the action stage also begin to acquire the behavioral and psychological tools necessary to sustain change and avoid relapse (Prochaska & Norcross, 2014).

After 6 months in the action stage, individuals move into *maintenance*. Maintenance can be lifelong and involves an ongoing commitment and practice of new behaviors, philosophies, and lifestyles to maintain whatever change was achieved (Prochaska & Norcross, 2014). Importantly, the stages of change model is not necessarily linear. Client may regress to earlier stages if they are unsuccessful at a certain stage (Prochaska & Norcross, 2014). As the stages of change model developed, a stage called *recycling* was added to describe times when a person regresses to or revisits an earlier stage before moving forward toward maintenance (Prochaska & Norcross, 2014). A widely used research tool to measure clients' stage of change is the University of Rhode Island Change Assessment (URICA; DiClemente & Hughes, 1990). This instrument is widely available on the web (for example here: https://habitslab.umbc.edu/urica/) and free. Its scoring is quite simple; the instrument can be scored to yield individual stage scores or a "readiness to change" score. The "readiness to change" score can be helpful to clinicians trying to determine their clients' change over time relative to attitude.

The stages of change model may be most clearly seen in a case example. John was a 15-year-old client who arrived at a short-term residential treatment center. He explained that his parents saw his marijuana use as a problem, but that he did not. John defined himself as having no problems with substance use. He was clearly at *precontemplation* stage. While he described that he smoked pot many times each day (including at school), he framed his use of pot as unproblematic, explaining "you can't be addicted to pot." He described that he had used a few other drugs, including LSD, ecstasy, cocaine, and pills when pot was not available. However, he believed that his overinvolved parents were his problem—not his substance use. During the course of his 2-month treatment, John described that he realized that, in order for him to manage his life, he needed to not smoke marijuana. He explained that he was planning on not smoking when he went home—only drinking. We can understand his treatment as helping him to move toward preparation stage. As happens in preparation stage, he intended to take action to make changes in his life. However, when John went home, he immediately began drinking to excess. His parents phoned me (JEB) to explain that he was leaving school mid-day and breaking into the family home to get into his parent's alcohol cabinet. He was showing up at his high school drunk and was close to getting expelled from school. John's plan for action was clearly flawed, but he was unable to recognize his cognitive errors. While he became somewhat motivated to change during treatment, his action plan was poor. He failed to recognize that, for him, substituting one substance for another was not an effective course of action. He failed to recognize his own addiction to substances.

Assessment of Substance Use

In order to create a treatment plan that will best fit the client, it is important to assess substance use among clients. Using previously developed, standardized client self- report measures within a thorough mental health assessment is one effective approach. Standardized substance use assessment measures in the NIH Toolbox and PROMIS websites require no additional training and take only a few minutes to complete. Free substance use assessment measures are here in the NIH Toolbox: http://www.healthmeasures.net/explore-measurement-systems/nih-toolbox/intro-to-nih-toolbox/ They are also on the PROMIS website, a site hosted by Northwestern University and funded by NIH: http://www.healthmeasures.net/explore-measurement-systems/promis/obtain-administer-measures We strongly encourage you to integrate standardized substance use measures into your mental health assessments for all adolescent clients.

Evidence-Based Treatments

The U.S. National Institute on Drug Abuse (NIDA) lists four categories of evidence-based approaches to adolescent SUDs: behavioral approaches, family-based interventions, recovery support services, and addiction medications (NIDA, 2014). The behavioral approaches that NIDA endorses include interventions such as group therapy CBT, individual psychotherapy CBT, motivational enhancement therapy, and 12-step programs (NIDA, 2014). Their endorsed family-based approaches include brief strategic family therapy, family behavior therapy, functional family therapy, multidimensional family therapy, and multisystemic therapy (NIDA, 2014). Their endorsed recovery support services aim to reinforce progress made in treatment and to improve quality of life for adolescents in substance use recovery (NIDA, 2014); these peer-based and agency-based recovery support services include 12-step groups such as Alcoholics Anonymous and Narcotics Anonymous, peer recovery support groups, peer mentorship or coaching, and recovery schools designed to support adolescents in early recovery from substance abuse (NIDA, 2014).

Addiction medications are recommended with caution: most medications have only been studied in individuals 18 years of age or older; only limited evidence exists to support the safety and effectiveness of addiction medications for adolescents under 18 (NIDA, 2014). Addiction medications may also have implications for adolescents' neurological development, as yet unstudied (NIDA, 2014). Due to these risk factors, we do not review addiction medications in this chapter.

The NIDA website is an excellent resource for clinicians seeking a brief overview of the evidence based treatments listed above. However, existing literature concludes that two interventions for adolescent substance use are the most efficacious: motivational interviewing and family-based approaches (Tanner-Smith, Wilson, & Lipsey, 2013).

Motivational Interviewing

Motivational interviewing (MI; Rollnick & Miller, 1995), is a client-centered intervention in which the clinician strives to collaborate with her client using a specific type of conversation to address ambivalence about change (Miller & Rollnick, 2013). MI places a great emphasis on language of change to strengthen client motivation and commitment to goals (Miller & Rollnick, 2013). For example, if an adolescent client indicates that his motivation for change is as low as 2 out of 10, the clinician may inquire why it is a 2 rather than a 1—instead of asking why their motivation is so low. This approach encourages clients to talk about why they are motivated in positive terms.

Research suggests that this approach may be especially well suited for adolescents because it respects their autonomy and provides choices (Brown et al., 2015). Studies substantiate MI as efficacious for adolescents with SUDs (Jensen et al., 2011). A 2011 review of MI for adolescent SUDs found that even one session of MI produced small but statistically significant reductions in use across many substances including tobacco, alcohol, marijuana, and other drugs (Jensen et al., 2011). MI continued to have a significant impact after treatment, in follow-ups ranging from 1 month to 2 years post-treatment (Jensen et al., 2011).

MI may also help adolescents with comorbid psychiatric and substance use issues (Brown et al., 2015). A randomized control trial which compared a two-session MI intervention to treatment as usual for adolescents with comorbid mental health and SUDs in a psychiatric hospital found that those who received the MI intervention went longer without using substances post-discharge than their peers who received treatment as usual (Brown et al., 2015).

For clinicians seeking training in MI, we recommend the textbook *Motivational interviewing: Helping people change* (3rd ed.) by William R. Miller and Stephen Rollnick, MI's creators. The SAMHSA website lists resources for additional training options: http://www.integration.samhsa.gov/clinical-practice/motivational-interviewing.

A variant of MI is the manualized treatment motivational enhancement therapy (MET). MET is a manualized brief psychotherapy intervention designed to enhance motivation to change (Miller, Zweben, DiClemente, & Rychtarik, 1992). Treatment typically involves an assessment, followed by two to four treatment sessions. Randomized controlled studies of MET for adolescents with no-treatment control groups found statistically significant improvements from pre- to post-treatment (Tanner-Smith, Wilson, & Lipsey, 2013). Further, a meta-analysis comparing family therapy, MET, CBT, group/mixed therapy and other interventions for adolescents found that only MET and family therapy showed statistically significant improvements over time, indicating they were more effective interventions than the others (Tanner-Smith et al., 2013).

Family-Based Approaches

Family-based interventions attempt to address systemic issues that may be impacting adolescent substance use. Research shows family-based risk and protective factors can predict adolescent substance use (Horigian, Anderson, & Szapocznik, 2016). For example, familial conflict, child abuse, and parental substance use are all risk factors for adolescent substance use (Horigian et al.,

2016). Similarly, positive parenting, familial antidrug rules and norms, and effective parent-teen communication link to a lower risk of substance use in adolescence (Horigian et al., 2016). A recent meta-analysis found family therapy to be more effective than other individual and group treatment modalities for adolescents with SUDs (Tanner-Smith et al., 2013).

While there are a variety of family interventions a clinician can utilize, family interventions typically address family communication and conflict; co-occurring behavioral, mental health, and learning disorders; problems with school or work; and social relationships (NIDA, 2014). NIDA (2014) endorses brief strategic family therapy, family behavior therapy, functional family therapy, multidimensional family therapy, and multisystemic therapy as effective interventions for family based adolescent substance use treatment. Chapter 13 of this book presents functional family therapy in depth, while Chapter 8 presents thorough descriptions of the mutisystemic therapy and multidimensional family therapy models. For more information on all of these modalities and information on training resources, clinicians can also consult the NIDA website at https://www.drugabuse.gov/publications/principles-adolescent-substance-use-disorder-treatment-research-based-guide/evidence-based-approaches-to-treating-adolescent-substance-use-disorders/family-based-approaches.

To illustrate the impact of working with the family as a system, we will describe the philosophy and practice of brief strategic family therapy (BSFT) here. BSFT focuses on relational interactions associated with adolescent substance use and behavioral problems (Horigian et al., 2016). BSFT hypothesizes that adolescent symptoms are generated by maladaptive family interactions such as overly rigid or loose boundaries, inappropriate family alliances, and the false belief that one individual is responsible for the family's issues (Horigian et al., 2016). BSFT does not focus on family discussion content, but rather how the family communicates and manages conflict (NIDA, 2003). Clinicians using BSFT focus on building therapeutic alliance with each family member and the family as a whole, and then work with them to identify family strengths and problems together. Clinicians help families develop conflict resolution skills, practice assertive communication, and develop mutually supportive relationships (Horigian et al., 2016). BSFT appears to be effective in reducing adolescent substance use and associated psychosocial consequences such as incarceration in diverse populations, while improving family function (Horigian et al., 2015; Valdez, Cepeda, Parrish, Horowitz, & Kaplan, 2013).

Research suggests that family-based approaches for adolescent SUDs are often more effective than individual or group work alone (Tanner-Smith et al., 2013). Thus, we encourage clinicians to consult the NIDA and SAMHSA websites (www.nida.gov and www.samhsa.gov) for a complete list of approved interventions and to work within their agencies to secure adequate training to deliver empirically validated family-based interventions.

Treatment for Co-Occurring Mental Health and SUDs

There is little consensus in the research literature regarding treatment of adolescents with co-occurring disorders. Oftentimes, clients receive treatment for mental health disorders while their SUDs go untreated or visa versa (SAMHSA, 2016). Some providers are unwilling to provide a client services until substance use has ceased and associated symptoms controlled (Hawkins, 2009). Some SUD treatment providers are cautious of treating clients with active mental health symptoms or who are on psychotropic medication, as they believe that any drug use, including prescription use, can be harmful (Hawkins, 2009). In the past, these contrasting views prevented an integrative treatment approach, with clinicians often opting for serial or parallel treatment methods (Bride, Sammuel, & Webb-Robbins, 2006).

Integrative approaches strive to treat co-occurring disorders, providing coordination between treatment systems to address disorders concurrently, providing treatment in a single setting with clinicians cross-trained in mental health and SUDs (Hawkins, 2009; Bride, et al., 2006). SAMSHA suggests that adolescents with co-occurring disorders are best treated using this kind of an integrated approach where substance use and mental disorders are treated simultaneously (SAMHSA, 2016). Integrated treatment links to better outcomes at a lower cost because a clinic or a team develops a treatment plan together, usually within the same treatment facility (Hawkins, 2009). Research suggests that this kind of integrated treatment results in increased adolescent quality of life, improved mental health symptoms and functioning due to stronger social supports, improved coping mechanisms learned during treatment, and decreased risk of hospitalization, suicidality, and homelessness (SAMHSA, 2017; Wu et al., 2016).

- When you are treating adolescents with *co-occurring disorders*, think of both diagnoses as primary.
- Treat co-occurring disorders in tandem using evidence-based models to treat both diagnoses (Hawkins, 2009).
- Include services that incorporate social supports and interventions which promote motivation toward positive change.
- Utilize a comprehensive and multisystem approach that incorporates a multidisciplinary team implementing a single unified treatment plan.
- Incorporate a long-term perspective that incorporates transition, aftercare, and support services.
- Emphasize risk reduction to prevent relapse and support the adolescent's reintegration into their life outside treatment (Hawkins, 2009).

For adolescents with co-occurring disorders, CBT, motivational enhancement interventions, motivational interviewing, and family therapies evidence the strongest treatment outcomes (Wu et al., 2016; Hawkins, 2009). In one study, adolescents with major depressive disorder and alcohol use disorder showed the biggest treatment gains when receiving CBT coupled with MET (Wu et al., 2016). In another study, adolescents who received a combination of MET and CBT reported decreased substance use at follow-ups up to a year (Hawkins, 2009; Dennis et al., 2004). Other research suggests that adolescents with co-occurring disorders who received CBT combined with MET showed immediately decreases in substance use, as well as at 1 year follow-up (Dennis et al., 2004). However, two thirds of adolescents in the study reported some substance use or related problems at or after the 12-month follow-up, suggesting that co-occurring disorders may be thought of as chronic conditions. Clinicians should always utilize relapse prevention interventions (Hawkins, 2009; Dennis et al., 2004).

Family-based approaches for adolescents with co-occurring disorders appear to improve family engagement and maintenance in treatment, decrease adolescent substance use, increase adolescent school attendance and performance, and improve family functioning (Hawkins, 2009). Family behavior therapy (FBT), multidimensional family therapy (MDFT), and multisystemic therapy (MST) are three integrative family therapy models that show efficacy for adolescents with co-occurring disorders (Hawkins, 2009).

A case example will help illuminate what treatment for co-occurring disorders can look like. Alex was a 16-year-old white young man from the southeastern United States whose parents brought him to a residential treatment center. They were concerned about his heavy drinking and dropping school grades. His previous response to therapy with several different outpatient therapists was poor, resulting in little treatment engagement and no behavior change. Alex's family history was positive for SUDs which appeared in both his maternal and paternal extended families.

Alex described in his initial session with me (JEB) that he thought his parents were "off their rockers. My life is just fine." Alex described a happy childhood with his married homosexual parents in a middle-class lifestyle where he shared a home also with two older brothers. Alex, however, described living through numerous hurricanes, the most recent of which had devastated his city. He described that he hid in the basement of an apartment building during previous hurricanes and was scared but protected from most details by the adults around him. However, he detailed that, a year earlier, the most recent hurricane had lasted for hours and was terrifying. He explained that he survived the hurricane by lying in a bathtub with one parent, hearing their apartment dissemble and building materials crash around them. He showed little emotion as he detailed subsequent scenes which included mass casualties and community devastation.

Ever since the most recent hurricane, Alex had ramped up his drinking. While he used to drink only on the weekends with his buddies, he was now drinking every day before school and smoking marijuana whenever he could get his hands on it. Alex described himself now as a daily drinker and smoker, explaining that he was too jittery without it. Since the hurricane, he had given up participation on the high school soccer team, spending time with his friends who wanted, like him, to drink all day. He reported tolerance and withdrawal symptoms related to his alcohol use. He reported that he sometimes drove his parents' car when drunk or high.

Alex also endorsed numerous symptoms of PTSD, including recurrent and distressing memories of the hurricane, recurrent nightmares about it, panic symptoms when he heard weather reports of strong storms headed toward his community, persistent negative beliefs about himself ("I won't live to see 18"), ruminative guilt about his inability to protect one parent who received minor injuries during the hurricane, and feelings of detachment from his family relationships. He also reported difficulty concentrating at school and sleep disturbances (difficulty falling asleep and staying asleep unless he was stoned).

Alex appeared to meet criteria both for alcohol use disorder with moderate severity and PTSD, both disorders which seemed to manifest in the previous year. He also appeared to have cannabis use disorder of mild severity. Consistent with Carliner et al. (2016), Alex's trauma from the hurricane appeared linked to his increased substance abuse. He seemed to be self-medicating his PTSD symptoms with alcohol and marijuana, aiming to blunt his emotionally dysregulating symptoms.

When I met Alex upon his arrival at the adolescent residential treatment center, he struck me as smart, engaging, charming, and funny. He liked to make his peers laugh and seemed equally comfortable with both male and female peers. He engaged easily in both individual and group treatment in the center, but denied that anything in his life needed changing. Using Prochaska's stages of change model, we can think of Alex as residing in the precontemplation stage at that point. He explained that his life functioned well. He believed that, when he failed out of school, he would get a job as a food service worker in a local restaurant, a job that some of his friends held. He detailed how much money he would make, the apartment he was planning on getting with his friends, and the easy-going life he would have without his parents breathing down his neck about his dropping grades. Alex drew a picture of a blissful, easy life—one he thought he could create if only his parents would back off.

In crafting his treatment plan, I worked with Alex and his parents, as well as Alex's entire treatment team at the residential center. We drafted a treatment plan in which Alex's dual diagnoses were both primary. We aimed to treat both diagnoses in tandem, using the evidence-based approach TF-CBT to work with Alex's PTSD in group and individual treatment and the evidence-based motivational interviewing and family therapy to address his alcohol use and cannabis use disorders. In his treatment plan, we incorporated the important role of social supports in his environment, building on Alex's strong social skills by structuring supportive group involvement within the residential treatment center. The aim here was to provide him with a supportive, sober living environment among his adolescent peers.

Alex's treatment plan included his family's involvement and treatment as well. We held twice-weekly videoconferences with Alex's parents, during which we focused on how his parents could support his sober choices and modify their own behaviors, including their substance use, to improve their relationships with him. His parents and siblings also came to the treatment center for several intensive family therapy weekends, during which improving familial communication and rebuilding strong, authentic relational connections was the focus. Alex shared with his parents during one of these weekends his feelings of guilt for not protecting them from injury during the hurricane. In one family therapy session that weekend, he and his parents cried together, sharing stories about their survival through the storm and its impact on them.

Some family therapy approaches view adolescent substance use as resulting from a combination of individual characteristics, family behaviors, school experiences, and neighborhood cultures (NIDA, 2014). This perspective acknowledges the multiple systems that influence adolescents' behaviors and leverages familial strengths to create a plan for recovery (Horigian et al., 2016). This kind of thinking impacted me in creating Alex's treatment plan. We conceptualized Alex's recovery as critically impacted by his family relationships. His substance use took place within the context of his PTSD, home community, school, peers, and other influences. Thinking about the various systems which impacted Alex and his substance use at home helped me to design a treatment plan which included addressing issues each of those systems.

Alex stayed in the residential treatment center for a year, after which he transitioned home with a strong aftercare plan including weekly individual therapy, daily 12-step meetings in his community, and an alternative high school with supportive case managers embedded in the school. Alex's time in the residential treatment center had its highs and lows, including him smuggling in contraband cigarettes and marijuana after a home visit. However, his time at the treatment center appeared to help him to move through Prochaska's stages of change and begin to address his PTSD symptomology and avoidance of triggers. While slow, Alex's symptom reduction was likely aided by his strong relationships with his peers and his rebuilt relationships with his parents. He saw these others as allies in his treatment process. His family's support served as a critical component of treatment, enabling him to transition home with few hiccups.

I heard from Alex's parents a year after he went home in an email in which his parents expressed appreciation for his time at the residential treatment center. They explained that, while he had relapsed several times since arriving home, the strengthened familial relationships and the skills he learned while at the residential program enabled him to disclose his relapse to his parents and recommit to a sober life. Alex's parents described themselves as "hopeful" and "optimistic that our son will live the long life he deserves." As Hawkins (2009) and Dennis et al. (2004) observe, adolescents' co-occurring disorders perhaps should be regarded as chronic conditions, needing support and relapse prevention interventions throughout the life span.

Alex's case illuminates an adolescent with dual diagnoses in which tandem treatment was key. Alex's SUDs and PTSD were treated simultaneously, involving evidence-based interventions and multisystemic approaches. This chapter reviewed the prevalence of adolescent SUDs, the risk factors and consequence for these disorders, the stages of change model, and finally SUDs assessment and treatment. Adolescents' SUDs can be difficult to treat, as many adolescents do not identify their substance use as a problem while family members do. Treatment of adolescent SUDs needs to involve high levels of clinical skill, evidence-based approaches, and a commitment to life-long support for these clients.

References

Bava, S., Frank, L., McQueeny, T., Schweinsburg, B., Schweinsburg, A., & Tapert, S., (2009). Altered white matter microstructure in adolescent substance abuse. *Psychiatry Research: Neuroimaging, 173,* 228–237. doi:10.1016/j.pscychresns.2009.04.005

Bava, S., & Tapert, S., (2010). Adolescent brain development and the risk for alcohol and other drug problems. *Neuropsychology Review, 20,* 398–413. doi:10.1007/s11065-010-9146

Bride, B., Sammuel, A., & Webb-Robbins, L., (2006). Is integrated treatment of co-occurring disorders more effective than nonintegrated treatment? *Best Practices in Mental Health, 15,* 43–57.

Brown, R. A., Abrantes, A. M., Minami, H., Prince, M. A., Bloom, E. L., Apodaca, T. R., . . . Hunt, J. I. (2015). Motivational interviewing to reduce substance use in adolescents with psychiatric comorbidity. *Journal of Substance Abuse Treatment, 59,* 20–29. doi:10.1016/j.sat.2015.06.016

Carliner, H., Keyes, K. M., McLaughlin, K. A., Meyers, J. L., Dunn, E. C., & Marins, S. S. (2016). Childhood trauma and illicit drug use in adolescence: A population- based national comorbidity survey replication—adolescent supplement study, *Journal of the American Academy of Child and Adolescent Psychiatry, 55,* 701–708. doi:10.1016/j.jaac.2016.05.010

Centers for Disease Control. (2015). Trends in the prevalence of alcohol use national YRBS: 1991–2015. Retrieved from https://www.cdc.gov/healthyyouth/factsheets.htm

Centers for Disease Control (2015). Trends in the prevalence of marijuana, cocaine, and other illegal drug use national YRBS: 1991–2015. Retrieved from https://www.cdc.gov/healthyyouth/factsheets.htm

Casey, B., & Jones, R., (2010). Neurobiology of the adolescent brain and behavior: Implications for substance use disorders. *Journal of American Academy of Child & Adolescent Psychiatry, 49,* 1189–1201. doi:10.1016/j.jaac.2010.08.017

DeBellis, M., Clark, D., Beers, S., Solof, P., Boring, A., Hall, J., . . . Keshavan, M. (2000). Hippocampal volume in adolescent-onset alcohol use disorders. *American Journal of Psychiatry, 157,* 737–744.

Dennis, M., Godley, S., Diamond, G., Tims, F., Babor, T., Donaldon, J., . . . Funk, R. (2004). The cannabis youth treatment (CYT) study: Main findings from two randomized trails. *Journal of Substance Abuse Treatment, 27,* 197–213. doi:10.1016.j.sat.2003.09.005

DiClemente, C. C. & Hughes, S. O. (1990). Stages of change profiles in alcoholism treatment. *Journal of Substance Abuse, 2,* 217–235.

Eme, R. (2016). ADHD and risky substance use in male adolescents. *ADHD Report, 24,* 1–8. doi:10.1521/adhd.2016.24.3.1

Hawkins, E. (2009). A tale of two systems: Co-occurring mental health and substance abuse disorders treatment for adolescents. *Annual Review of Psychology, 60,* 197–227. doi:10.1146/annurev.psych.60.110707.163456

Horigian, V. E., Anderson, A. R., & Szapocznik, J. (2016). Family-based treatments for adolescent substance use. *Child and Adolescent Psychiatric Clinics of North America, 25,* 603–628. doi:10.1016/j.chc.2016.06.001

Horigian, V. E., Feaster, D. J., Robbins, M. S., Brincks, A. M., Ucha, J., Rohrbaugh, M.J., . . . Szapocznik, J. (2015). A cross-sectional assessment of the long-term effects of brief strategic family therapy for adolescent substance use. *The American Journal on Addictions, 24,* 637–645. doi:10.1111/ajad.12278

Irons, D. E., Iacono, W. G., & McGue, M. (2015). Tests of the effects of adolescent early alcohol exposures on adult outcomes. *Addiction, 110,* 269–278. doi:10.1111/add.12747

Jensen, C. D., Cushing, C. C., Aylward, B. S., Craig, J. T., Sorell, D. M., & Steele, R. G. (2011). Effectiveness of motivational interviewing interventions for adolescent substance use behavior change: A meta-analytic review. *Journal of Consulting and Clinical Psychology, 79,* 433–440. doi:10.1037/a0023992

Johnson, S. B., Blum, R. W., & Giedd, J. N. (2009). Adolescent maturity and the brain: The promise and pitfalls of neuroscience research in adolescent health policy. *Journal of Adolescent Health, 45,* 216–221. doi:10.1016/j.jadohealth.2009.05.016

Kennedy, K., & Gregoire, T.K. (2009). Theories of motivation in addiction treatment: Testing the relationship of the transtheoretical model of change and self-determination theory. *Journal of Social Work Practice in the Addictions, 9,* 163–183. doi:10.1080/15332560902852052

Kessler, R. (2004). The epidemiology of dual diagnosis. *Biological Psychiatry, 56,* 730–737. doi:10.1016/j.biopsych.2004.06.034

Libby, A., Orton, H., Stover, S., Riggs, P. (2005). What came first, major depression or substance use disorder? Clinical characteristics and substance use comparing teens in a treatment cohort. *Addictive Behaviors, 30,* 1649–1662. doi:10.1016/j.addbeh.2005.07.012

Lichtenstein, D. P., Spirito, A., & Zimmermann, R. P. (2010). Assessing and treating co-occurring disorders in adolescents: Examining typical practice of community- based mental health and substance use treatment providers, *Community Mental Health Journal, 46,* 252–257. doi:10.1007/s10597-009-9239-y

Medina, K., Hanson, K., Schweinsburg, A., Cohen- Zion, M., Nagel, B., & Tapert, S., (2007). Neuropsychological functioning in adolescent marijuana users: Subtle deficits detectable after a month of abstinence. *Journal of the International Neuropsychological Society, 13,* 807–820. doi:10.1017/S1355617707071032

Medina, K., McQueeny, T., Nagel, B., Hanson, K., Schweinsburg, A., & Tapert, S., (2008). Prefrontal cortex volumes in adolescents with alcohol use disorders: Unique gender effects. *Alcoholism: Clinical and Experimental Research, 3,* 386–394. doi:10.1111/j.1530-0277.2007.00602.x

Medina, K., Nagel, B., & Tapert, S., (2010). Abnormal cerebellar morphometry in abstinent adolescent marijuana users. *Psychiatry Research: Neuroimaging, 182,* 152–159. doi:10.1016/j.pscychresns.2009.12.004

Miller, W. R., & Rollnick, S. (2013). *Motivational interviewing: Helping people change* (3rd ed.). New York, NY: Guilford Press.

Miller, W. R., Zweben, A., DiClemente, C. C., & Rychtarik, R. G. (1992). Motivational enhancement therapy manual: A clinical research guide for therapists treating individuals with alcohol abuse and dependence. *NIAAA Project MATCH monograph series* (Vol. 2, pp. 1–120). Rockville, MD: National Institute on Alcohol Abuse and Alcoholism.

National Institute on Drug Abuse. (2003). Brief strategic family therapy for adolescent drug abuse. *Therapy Manuals for Drug Abuse, Manual 5.* Retrieved from https://archives.drugabuse.gov/pubs/index.html

National Institute on Drug Abuse (2014). Principles of adolescent substance use disorder treatment: A research-based guide. Retrieved from https://www.drugabuse.gov/publications/principles-adolescent-substance-use-disorder-treatment-research-based-guide/evidence-based-approaches-to-treating-adolescent-substance-use-disorders/behavioral-approaches

Peiper, N. C., Ridenour, T. A., Hochwalt, B., & Coyne-Beasley, T. (2016). Overview on prevalence and recent trends in adolescent substance use and abuse. *Child and Adolescent Psychiatric Clinics of North America, 25,* 349–365. doi:10.1016/j.chc.2016.03.005

Poudel, A., & Gautam, S. (2017). Age of onset of substance use and psychosocial problems among individuals with substance use disorders. *BMC Psychiatry, 17,* 1–7. doi:10.1186/s12888-016-1191-0

Prochaska, J. (1979). *Systems of psychotherapy: A transtheoretical analysis.* Homewood, IL: Dorsey.

Prochaska, J. O., & DiClemente, C., (1983). Stages and processes of self-change of smoking: Toward an integrative model of change. *Journal of Consulting and Clinical Psychology, 51,* 390–395.

Prochaska, J. O., & Norcross, J. C. (2014). Comparative conclusions: Toward a transtheoretical therapy. In J. O. Prochaska, & J. C. Norcross, (Eds.), *Systems of Psychotherapy: A Transtheoretical Analysis* (pp. 453–481). United States: Cengage Learning

Rollnick, S., & Miller, W.R. (1995). What is motivational interviewing? *Behavioral and Cognitive Psychotherapy, 23,* 325–334.

Rosner, R., (2013). *Clinical Handbook of Adolescent Addiction.* Hoboken, NJ: Wiley.

Siddiqui. S., Chatterjee, U., Kumar, D., Siddiqui A., & Goyal, N., (2008). Neuropsychology of prefrontal cortex. *Indian Journal of Psychiatry, 3,* 202–208. doi:10.4103/0019-5545.43634

Silveri, M., Dager, A., Cohen-Gilbert, J., & Sneider, J., (2016). Neurobiological signatures associated with alcohol and drug use in the human adolescent brain. *Neuroscience & Biobehavioral Reviews, 70,* 244–259. doi:10.1016/j.neubiorev.2016.06.042

Squeglia, L., Jacobus, J., & Tapert, S., (2009). The influence of substance use on adolescent brain development. *Clinical EEG and Neuroscience, 40*, 31–38. doi:10.1177/155005940904000110

Stone, A. L., Vander Stoep, A., & McCauley, E. (2016). Early onset substance use in adolescents with depressive, conduct, and comorbid symptoms. *Journal of Early Adolescence, 36,* 729–753. doi:10.1177/0272431615586463

Substance Abuse and Mental Health Services Administration. (2013). Results from the 2012 national survey on drug use and health: Summary of national findings. Retrieved from: https://www.samhsa.gov/data/sites/default/files/NSDUHresults2012/NSDUHresults2012.pdf

Substance Abuse and Mental Health Services Administration. (2015). Behavioral health trends in the United States: Results from the 2014 national survey on drug use and health. Retrieved from https://www.samhsa.gov/data/sites/default/files/NSDUH-FRR1-2014/NSDUH-FRR1-2014.pdf

Substance Abuse and Mental Health Services Administration. (2016). Co-occurring disorders. Retrieved from https://www.samhsa.gov/disorders/co-occurring

Substance Abuse and Mental Health Services Administration. (2017). Behavioral health treatments and services, treatment for co-occurring mental and substance use disorders. Retrieved from https://www.samhsa.gov/treatment#co-occurring

Substance Abuse and Mental Health Services Administration. (2017). Quick guide for clinicians: Tip 31, screening and assessing adolescents for substance use disorders. Tip 32, treatment of adolescents with substance use disorders. Retrieved from: http://store.samhsa.gov/shin/content//SMA01-3596/SMA01-3596.pdf

Tanner-Smith, E. E., Wilson, S. J., & Lipsey, M. W. (2013). The comparative effectiveness of outpatient treatment for adolescent substance abuse: A meta-analysis. *Journal of Substance Abuse Treatment, 44,* 145–158. doi:10.1016/j.sat.2012.05.006

Tapert, S., Granholm, E., Leedy, N., & Brown, S., (2002). Substance use and withdrawal: Neuropsychological functioning over 8 years in youth. *Journal of International Psychological Society, 8,* 873–883. doi:10.1017/S1355617702870011

Valdez, A., Cepeda, A., Parrish, D., Horowitz, R., & Kaplan, C. (2013). Adapted brief strategic family therapy for gang-affiliated Mexican American adolescents. *Research on Social Work Practice, 23,* 383–396. doi:10.1177/1049731513481389

Van Gastel, W. A., Tempelaar, W., Bun, C., Schubart, C. D., Kahn, R. S., Plevier, C., & Boks, M. P. M. (2013). Cannabis use as an indicator of risk for mental health problems in adolescents: A population-based study at secondary schools. *Psychological Medicine, 43,* 1849–1856. doi:10.1017/S0033291712002723

Wu, S. S., Schoenfelder, E., & Hsiao, R. C. J. (2016). Cognitive behavioral therapy and motivational enhancement therapy. *Child and Adolescent Psychiatric Clinics, 25,* 629–643.doi:10.1016/J.CHC.2016.06.002

Zullig, K. J., Divin, A. L., Weiler, R. M., Haddox, J. D., & Pealer, L.N. (2015). Adolescent nonmedical use of prescription pain relievers, stimulants, and depressants, and suicide risk. *Substance Use & Misuse, 50,* 1678–1689. doi:10.3109/10826084.2015.1027931

SECTION III
SPECIAL POPULATIONS AND APPROACHES

11

Working With LGBTQ Adolescents

Katherine V. Ovrom, Jerry Buie, and Joanna E. Bettmann

The process of realizing sexual orientation and solidifying gender identity is an important aspect of adolescence. A significant portion of the U.S. population experiences same-sex attraction, others find that their biological sex does not fit with their gender identity, and some wrestle with where they fall on the spectrums of sexual orientation and identity. For those adolescents who do not identify with their birth gender or whose sexuality does not conform to heteronormativity, confusion and fear can develop.

Clinicians working with adolescents need to be familiar with the challenges faced by lesbian, gay, bisexual, transgender, and queer (LGBTQ) individuals. This chapter will address LGBTQ youth's increased risk of victimization, physical violence, mental health disorders, homelessness, and suicide. These increased risks reflect, in part, societal prejudices and inequalities against LGBTQ populations. Before exploring LGBTQ youth and their particular needs, we will establish some working definitions of sexuality and gender identity.

Sexual Orientation, Sexual Behavior, and Gender Identity

The American Psychological Association defines sexual orientation as

> an enduring pattern of emotional, romantic, and/or sexual attractions to men, women, or both sexes. Sexual orientation also refers to a person's sense of identity based on those attractions, related behaviors, and membership in a community of others who share those attractions. (2008, p. 1)

Important parts of this definition include the enduring pattern of attraction and the sense of identity. Sexual behavior does not define sexual orientation.

For example, if an adolescent male discloses a sexual experience with another male to his therapist, that does not indicate that this client is gay. If the client discovers that he prefers relationships and sexual experiences only with men, he may eventually decide to identify as a gay male. However, one same-sex experience does not, in itself, correlate with any sexual orientation. While sexual behavior may inform sexual orientation, it does not define it.

Clinicians also should understand that the expressions of human gender identity and sexual orientation are diverse and fluid (Diamond, 2008, 2012, 2014). Lesbian, gay, and bisexual are the most common nonheterosexual orientations. However, sexual orientation is a complex component of human sexuality that often defies categorization. Several lesser-known sexual orientations have gained more attention in recent years; these include pansexual and asexual identities. Pansexual is a term used to describe an individual for whom gender does not matter in the context of sexual attraction. The key difference between bisexual and pansexual is that pansexual individuals may be attracted to those who identify as transgender or may be unconcerned about the biological sex and gender identity of their partner when it comes to sexual partnership. Asexual individuals do not experience sexual attraction and may experience pressure from society to engage in intimate relationships when they are not inclined to do so. These sexualities are less common than lesbian, gay, and bisexual orientations, but clinicians must be aware that many adolescent clients experience complex transitions as they become aware of their sexual orientation and identities.

Gender identity is a distinct form of identity. Gender identity has been defined as "a person's self-perception or self-acceptance of being male, female, both, or neither (androgynous)" (Campos, 2005, p. 107). An individual may identify as transgender when their biological sex does not match their psychological sense of gender identity (Mayo, 2014). Gender identity experts argue that the term "transgender" is limiting and propose using the term "transgender and gender nonconforming" or "gender non-binary" as umbrella terms to describe people for whom the labels "man" or "woman" are not accurate or sufficient for describing their gender identities (Chang, Singh, & Rossman, 2017). For example, individuals born with characteristics of both biological sexes, commonly referred to as intersex (Mayo, 2014), are often lumped into the category of transgender. There are also many sub-categories that fall under the term transgender, such as male to female and female to male, which add complexity and depth to this label. Labels such as transgender, bisexual, and so forth are social constructs that allow for the categorization of individuals who may or may not agree with the definitions of those social constructs. The DSM-5 uses the diagnosis "gender dysphoria" to refer to those who have "a marked incongruence between one's experienced/expressed gender and assigned gender" (American Psychiatric Association, p. 452). However, this diagnostic terminology is offensive to some in the transgendered community, who object to having gender dysphoria defined as pathological.

The intention here is not to define every possible gender identity and sexual orientation, as these can be fluid and vary across cultures and contexts. Instead, we emphasize that human sexuality and gender identification contain a spectrum of options. As clinicians, our work is to support adolescent clients in their identity development across a variety of domains, including sexual orientation and gender identity.

Prevalence

The prevalence of LGBT adolescents is unclear because most surveys that include sexual orientation focus on adults. In one survey of more than 120,000 U.S. young adults aged 18–29, 3.4% identified as lesbian, gay, bisexual, or transgender, while 4.4% were unidentified or refused to answer (Gates & Newport, 2012). A Gallup survey found that 4% of U.S. adults identified as lesbian, gay, bisexual, or transgender, while 5.6% of adults 18–44 self-identified in one of the LGBT categories (Gates, 2014). Notably, there are contextual pressures that call into question the accuracy of these data. Many individuals who identify as nonheterosexual may decline to answer or may falsely identify as heterosexual due to ongoing cultural stigma (Gates & Newport, 2012). Therefore, we should consider the percentages cited above as the minimum percentages of U.S. adolescents and adults who openly identify as LGBTQ.

LGBTQ Adolescent Development

Adolescents who have LGBTQ experiences, identify as LGBTQ, or question their sexual identities undergo the same physical and psychosocial developmental processes as their heterosexual, gender-conforming peers. The formation of a sexual identity and the confirmation or questioning of gender identity is a normal part of adolescent development. Sexual identity development is described as the recognition that one is a sexual being, the process of engaging in sexual behaviors, the formation of attitudes and beliefs around sexuality, and working through the socioemotional challenges of sexual behavior (Graber & Archibald, 2001). For LGBTQ adolescents, the experience of developing and defining their sexual orientation and/or gender identity is distinct from that of their heterosexual peers (Graber & Archibald, 2001).

Researchers have proposed a series of developmental milestones unique to LGBTQ individuals as they form their sexual and gender identity (Campos, 2005; D'Augelli & Patterson, 2001). Many of these milestones are shaped by the societal forces of stigma and homophobia that play an active role in U.S. culture (Baunach, 2012; Campos, 2005). For adolescents who grow up in an accepting familial and cultural environment, some of these stigmas may not apply. For those who grow up in circumstances where there is significant stigma toward the LGBTQ community, they may never reach or consider the later steps of embracing their LGBTQ identity. However, this model serves as a useful illustration of one LGBTQ developmental trajectory.

The first step proposed by this model is awareness of stigma (Campos, 2005). In this stage, a young person, who likely is not yet aware of their sexual orientation, receives messages from external sources such as peers, adults, cultural institutions, and the media, that anything other than a gender in line with biological sex and heterosexuality are in some way wrong, or less than (Campos, 2005). For example, a child may hear a religious figure say that gay people will go to hell or overhear a friend call another person "gay" as an insult. These early moments effectively transmit the cultural stigma around homosexuality and alternative gender identities.

The next step described in literature is an individual's realization that he/she/they are somehow different (Campos, 2005). Many LGBTQ adults describe early awareness that they were different from the majority of their peers. At the time of this realization, most were still not aware of their sexual identity or orientation, but nonetheless felt a sense of difference, and in some cases, separateness from their social, familial, or cultural groups. Some children may express their sense of difference to those around them. But many children keep that to themselves and only divulge that experience after they have come out publicly as LGBTQ.

Next, the child or adolescent is able to connect their gender or sexuality to this sense of difference (Campos, 2005). Where before they were unable to identify why they felt different, they later become aware of feelings of sexual attraction toward the same-sex, or a gender identity that does not match their biological sex, and connect those feelings to the sense of difference.

At this point, many adolescents experience denial or resistance toward their sexual orientation or gender identity (Campos, 2005). Here external forces including those of culture, religion, and family play a significant role in whether adolescents feel the need to deny or resist their sexual identity. Those who have internalized significant stigma toward LGBTQ identities may try to distance themselves from feelings of same-sex attraction or non-normative gender identity. Youth who belong to a religion that believes heterosexuality is the only acceptable sexual orientation may face extreme internal conflict, as the belief system in which they were raised rejects a part of who they are. Adolescents who do experience this denial or resistance may avoid their sexual feelings or identity by engaging in heterosexual dating or channeling their energy into academics or athletics. This period of resistance does not happen for all LGBTQ adolescents, but does for many. As clinicians, we can work with adolescent clients to identify strategies they use to deny or resist their own identities. However, clinicians must be vigilant to ensure that adolescent clients are able choose to own their identification, rather than insisting such adolescents are in denial if they have engaged in homosexual behaviors.

The final two proposed milestones are realization of sexual orientation, followed by acceptance of sexual orientation (Campos, 2005). The exact time when an adolescent is able to identify with a specific sexual orientation varies. However, most land on their specific sexual identity by late adolescence (Campos, 2005). Individuals who move past denial and into acceptance may choose to disclose their sexual identity by coming out or engaging in a relationship with a partner of choice. The research that underlies this trajectory of sexual identity development is based on interviews of a large number of LGBTQ adults (Campos, 2005; D'Augelli & Patterson, 2001). Thus, as mainstream U.S. society becomes more accepting of LGBTQ populations, this process may change.

Limitations of Developmental Models

Several critiques have been levied against the concept of developmental models for sexual orientation and gender identity exploration. One common critique is that these milestones either do not occur, occur in a different order, or move back and forth between stages over the course of years (Bosse & Chiodo, 2016; Diamond, 2000). Further, some scholars call into question whether such models are not more representative of a male, rather than female, experience (Diamond, 2000). These scholars state that many women's experiences contradict the developmental narrative of sexual orientation as an early-appearing trait, noting that female cases are often ignored or considered exceptional since they go against the norm (Diamond & Savin-Williams, 2000). In fact, research has found that many women experience a greater degree of fluidity in the process of sexual orientation development than a linear stage model captures (Diamond, 2000, 2008, 2012). Sexual fluidity, meaning situational flexibility or change in sexuality over time and social context, is a common experience for many adolescents and adults (Diamond 2008, 2012, 2014).

Finally, linear models such as the one presented above make cultural assumptions that may not take into account the varying cultural and spiritual factors that influence the development of LGBT adolescents from minority racial or ethnic groups (Sánchez, 2015). Thus, while the above model can serve as a rough blueprint that describes common experiences for some LGBTQ youth, each individual should be assessed in the context of their culture, family, spirituality, and other domains that interact with the heterosexual white dominant culture of the United States.

Coming Out

The process of coming out for those adolescents who do so, and the responses of families, societies, and institutions to them, has significant impact upon adolescents' sense of identity, well-being, and mental health. While coming out is most often used to describe an individual verbally sharing their LGBTQ identity, that verbal sharing is only one aspect of this process. The American Psychological Association defines coming out as: "self-awareness of same-sex attractions; the telling of one or a few people about these attractions; and identification with the lesbian, gay, and bisexual community" (2008, p. 3). Another working definition of coming out begins with the recognition of an LGBTQ identity and the eventual disclosure of this identity with other people, communities, or the public at large (Biegel, 2010). How and to what degree an individual chooses to come out varies. Some adolescents come out to friends or peers and not to their families. Others share their identities with one parent and not the other for fear of rejection. Still others share their identities freely at school and in the community. For some, being out can create a statement of social advocacy. By publicly sharing their LGBTQ identity, adolescents can serve as a model for other peers and can combat societal prejudice by placing a human face to a stigmatized label.

Being out, meaning that an individual shares and integrates their LGBTQ identity into their daily life, links to increased psychosocial well-being in adulthood (Russell, Toomey, Ryan, & Diaz, 2014). Even after accounting for the increased risk of victimization at school, adolescents who came out in high school or earlier showed better psychosocial adjustment in young adulthood (Russell et al., 2014). The American Psychological Association (2008) confirms that those individuals who come out generally feel better able to integrate that aspect of their identity, which leads to greater well-being. Coming out may also lead to increased social support from friends and family once they are aware of an individual's LGBTQ identity (American Psychological Association, 2008). Unfortunately for many, coming out does not lead to increased social support, but puts them at greater risk for bullying, discrimination, and physical violence.

The Consequences of Stigma

Victimization

Adolescents who identify or are perceived as LGBTQ are at a higher risk for many negative experiences. One tragically common experience for LGBTQ adolescents is victimization or bullying (Greene, Britton, & Fitts, 2014; Marx & Kettrey, 2016). Nearly 9 out of 10 ten LGBT students reported experiencing harassment at school in the last year in a 2009 national school survey, and, of those, a third felt so unsafe at school that they reported having missed school for at least a day in the last month for fear of harassment (Kosciw, Greytak, Diaz, & Barkiewicz, 2010). Common types of bullying include verbal insults and physical harassment such as pushing or even assault (Huebner, Thoma, & Neilands, 2015).

The Human Rights Campaign (2016) conducted a large scale survey of over 10,000 adolescents from a wide variety of communities in the United States, which explored their experiences at home, in school, and in their communities. Their survey found that over half of LGBTQ students had experienced verbal harassment at school. LGBTQ youth in their study were twice as likely as their heterosexual counterparts to experience verbal harassment, physical assault, and exclusion from peer groups in school (Human Rights Campaign, 2016). Further, when asked to identify the most important problem facing them at the time of the survey, school/bullying problems came in second only to nonaccepting families (Human Rights Campaign, 2016).

Mental Health and Substance Abuse

The prevalence and frequency of sexual or gender-based victimization and bullying has severe consequences. Internalizing dynamics, such as depressive and anxious feelings, are more prevalent in LGBTQ youth, especially those who have experienced bullying, than in their heterosexual peers (Marx & Kettrey, 2016; McConnell, Birkett, & Mustanski, 2016; Russell, Ryan, Toomey, Diaz, & Sanchez, 2011). LGBTQ adolescents are 3 to 4 times more likely to meet criteria for an internalizing disorder, such as depression or anxiety, than heterosexual youth (Goldbach & Gibbs, 2015). Further, increasing levels of victimization during adolescence lead to increased risk for both depression and post-traumatic stress disorder (Mustanski, Andrews, & Puckett, 2016). Another study found victimization was correlated with not only increased mental health issues, but also shame-based coping strategies including self-attack via internalized homophobia, self-blame for bullying and other negative events, and withdrawal (Greene, Britton, & Fitts, 2014).

Some research links sexual or gender-based victimization and substance use in adolescents (Huebner et al., 2015). In one study, those who identified as LGBTQ were twice as likely to have tried alcohol or drugs as their heterosexual peers (Human Rights Campaign, 2016). The increased levels of substance abuse in this population may link to perceived stigmatization, familial rejection, and/or homelessness (McConnell, Birkett, & Mutanski, 2016; Ray, 2006).

Homelessness

LGBTQ youth disproportionately experience homelessness in comparison with their heterosexual peers. LGBTQ youth comprise between 20 and 40% of all homeless youth (Ferguson & Maccio, 2015; Ray, 2006). There are multiple reasons why an LGBTQ adolescent may experience homelessness; by far, the most common is a negative response from their family toward their sexual identity or gender expression (Ferguson & Maccio, 2015). Negative responses may include parental rejection, verbal and psychological abuse, physical abuse, and/or being forced to leave the family home (Fergunson & Maccio, 2015). LGBTQ youth are at a higher risk for mental disorders, substance abuse, and suicidality than their heterosexual peers. But homelessness compounds these risk factors: homeless LGBTQ youth have even higher rates of mental disorders and substance use problems (Keuroghlian, Shtasel, & Bassuk, 2014). Homeless LGBTQ adolescents are also more likely to experience violent physical and sexual assault; their risk for experiencing sexual assault is nearly double that for heterosexual homeless youth (Keuroghlian et al., 2014; National Coalition for the Homeless, 2009). Recent research stresses the importance of recognizing the increased risks to LGBTQ youth brought by stigma, victimization, familial rejection, and internalized oppression (Ferguson & Maccio, 2015; Keuroghlian et al., 2014). Suicide attempts are more common among homeless youth. Between 20 and 40% of homeless youth have attempted suicide in their lifetime (Moskowitz, Stein, & Lightfoot, 2013).

LGBTQ Youth Suicide

Rates of suicidal ideation and suicide attempts are alarmingly high among the LGBTQ youth population as a whole (American Medical Association, 2016). In 2016, the American Medical Association reported that suicide was the leading cause of death for LGBTQ youth in the United States. In one study, 43% of LGB-identified high school students reported suicidal ideation in the past year compared to 15% of heterosexual students. Of those 43%, 29% made an actual suicide attempt, almost 5 times as many as their heterosexual peers (CDC, 2015). Notably, transgender youth were not identified in this survey, leading to a lack of information regarding the risks they face.

Some research identifies victimization or bullying as the second strongest predictor of both self-harm and suicidal ideation after a previous suicide attempt (Liu & Mutanski, 2012). In fact, victimization on the basis of sexual orientation or gender identity corresponded to a 250% increased risk of self-harm (Liu & Mutanski, 2012). Other factors associated with psychosocial risks including suicidal ideation are the negative responses of other people to nonconforming gender behavior, high-risk sexual behaviors, conflicts with family in relation to coming out or sexual identity, and mistreatment in the community and at school (Marshal et al., 2011). Further, the sense of isolation or lack of social support that many LGBTQ youth experience from family or peers due to stigma may also contribute to a heightened risk for suicidality (Mutanski & Liu, 2013). Importantly, homophobic victimization, meaning victimization based on an individual's sexual orientation, is more strongly linked to depression and suicidal ideation than nonhomophobic victimization (Patrick et al., 2013). Although LGBTQ youth are currently at an elevated risk for depression and suicidality because of the stigma surrounding their sexual identity, protective factors, including the support of family, can mitigate these risks.

Sources of Resiliency

A strong body of evidence supports the fact that increased mental health and psychosocial risks faced by LGBTQ youth are not a result of intrinsic characteristics, but rather high levels of adversity generated by cultural stigma and homophobia (Herrick, Egan, Coulter, Friedman, & Stall, 2014). Despite the increased risks for this population, the majority of LGBTQ youth do not experience negative health or mental health outcomes; instead, they exhibit remarkable resiliency in the face of adversity (Herrick et al., 2014). Recent literature identifies several sources of resiliency that include both personal characteristics and social factors (Herrick et al., 2014).

One personal source of resiliency is the ability to accept and integrate one's sexual or gender identity. Research investigating LGBTQ youth development found that acceptance of sexual or gender identity empowers individuals to better recognize stigma and in so doing, to avoid internalized shame or guilt that can contribute to the development of mental disorders or substance use disorders (Herrick et al., 2014). Coming out and embracing one's identity allows LGBTQ youth to access a community of other sexual minority youth within which they can share experiences, cultural events, identity, and mentors who support their development and well-being (Herrick et al., 2014). Integration into sexual minority communities links to increased resilience among LGBTQ youth (Herrick et al., 2014). Peers and family are another important source of support that may buffer the impact of societal stigma and prejudice.

Peers

Many LGBTQ adolescents come out to close friends even before they share their sexual orientation with family (Potoczniak, Crosbie-Burnett, & Saltzburg, 2009). Some schools have utilized the power of peer support to improve the experience and safety of LGBTQ adolescents. One model of school-based peer support, Gay-Straight Alliances, can have a particularly powerful effect. A recent meta-analysis exploring Gay-Straight Alliances established a strong association between the presence of Gay-Straight Alliances in schools and significant reduction in LGBTQ-directed bullying and victimization (Marx & Kettrey, 2016). Gay-Straight Alliances also have the freedom to provide a wide range of support and opportunities for advocacy to LGBTQ youth and their heterosexual allies. For example, some Alliances offer individual peer counseling while others develop school or community based projects designed to raise awareness and acceptance of LGBTQ youth (Marx & Kettrey, 2016).

Family

Families who support and accept their LGBTQ children can bolster resilience and protect those children from some of the effects of victimization and its associated risks for mental disorders and substance abuse issues (McConnell et al., 2016; Ryan, Russell, Huebner, Diaz, & Sanchez, 2010). Family support and acceptance is also associated with reduced risk for lifetime suicide attempts in LGBTQ youth (Mutanski & Liu, 2013). Family support of sexuality reduces distress in LGBTQ adolescents, and family acceptance is associated with higher self-esteem, as well as physical and mental health (McConnell et al., 2016). In fact, family support in adolescence is so powerful that the positive outcomes of higher self-esteem, social support, and general health persist into adulthood (Ryan et al., 2010).

One area in which the family can be critical is in their response to coming out disclosures. Many adolescents who are considering coming out fear that, by disclosing their sexual identities, they risk changing, weakening, or losing their relationships with family members (Potoczniak et al., 2009). Notably, LGBTQ youth with lower levels of familial support report significantly more feelings of loneliness, depression, psychosomatic distress, and suicidality (McConnell et al., 2016). In some cases, familial rejection can be so severe as to lead to homelessness. From a resiliency perspective, personal acceptance of identity, as well as support from family, peers, and community can buffer the impact of societal stigma and homophobia on LGBTQ adolescents.

Implications for Treatment

The relationship between the many factors that shape the experience of an LGBTQ adolescent is nuanced and interdependent. Lack of familial support can lead to mental disorders and homelessness, while homelessness itself can lead to more mental health problems, substance use disorders, or suicide. Clinicians need to recognize the risks faced by LGBTQ youth that can exacerbate mental health conditions and suicidality (Marshal et al., 2011). When working with LGBTQ youth, clinicians can offer supportive individual counseling but should be aware that family therapy and peer support may be critical components of treatment. Interventions that engender the adolescent's family support may be more effective than individual therapy alone (Mutanski & Liu, 2013). Further, linking LGBTQ youth to peer-based support such as school-based Gay-Straight Alliances may reduce the likelihood of adolescent victimization at school and strengthen peer support.

Case Study

The case study presented below highlights many of the complexities of working with an adolescent exploring gender identity. The case study also highlights the significant impact of familial responses on adolescent behavior and wellbeing.

Stephanie (a pseudonym) was a 14-year-old biological female with a male appearance. The second author's work with her began when Stephanie's mother called to say that her daughter wanted to begin hormone therapy to become male. Her mother reported, "this fascination with becoming male has been ongoing for over a year and we have no idea what to do." Stephanie's mother expressed concern that Stephanie was exhibiting depression and suicidal feelings. This concern prompted her to bring Stephanie into therapy to determine a course of action. On the phone, the mother did not rule out medical treatment but wanted to be sure that Stephanie was not going through a "phase." The mother indicated that Stephanie preferred male pronouns and the name Stephen. Through the rest of this case scenario, Stephanie will be referred to with male pronouns and by the name Stephen.

As part of the initial assessment on the phone, Stephen's mother reported that Stephen was often depressed, had withdrawn from the family, was not talking about his feelings, and seemed to be isolating himself at school. He was spending a great deal of time on the internet and became hostile when his parents initiated communication. Stephen's mother expressed fear of the social consequences of her child transitioning in a religiously and politically conservative community. She worried that the transition would be dramatic and could invite potential acts of violence. She stated, "there is no way in hell I'm going to use my insurance to change my little girl into a boy."

When the second author met Stephen, he had a slight build, wore jeans and a typically masculine shirt, and his hair was cut and styled in a short, fashionable manner (self-styled and cut to look more masculine). Stephen shared that he had always felt trapped in the wrong body and rejected the social constructs around the idea of himself as female. He detested his breasts and bound them to minimize their appearance. He referred to them as birth defects. He discussed what he knew about breast removal and hormone treatment, indicating that he had already done considerable research online on this topic. He reported that he had recently come out to his parents because, prior to his online research, he had little idea of how to articulate his identity. He reported (and his parents later confirmed) that he never identified as a female, with a strong preference for typically masculine modes of dressing and hobbies. He showed no interest in relating to his body in terms of feminine issues or needs. He was unsure and confused about his sexual orientation. To date, he had only discussed his gender dysphoria with a few close friends and his parents. He felt his friends supported him, but his parents were struggling since they still referred to him as Stephanie and used feminine pronouns. He had a male avatar online that allowed him to play out a male character and build online relationships as a male.

During Stephen's initial psychotherapy appointment, he attributed part of his depression and withdrawal from the family to his perception that his parents could not or would not understand him or allow him to participate in hormone treatment. He felt frustrated with their use of his female name and female pronouns in referring to him. He felt stuck in his female body and unable to express his identity in a way that felt comfortable and fulfilling for him. Stephen spent several sessions talking about his gender identity and sorting through confusion between gender expression and sexual orientation. Eventually, with some encouragement from the second author, he expressed the desire to have more dialogue and discussion with his parents. The second author explained to Stephen that his parents' confusion could be a result of his unwillingness to openly discuss issues. Up until this point, his parents had avoided participating in therapy, but would bring him to his individual sessions and be cordial in the waiting room. The second author sensed that there was a family dynamic of avoiding difficult discussions which made this issue hard for them to explore. Stephen and the second author agreed it was time to bring his parents into the process to discuss his gender identity openly.

With Stephen's consent, the second author spoke with his parents alone so they could have space to express their feelings openly concerning Stephen's gender identity. The second author encouraged them to process their concerns and feelings about Stephen's behaviors and experiences. The second author referred to Stephanie as Stephen (modeling the correct way to address Stephen) and used male pronouns. The parents stated the name change and pronouns were difficult for them. The second author provided some psychoeducation to help them understand gender dysphoria and issues related to being transgender.

In this session, Stephen's mother reported her significant grief and her sense that she lost a daughter. She expressed, "she will always be my daughter no matter what she does to her body." She stated, "nothing will happen until she's 18 and can make her own decisions." She also expressed considerable concern about "what will the neighbors think, this is a conservative community, I don't want her to be bullied." However, while she expressed difficulty accepting Stephen, she also said that she understood that her support was critical for his well-being. Stephen's father was more open to Stephen's wishes and said that he wanted what was best for his child. He stated that he was beginning to appreciate that he would gain a son through this process. The second author noticed that as Stephen's father began to show more signs of acceptance, this seemed to give Stephen's mother permission to explore alternative ways of thinking about Stephen's identity. The second author met with the parents several more times to let them explore, grieve, and adapt to Stephen's transition. During this time, Stephen was eager to move forward, becoming frustrated that his parents were still not responding to his requests to begin hormone therapy.

After several sessions with Stephen's parents, Stephen's older sister came home from college for a visit. She participated in a psychotherapy session with Stephen. During that session, they discussed how to approach his parents. Stephen's sister encouraged him to give their parents time to better understand his transition. Her words seemed to help him understand why waiting for his parents to support him might be beneficial. Eventually, the second author held a family session with both parents, sister, and Stephen. By this time, Stephen had been in therapy for over a year and was becoming more despondent and depressed. His parents still would not allow him to begin hormone therapy. While his parents were showing signs of acceptance including the use of male pronouns, they still expressed significant fear around medical treatment to transition and insisted Stephen would have to wait until he graduated high school.

Unable to move forward with his transition, Stephen began to discuss his feelings of suicidality. His parents expressed concern for his mental health. The second author communicated his professional opinion to the parents that, because Stephen could not access medical treatment to bring his biological sex into congruency with his gender identity, his gender dysphoria was contributing significantly to his depression and suicidality. As a family intervention, the second author invited Stephen and his parents to attend a conference on transgender issues held by local LGBTQ community leaders. The family agreed to attend, marking a turning point for Stephen and his family.

At the conference, Stephen met other transgender youth and learned about community resources for transgender youth. Prior attempts by the second author to link Stephen's parents to parent support groups or link Stephen to support groups had been met with little interest. But at the conference, Stephen's parents listened to other parents in similar circumstances and heard how their children were coping pre- and post-medical treatment. Stephen's parents also met with medical professionals who worked with individuals in transition and heard from youth who utilized those services.

After the conference, Stephen's parents began to talk about permitting him to begin hormone therapy with a doctor who specialized in transgender care. Stephen's mother moved from tolerating Stephen's gender identity to advocating for her son. With permission from both parents, Stephen began hormone therapy. Within months of starting that treatment, Stephen showed improved mental health. He began to engage with his family and school more proactively. Stephen's entire family experienced growth in parallel to Stephen's transition. His mother began volunteering at the local LGBTQ community center. Stephen's friends at school adapted easily to his new identity. Stephen reported he felt finally integrated into his school, family, and community. During an individual psychotherapy session after he began hormone therapy, Stephen described a feeling of physiological change, explaining that he finally felt more at home in his body.

Case Analysis

The case above illustrates some of the difficult dynamics inherent in transgender adolescent transition. Stephen's gender dysphoria made him vulnerable to isolative behaviors, depression, and suicidality. While he had the support of some peers, he felt rejected by his family, not supported for who he recognized himself to be. Stephen's treatment began as individual psychotherapy, but evolved to include family therapy and community resource referrals. These adjunctive interventions enabled the clinician to assist Stephen's family in learning more about gender dysphoria and transgender identity, a process which led to their full support of his transition. Clinicians working with LGBTQ adolescents should consider such adjunctive interventions critical to good care.

Stephen's case also highlights an important legal reality which faces LGBTQ adolescents. In the United States, adolescents do not have the legal right to make their own medical decisions. Historically, state and federal statutes have asserted that "all persons are equally possessed of fundamental individual rights and theoretically enjoy equal access to established remedies for the enforcement of those rights. Nonetheless, not all classes of individuals enjoy the same rights or, concomitantly, the same remedies" (Moore, 1994, p. 261). Citizens under 18 cannot vote, drink alcohol, or consent to certain types of medical treatment. For example, the law holds that "minors do not have the capacity to wisely exercise the franchise" (Moore, p. 261). In these cases, "the law presumes that the interests of children will be protected by the adult members of the community who hold the franchise," typically their parents or guardians (Moore, p. 261). But what about the case of LGBTQ adolescents whose parents wish to deny them medical treatment for gender dysphoria or LGBTQ adolescents whose parents who would like to engage them in conversion therapy in an attempt to change their sexual orientation?

In 1971, U.S. Supreme Court Chief Justice Warren Burger wrote, " 'The law's concept of the family rests on a presumption that parents possess what a child lacks in maturity, experience, and capacity for judgment required in making life's difficult decisions. . . . Most children, even in adolescence, simply are not able to make sound judgments concerning many decisions, including their need for medical care or treatment'" (Burger as cited in Levine, 2000, p. 205). But the case of Stephen highlights an important component of LGBTQ treatment: the dilemma that presents itself to the clinician when the parents want something different than the adolescent client wants. What if the clinician had advocated for the parents' perspective to Stephen, encouraging him to live as a woman and avoid the bullying and scrutiny his mother worried about? Might his suicidality increased, his depression exacerbated, his mental health worsened? We will never know.

However, Stephen's mental distress seems so clearly linked to his gender dysphoria, to his sense that he was living life in the wrong body and with the wrong gender identity. When the clinician supported Stephen, advocated for him, and helped his family to learn more about transgendered transition and identity, Stephen's mental health improved dramatically. While LGBTQ adolescents face many risk factors and stressors—suicidality, homelessness, bullying, stigmatization—they can thrive when their resiliency is supported, their families stand behind them, and their social networks are strong. The case of Stephen shows us a conflicted adolescent with gender dysphoria who, with the support and interventions of his clinician, thrived.

References

American Medical Association (2016). *LGBT youth suicide prevention resources.* Retrieved from: http://www.ama-assn.org/ama/pub/about-ama/our-people/member-groups-sections/glbt-advisory-committee/glbt-resources/lgbt-youth-suicide-prevention.page

American Psychiatric Association. (2013). *Diagnostic and Statistical Manual of Mental Disorders* (5th ed,). Washington, DC: Author.

American Psychological Association. (2008). *Answers to your questions: For a better understanding of sexual orientation and homosexuality.* Washington, DC: Author. Retrieved from www.apa.org/topics/sorientation.pdf.

Baunach, D. M. (2012). Changing same-sex marriage attitudes in America from 1988 through 2010. *Public Opinion Quarterly, 76,* 364–378. doi:10.1093/poq/nfs022

Biegel, S. (2010). *The right to be out.* Minneapolis, MN: University of Minnesota Press.

Bosse, J. D., & Chiodo, L. (2016). It is complicated: Gender and sexual orientation identity in LGBTQ youth. *Journal of Clinical Nursing, 25,* 3665–3675. doi:10.1111/jocn.13419

Campos, D. (2005). *Understanding gay and lesbian youth: Lessons for straight school teachers, counselors, and administrators.* Lanham, MD: Rowman & Littlefield Education.

Centers for Disease Control and Prevention. (2016). *Health risks among sexual minority youth.* Retrieved from http://www.cdc.gov/healthyyouth/disparities/smy.htm

Chang, S. C., Singh, A. A., & Rossman, K. (2017). Gender and sexual orientation diversity within the TGNC community. In A. A. Singh, & L.M. Dickey (Eds.), *Affirmative counseling and psychological practice with transgender and gender nonconforming clients* (pp. 19–40). Washington DC: American Psychological Association.

D'Augelli, A. R. & Patterson, C.J . (2001). *Lesbian, gay, and bisexual identities and youth: Psychological perspectives*. New York, NY: Oxford University Press.

Diamond, L. M. (2000). Sexual identity, attraction, and behavior among young sexual minority women over a 2-year period. *Developmental Psychology, 36,* 241–250.

Diamond, L. M. (2008). Female bisexuality from adolescence to adulthood: Results from a 10-year longitudinal study. *Developmental Psychology, 44,* 5–14. http://dx.doi.org/10.1037/0012-1649.44.1.5

Diamond, L. M. (2012). The desire disorder in research on sexual orientation in women: Contributions of dynamical systems theory. *Archives of Sexual Behavior, 41,* 73–83. http://dx.doi.org/10.1007/s10508-012-9909-7

Diamond, L. M. (2014, February). *"I was wrong! Men are pretty darn sexually fluid too."* Presentation at the meeting of Sexuality Preconference of the Society for Personality and Social Psychology, Austin, TX.

Diamond, L. M., & Savin-Williams (2000). Explaining diversity in the development of same-sex sexuality among young women. *Journal of Social Issues, 56,* 297–313.

Ferguson, K. M., & Maccio, E. M. (2015). Promising programs for lesbian, gay, bisexual, transgender, and queer/questioning runaway and homeless youth. *Journal of Social Service Research, 41,* 659–683. doi:10.1080/01488376.2015.1058879

Gates, G. J. (2014). *LGBT demographics: Comparisons among population-based surveys.* Los Angeles, CA: The Williams Institute, UCLA School of Law.

Gates, G. J. & Newport, F. (2012). *Special report: 3.4% of U.S. adults identify as LGBT.* Inaugural Gallup findings based on more than 120,000 interviews. Retrieved from http://www.gallup.com/poll/158066/special-report-adults-identify-lgbt.aspx

Goldbach, J. T., & Gibbs, J. (2015). Strategies employed by sexual minority adolescents to cope with minority stress. *Psychology of Sexual Orientation and Gender Diversity, 2,* 297–306. doi:http://dx.doi.org/10.1037/sgd0000124

Graber, J. A., & Archibald, A. B. (2001). Psychosocial change at puberty and beyond: Understanding adolescent sexuality and sexual orientation. In A. R. D'Augelli & C. J. Patterson (Eds.), *Lesbian, gay, and bisexual identities and youth: Psychological perspectives* (pp. 3–26). New York, NY, US: Oxford University Press.

Greene, D. C., Britton, P. J., & Fitts, B. (2014). Long-term outcomes of lesbian, gay, bisexual, and transgender recalled school victimization. *Journal of Counseling & Development, 92,* 406–417. doi:10.1002/j.1556-6676.2014.00167.x

Herrick, A. L., Egan, J. E., Coulter, R. W. S., Friedman, M. R., & Stall, R. (2014). Raising sexual minority youths' health levels by incorporating resiliencies into health promotion efforts. *American Journal of Public Health, 104,* 206–210. doi:10.2105/AJPH.2013.301546

Huebner, D. M., Thoma, B. C. & Neilands, T. B. (2015). School victimization and substance use among lesbian, gay, bisexual, and transgender adolescents. *Society for Prevention Science, 16,* 734–743. doi:10.1007/s11121-014-0507-x

Human Rights Campaign. (2016). *Growing up LGBT in America: HRC youth survey report key findings.* Retrieved from: www.hrc.org/youth-report

Keuroghlian, A. S., Shtasel, D., & Bassuk, E. L. (2014). Out on the street: A public health and policy agenda for lesbian, gay, bisexual, and transgender youth who are homeless. *American Journal of Orthpsychiatry, 84*, 66–72. doi:10.1037/h0098852

Kosciw, J. G., Greytak, E. A., Diaz, E. M., & Bartkiewicz, M. J. (2010). The 2009 national school climate survey: The experiences of lesbian, gay, bisexual and transgender youth in our nation's schools. Retrieved from: http://glsen.org.nscs

Levine, S. (2000). Informed consent of minors in crucial and critical health care decisions. In A. H. Esman (Ed.), *Adolescent Psychiatry: Developmental and Clinical Studies, Volume 25, Annals of the American Society for Adolescent Psychiatry* (pp. 203–217). Hillsdale, NJ: Analytic Press.

Liu, R. T., & Mustanski, B. (2012). Suicidal ideation and self-harm in lesbian, gay, bisexual, and transgender youth. *American Journal of Preventive Medicine, 42*, 221–228.

Marshal, M. P., Dietz, L. J., Friedman, M. S., Stall, R., Smith, H. A., McGinley, J., . . . Brent, D. A. (2011). Suicidality and depression disparities between sexual minority and heterosexual youth: A meta-analytic review. *Journal of Adolescent Health, 49*, 115–123. doi:10.1016/j.jadohealth.2011.02.005

Marx, R. A., & Kettrey, H. H. (2016). Gay-straight alliances are associated with lower levels of school-based victimization of LGBTQ+ youth: A systematic review and meta-analysis. *Journal of Youth & Adolescence, 45*, 1269–1282. doi:10.1007/s10964-016-0501-7

Mayo, C. (2014). *LGBTQ youth and education: Policies and practices.* New York, NY: Teachers College Press.

McConnell, E. A., Birkett, M., & Mustanski, B. (2016). Families matter: Social support and mental health trajectories among lesbian, gay, bisexual, and transgender youth. *Journal of Adolescent Health, xxx*, 1–7. doi:http://dx.doi.org/10.1016/j.jadohealth.2016.07.026

Moore, D. J. (1994). Legal issues in adolescent inpatient psychiatry. In H. S. Ghuman & R. M. Sarles (Eds.), *Handbook of adolescent inpatient psychiatric treatment* (pp. 261–276). Philadelphia, PA: Brunner/Mazel.

Moskowitz, A., Stein, J. A., & Lightfoot, M. (2013). The mediating roles of stress and maladaptive behavior on self-harm and suicide attempts among runaway and homeless youth. *Journal of Youth and Adolescence, 42*, 1015–1027. doi:10.1007/s10964-012-9793-4

Mutanski, B. & Liu, R. T. (2013). Longitudinal study of predictors of suicide attempts among lesbian, gay, bisexual, and transgender youth. *Archives of Sexual Behavior, 42*, 437–448. doi:10.1007/s10508-012-0013-9

Mustanski, B., Andrews, R., & Puckett, J. A. (2016). The effects of cumulative victimization on mental health among lesbian, gay, bisexual, and transgender adolescents and young adults. *American Journal of Public Health, 106*, 527–533. doi:10.2105/AJPH.2015.302976

National Coalition for the Homeless. (2009). *LGBTQ Homelessness.* Retrieved from: http://www.nationalhomeless.com

Patrick, D. L., Bell, J. F., Huang, J. Y., Lazarakis, N. C., & Edwards, T. C. (2013). Bullying and quality of life in youths perceived as gay, lesbian, or bisexual in Washington State, 2010 [Abstract]. *American Journal of Public Health, 103*, 1255–1261. doi:10.2105/AJPH.2012.301101

Potoczniak, D., Crosbie-Burnett, M., & Saltzburg, N. (2009). Experiences regarding coming out to parents among African American, Hispanic, and White gay, lesbian, bisexual, transgender, and questioning adolescents. *Journal of Gay & Lesbian Social Services, 21,* 189–205.

Ray, N. (2006). An epidemic of homelessness. *National, Gay and Lesbian Task Force Policy Institute, National Coalition for the Homeless.*

Russell, S. T., Ryan, C., Toomey, R. B., Diaz, R. M., & Sanchez, J. (2011). Lesbian, gay, bisexual, and transgender adolescent school victimization: Implications for young adult health and adjustment. *Journal of School Health, 81,* 223–230.

Russell, S. T., Toomey, R. B., Ryan, C., & Diaz, R. M. (2014). Being out at school: The implications for school victimization and young adult adjustment. *American Journal of Orthopsychiatry, 84,* 635–643. http://dx.doi.org/10.1037/ort0000037

Ryan, C., Russell, S. T., Huebner, D., Diaz, R., & Sanchez, J. (2010). Family acceptance in adolescence and the health of LGBT young adults. *Journal of Child and Adolescent Psychiatric Nursing, 23,* 205–213. doi:10.1111/j.1744-6171.2010.00246.x

Sánchez, F. (2015). Assessing sexual orientation and gender identity issues among Latinos. In K. F. Geisinger (Ed.), *Psychological testing of Hispanics: Clinical, cultural, and intellectual issues* (pp. 291–308). Washington DC: American Psychological Association.

12

Working With Adopted Adolescents

Mindy J. Vanderloo and Joanna E. Bettmann

More than 2% of the U.S. population under 18 are adopted (Kreider & Lofquist, 2014). Adopted youth come from a range of backgrounds and have varied paths to adoption. This chapter will consider adolescents who were adopted domestically and internationally, adopted by relatives and unrelated families, adopted by step-parents, adopted into transracial families, adopted at birth and as older children, and adopted after contact with the child welfare system. Among adopted children in the United States, approximately 25% are adopted internationally, 37% through public foster care systems, and 38% through domestic private adoption (Vandivere, Malm, & Radel, 2009). These subgroups often have vastly different experiences; therefore, treatment approaches and interventions presented in this chapter should be adapted to fit individual clients and their circumstances.

Adopted individuals are more likely to come into contact with mental health professionals than their nonadopted peers (Juffer & van Ijzendoorn, 2005; Keyes, Sharma, Elkins, Iacono, & McGue, 2008; Miller et al., 2000). Thus, psychotherapists need to build competency in working with adopted children and their families (Bettmann, Freeman, & Parry, 2015). This chapter will provide an overview of adversities prevalent among adopted adolescents and effective treatment to address these issues. The chapter concludes with two case studies to illuminate treatment with different adopted adolescents.

Demographics

National U.S. data indicates adopted children are more likely to be female (53.4%) than male (46.6%; Kreider & Lofquist, 2014). Mirroring U.S. demographics, most adopted children in the United States are non-Hispanic Caucasian (49.0%), with smaller percentages Hispanic (18.8%), African American (16.1%), Asian American (10.0%), multiracial (6.5%), "other race"

(5.3%), American Indian or Native Alaskan (1.8%), and Native Hawaiian/ Pacific Islander (0.4%; Kreider & Lofquist, 2014). African American and Asian American children are overrepresented among adoptees. For example, 16.1% of U.S. African American children live with adoptive families, while 13.4% live with biological families (Kreider & Lofquist, 2014). Approximately 14.1% of adopted children live in poverty, lower than the 21.1% of children who live with their biological parents in poverty, suggesting that adoptive families may have higher socioeconomic status (Kreider & Lofquist, 2014).

Common Issues Faced

Some adopted adolescents arrive to therapy wanting to explore the reasons for their adoption or having incomplete or undesirable information about their birth family or reasons for adoption. Some feel different than their nonadopted peers or feel insecure, as though they may lose their adoptive family. Others want to connect with their birth families or want to reconcile their biological ethnic and cultural identity with that of their adoptive families. These issues can be explored in therapy to develop a healthy, integrated, and meaningful adoptive identity (Riley & Meeks, 2005).

While the majority of adopted youth and adults fare well and have comparable psychosocial outcomes to their nonadopted peers (Borders, Penny, & Portnoy, 2000; Burrow, Tubman, & Finley, 2004; Juffer & van Ijzendoorn, 2007), many adopted children experience social, educational, and psychological problems (Barroso, Barbosa-Ducharne, Coelho, Costa, & Silva, 2017; Feigelman, 2001; Juffer & van Ijzendoorn, 2005; Keyes et al., 2008; Miller et al., 2000; Simmel, 2007; van Ijzendoorn, Juffer, & Poelhuis, 2005). Compared to their nonadopted peers, adopted children have poorer school performance (van Ijzendoorn et al., 2005), more learning disabilities (van Ijzendoorn et al., 2005), higher rates of smoking and substance abuse (Miller et al., 2000), more internalizing symptoms and emotional distress (Juffer & van Ijzendoorn, 2005; Miller et al., 2000), more externalizing and behavioral problems (Barroso et al., 2017; Feigelman, 2001; Juffer & van Ijzendoorn, 2005; Keyes et al., 2008; Miller et al., 2000; Simmel, 2007), and more physical health problems (Miller et al., 2000).

However, there is significant variation in these outcomes by age. For example, children adopted between 6 months and 18 months tend to have fewer behavioral problems (Beckett et al., 2006), better school performance, and stronger physical development (van Ijzendoorn & Juffer, 2006) compared to their later-adopted peers. These findings are likely due in part to the important attachment relationships which are critical to healthy early childhood development (Thompson, 2008). Children adopted at younger ages likely experience fewer or less severe disruptions in these early important relationships.

Adoption and Attachment

Meta-analytic research indicates that adopted youth are more likely than their nonadopted peers to be insecurely attached (van den Dries, Juffer, van Ijzendoorn, & Bakermans-Kranenburg, 2009). Notably, children adopted between birth and 12 months of age show similar attachment security to nonadopted peers, while children adopted after 12 months of age are more likely to display insecure attachment than nonadopted children (van den Dries et al., 2009). Some adopted children may be more insecurely attached because of their early life experiences, such as the loss of a parent, divorce, multiple changes in caregivers, disrupted placements, neglect, and trauma (Beijersbergen, Juffer, Bakermans-Kranenburg, & van Ijzendoorn, 2012; Hussey, Falletta, & Eng, 2012; Nickman et al., 2005; Sroufe, 2005; van den Dries et al., 2009).

This attachment insecurity is problematic because secure attachment in adolescence links to a number of beneficial outcomes, including stronger emotional regulation skills, stronger peer relationships, stronger sense of self-worth, better stress management skills, and fewer behavioral and mental health problems (Cassidy & Shaver, 1999; Dykas, Woodhouse, Cassidy, & Waters, 2006; Harwood, Xin, & Yu, 2013; Laible, 2007; Seiffge-Krenke, 2006; Shoshani, Nakash, Zubida, & Harper, 2014). Not surprisingly, children who experience institutionalization, such as orphanage stays, display even greater attachment insecurity than adopted children who lived only with primary caregivers (Harwood et al., 2013; Tan, Marfo, & Dedrick, 2010). Given these findings, strengthening adopted adolescents' attachment relationships should be a focus of treatment when working with these clients and their families. One example of what this focus can look like will be presented later in this chapter, within one of the case studies.

Adolescent Identity and Adoption

An important developmental task of adolescence is identity formation (Erikson, 1968). Adolescents are typically figuring out who they are in relation to their families, identifying their own passions and interests separate from those of their families. However, some adopted adolescents experience particular identity problems relative to their adoptive status (Bettmann, Demong, & Jasperson, 2008; Grotevant, 1997; Riley & Meeks, 2005). A framework for understanding these identity problems is useful.

One framework cites adoptive identities as falling into one of four categories: *integrated, limited, unexamined,* and *unsettled* (Dunbar, 2003; Dunbar & Grotevant, 2004; Grotevant, Lo, Fiorenzo, & Dunbar, 2017). This framework considers six components in categorizing adolescents into these four groups: exploration, salience, consistency, flexibility, positive affect, and negative affect. Each of these components will be explained below.

Adopted adolescents with integrated adoptive identity show moderate levels of exploration of the meaning of adoption in their lives. They also indicate that their adoption influences their thoughts, feelings, behaviors, and decisions, showing high levels of salience. They have high levels of consistency around their adoptive identity, meaning that they display internally consistent narratives about their adoptive identity. They show high levels of flexibility in considering and integrating differing views, meaning that they have strong ability to view issues as others might see them. They also show high levels of positive affect and low levels of negative affect about their adoptions (Grotevant et al., 2017).

By contrast, individuals who are classified as having limited adoptive identity demonstrate low to moderate levels of exploration, low to moderate levels of salience, moderate levels of consistency, moderate levels of flexibility, moderate levels of positive affect, and low levels of negative affect (Grotevant et al., 2017). Individuals who are classified as having unexamined adoption identity development have low levels of exploration, low levels of salience, low to moderate levels of consistency, low to moderate levels of flexibility, and low levels of both positive and negative affect (Grotevant et al., 2017).

Individuals who are classified as having unsettled adoptive identity have high levels of exploration, high levels of salience, high levels of consistency, high levels of flexibility, and high levels of both positive and negative affect (Grotevant et al., 2017). Compared to those in the other three identity categories, adopted adolescents with unsettled adoptive identities struggle more with internalizing problems as they transition to adulthood. Unsettled individuals are distinguished by high level of salience, meaning their thoughts and feelings about their adoption influence them significantly and they spend substantial time thinking about their adoption. Though they may express some positive emotions about their adoption, they also express high levels of negative affect about their adoption. Thus, an unsettled individual may spend significant amounts of time ruminating about adoption, showing preoccupation with their birth parents or expressing negative feelings about their adoption or adoptive family (Grotevant et al., 2017).

This identity framework offers one lens for considering adopted adolescents in treatment. If you are working with an adopted adolescent, which identity category maps best onto your client's behavior and thoughts? What does that identity category suggest in terms of the treatment you provide? How might you adjust treatment goals to match your client's needs in terms of her adoptive identity category? Explore your client's feelings about being adopted. If your adopted client displays high levels of preoccupation and negative affect in relation to adoption, focus time in treatment on the adoption, what the client wishes for, and how he can move forward with the life he now has.

Transracial Adoption

Transracial adoption is the adoption of a child of one race by parents of a different race (Johnson, Mickelson, & Davila, 2013). Adoption experts suggest that adopted youth should have a strong connection to individuals from their same cultural and racial biological heritage (Evan B. Donaldson Adoption Institute, 2008). Notably, parents who support adopted adolescents in learning about their biological ethnic heritage, encourage pride in that ethnic heritage, and share ethnic experiences with them help both the adolescents and the parents to have positive views of adolescents' biological ethnic heritage (Feigelman & Silverman, 1984; Yoon, 2001). These experiences are likely to influence positively the adopted adolescent's self-esteem and well-being (Yoon, 2004).

Accordingly, you should encourage families with a transracially adopted child to support their child's exploration of biological racial and ethnic heritage. You can assist parents with this by suggesting how parents can find relevant community events, people, parades, or foods in your area. Encourage parents to take the lead from their children. Rather than push the adolescent to attend an event linked to their biological heritage, parents should ask their adopted child: "How can we support you in exploring your biological heritage to the extent that you want to?"

Adolescent Foster Children

U.S. child welfare agencies have three primary goals: enhancing children's safety, ensuring the permanency of children's placements, and safeguarding the well-being of children in foster care (Pecora, Whittaker, et al., 2009). Threat to children's safety is commonly the reason children enter the custody of state child welfare services. The majority of youth enter foster care because of neglect (61%), parental drug abuse (34%), parents' inability to cope (14%), physical abuse (12%), and youth behavioral problems (11%). Child welfare agencies are charged with removing children and adolescents from unsafe homes and working to prevent future problems such as child maltreatment.

Child welfare's goal of permanency engages the child welfare system in finding a legal permanent placement for youth (Pecora, Whittaker, et al., 2009). This may involve reunification with the family of origin, placement with related family members, or adoption. Depending on the agency's goal for the child, your interventions will vary. For example, if reunification with the family of origin is the goal for an adolescent, therapists will implement interventions to increase the parents' ability to maintain the adolescent's safety in the home, as well as interventions to address the adolescent's behavioral or mental health needs. If the adolescents' parents are unwilling or unable to provide a safe environment, the child welfare agency seeks kinship adoptive placements or nonkinship adoptive placements. Many adolescents emancipate from the custody of child welfare services prior to achieving a legal-permanent placement: in 2016, more than 20,000 youth emancipated by aging out of U.S. child welfare systems (U.S. Department of Health & Human Services, 2017). In such cases, the agency's goal is to provide adolescents with independent living skills.

Child welfare's broad goal of enhancing children's well-being involves improving children's mental health, behavioral health, education, physical health, and, for older youth, employment skills (Pecora, Whittaker, et al., 2009). Mental and behavioral health needs of youth in foster care are approximately five times greater than the needs of youth not involved with child welfare (Landsverk, Burns, Stambugh, & Rolls Reutz, 2006). Youth in foster care are less likely to complete high school (Pecora et al., 2006) and more likely to experience mental health problems (Courtney, Needell, & Wulczyn, 2004). They are also more likely to be unemployed (Naccarato, Brophy, & Courtney, 2010; Pecora et al., 2006), to be dependent on public assistance (Pecora et al., 2006), to be incarcerated (Reilly, 2003), to be homeless (Reilly, 2003), and to have teen pregnancies (Reilly, 2003). These outcomes are often worse for youth who age out of the system prior to obtaining a permanent family placement (Brown, Courtney, & Curtis McMillen, 2015; Courtney et al., 2007; Reilly, 2003).

A review of effective interventions for youth in foster care is beyond the scope of this chapter. Those interested in working with this population are encouraged to read works by McCauley, Pecora, and Rose (2006) and Pecora, Kessler, et al. (2009).

Assessment of Adopted Adolescents and Their Families

Given the range of mental health and behavioral issues which adopted youth and their families experience, you must conduct a comprehensive assessment of each adopted client and family (Murray & Sullivan, 2017). Assessments should include the following areas:

- Adolescent behavioral and socioemotional functioning, as well as age-appropriate functioning
- Parent-child relationship
- Parent functioning (parental stress, parental depression/anxiety/PTSD)
- Trauma exposure and traumatic stress
- Adoption-specific functioning (Murray & Sullivan, 2017)

To screen for the adolescent's functioning, you can utilize the biopsychosocial assessment structure explained in Chapter 4, "Assessment in Adolescent Treatment," or any of the standardized instruments referred to in that chapter. In assessing functioning, think about how the adolescent is meeting or not meeting basic expectations at home, school, with family members, with teachers, with peers. Is the adolescent running into trouble in each do-main (home, school, sports team, religious environment, community group, etc.) or is the adolescent exceeding expectations in each of those areas? Is the adolescent able to hold responsibilities similar to other adolescents who are the same/similar age or developmental level or failing to do so? Can the adolescent take responsibility for herself, a pet, or a family chore? Does the adolescent hold a job or bring money into the home? Does the adolescent get passing grades and show up to class on time, prepared for that day's material?

To assess the parent-child relationship, assess from both the perspective of the parent and the adolescent. Ask the parent: "How often do you feel close to your child?" "What makes you feel connected to her?" "How often do you feel angry or disconnected from her?" "What makes that anger or disconnection worse?" You should also assess the parent-child relationship from the adolescent's perspective. "How does your parent show that she/he cares about you deeply? How often does that happen?" "Does your parent listen to you carefully most of the time?" "How often does your parent yell at you or get angry with you?" "How often does your parent say something which makes you feel bad about yourself?"

Assessing for parental functioning may reveal important, underlying issues. Many useful, free tools are available here to assess these issues: http://www.healthmeasures.net/explore-measurement-systems/promis.   The PROMIS website provides many brief and empirically validated tools to evaluate adults' stress, mental health, psychological health, social engagement, and overall functioning.

Consider screening for the adolescent's trauma exposure and traumatic stress exposure using a standardized tool such as the trauma symptom checklist (Wherry, Huffhines, & Walisky, 2016) or using your own trauma-focused queries. The DSM-5 website has both a free PTSD screening tool, as well as early development and home screening tools available here: https://www.psychiatry.org/psychiatrists/practice/dsm/educational-resources/assessment-measures.

In assessing adoption-specific functioning, consider the client and family's grief and loss over the adoption, any unmet expectations, openness in the adoption, their understanding of adoption, racial and cultural identities of the parents and adolescent, and their perceptions of the adoption's permanence (Murray & Sullivan, 2017). As you assess for grief and loss, you are considering adolescents' potential grief over the loss of their birth family, as well as the adoptive parents' potential loss as a result of infertility. In terms of unmet expectations, evaluate the difference between parental expectations of adoption and their adopted child with the reality of the adoption and the adolescent.

For example, the therapist might ask, "All parents who adopt have expectations about their child and the adoption experience. What has been different from what you expected?" (Murray & Sullivan, 2017, p. 220). You might ask your later-adopted adolescent clients: "Is adoption what you thought it would be? What has been different or surprising?" (Murray & Sullivan, 2017, p. 220). In exploring for openness in adoption, assess if there is secrecy around the adolescent's birth family, adoption, or adoption-relation information. This secrecy could be harmful and engender mistrust in the parent-child relationship if the child later discovers the adoption. Additionally, secrecy could communicate that adolescents should be ashamed of their adoption or past (Murray & Sullivan, 2017). Assessing adopted adolescents involves exploring what they understand both about adoption generally and their own adoption specifically (Murray & Sullivan, 2017).

Exploring race and culture in the assessment involves evaluating racial and cultural differences between the adolescent and adoptive parents, gauging their perceptions of the adolescent's racial and cultural history, assessing how much exposure the adolescent has had to knowledge, people, and cultural activities of their biological heritage, as well as experiences of racism and bias experienced by the adolescent and/or family (Murray & Sullivan, 2017). Regarding adoption-specific issues, you should assess for the adolescent's perceptions of permanency. Does your client have concerns that he will not continue to live with his adoptive family or that their relationships will end after he turns 18? Similarly, ask the adolescent's parents: is this adoption permanent? What does that permanency mean to you?

Screening Tool

Funded by the U.S. Children's Bureau (an office of the U.S. Administration for Children and Families), AdoptUSKids created a screening tool for clinicians to gather information on adoptive families' needs. It is available here: http://www.nrcdr.org/_assets/files/AUSK/support-matters/support-matters-resource-guide.pdf. The tool is not a comprehensive assessment, but rather provides an initial screening for areas that may need clinical attention or further assessment. The following is a section of the AdoptUSKids screening tool focused on adoptive adolescent needs and parent-adolescent relationship. This section of the tool helps identify presenting problems the adopted adolescent might have.

Child's or Children's Needs

Do any of your adopted children or children in foster or kinship care have any of the following issues? If so, please rate the issue as mild, moderate, or severe. If you have only one adopted child or child in foster or kinship care, check only one box in each row. If you have more than one adopted child or child in foster or kinship care, you can check each box that applies (for example, if you have three children and one has a moderate physical disability and one has mild disability, you would check "At least one child has a mild version of this issue" and "At least one child has a moderate version of this issue").

	None of my children has this issue	At least one child has a mild version of this issue	At least one child has a moderate version of this issue	At least one child has a severe version of this issue
Physical health problem				
Neurological problem (autism spectrum disorder, Down syndrome, fetal alcohol spectrum disorder, etc.)				
Learning disability				
Emotional problem (reactive attachment disorder, oppositional defiant disorder, bipolar disorder, post-traumatic stress disorder, etc.)				
Behavioral problem (cruelty to animals, lying, hyperactivity, stealing, sexually acts out, etc.)				
Other problem (please list)				

WHAT ISSUES OR PROBLEMS WOULD YOU LIKE TO ADDRESS?

In general, do any of the children you are parenting through adoption, foster care, or kinship care have significant difficulties in the following areas? If you have multiple children through adoption, foster care, or kinship care, please consider all of the children together when choosing your answer.

	None of the time	Some of the time	Most of the time	All of the time
At home (including with your other children)				

In school				
In the community (for example, at church, in clubs or community centers, in the neighborhood)				
With peers				
Other (please list)				

RELATIONSHIP BETWEEN YOU AND YOUR ADOPTED CHILDREN OR CHILDREN IN FOSTER OR KINSHIP CARE

The following questions are about the relationship between any children you are parenting through adoption, foster care, or kinship care. Please check the response that best reflects your experience. If you have multiple children and they have different experiences, pick the answer that best represents your entire household.

Have you experienced any of the following concerns related to any children you are parenting though adoption, foster care, or kinship care? (Check all that apply.)

- At least one of my adopted children or children in foster or kinship care does not respect me.
- I have significant trouble trusting at least one of my adopted children or children in foster or kinship care.
- I have significant trouble communicating effectively with at least one of my adopted children or children in foster or kinship care.
- I have more than one child, and the children have significant difficulty getting along with one another.
- I have birth, step, or other children in the home, and there is significant tension between these children and at least one adopted child or child in foster or kinship care.
- I have birth, step, or other children in the home, and I feel I give them less time or attention than I should due to the complex needs of at least one adopted child or child in foster or kinship care.

Overall, would you describe the impact of parenting children through adoption, foster care, or kinship care on your family?

- Mostly positive
- Positive and negative—about equal
- Mostly negative

Reprinted with Permission of AdoptUSKids (https://adoptuskids.org). AdoptUSKids is operated by the Adoption Exchange Association and is made possible by grant number 90C01133 from the Children's Bureau. The contents of its publication are solely the responsibility of the Adoption Exchange Association and do not necessarily represent the official views of the Children's Bureau, ACYF, ACF, or HHS.

If the initial screening highlights needs related to the adopted adolescent, follow up with more in-depth assessments. For example, the initial screening may show evidence of emotional or behavioral problems in the adolescent. Then, follow up with an assessment of internalizing and/or externalizing problems, such as the Child Behavior Checklist (CBCL; Achenbach et al., 2013). The CBCL for 6- to 18-year-olds assesses functioning in the following domains: anxious/depressed, withdrawal/depressed, somatic complaints, social problems, thought problems, attention problems, rule-breaking behavior, and aggressive behavior. The CBCL must be purchased from the Achenbach System of Empirically Based Assessment (http://www.aseba.org/ordering/howtoorder.html).

Adoptive Parents

Working with adopted adolescents should always include assessment of their family systems. While adoption is a source of joy for many, many parents experience stress after adoption (Barth & Miller, 2000). Adoptive parents may have difficulty developing relationships with their adopted child or may have concerns about their adoptive child's problematic behavior (Carnes-Holt & Bratton, 2014). Adoptive parents sometimes express feelings of uncertainty or failure about their ability to parent their adoptive child (Bettmann et al., 2008; Carnes-Holt & Bratton, 2014; Riley & Meeks, 2005). They might feel like frauds, thinking that they struggle as parents because they are adoptive, rather than birth, parents. Some adoptive parents express anger or resentment for problems the adoptive child brings into their lives (Riley & Meeks, 2005). Others feel confused and rejected when their adoptive children show hostility in their relationship (Carnes-Holt & Bratton, 2014). Some adoptive parents feel grief if they are unable to have biological children (Bettmann et al., 2008; Foli, Hebdon, Lim, & South, 2017) or experience financial stress from adoption and providing for their child (Foli et al., 2017).

Family Assessments

The Stress Index for Parents of Adolescents (SIPA; Sheras et al., 2001) assesses both parenting stress and child functioning. The SIPA has four domains: the adolescent, the parent, the adolescent-parent relationship, and life stressors. The adolescent domain assesses adolescents' moodiness/emotional lability, social isolation/withdrawal, delinquency/antisocial, and failure to achieve or persevere. The parent domain assesses parents' life restrictions, relationship with spouse/partner, social alienation, and incompetence/guilt. A composite score for total parenting stress is also provided. The SIPA must be purchased for use (https://www.parinc.com/Products/Pkey/412).

Initial assessment may highlight problems related to the family system or the parent-child relationship. In this case, clinicians could administer the McMaster Model of Family Functioning Family Assessment Device (FAD; Miller, Epstein, Bishop, & Keitner, 1985). This instrument has seven subscales measuring general family functioning: communication, affective responsiveness, problem solving, behavioral control, affective involvement, and roles. The instrument is free, available here: http://www.nctsn.org/content/family-assessment-device.

There are many other assessments that may be appropriate for adopted adolescents and their families. The California Evidence-Based Clearinghouse (http://www.cebc4cw.org/assessment-tools/measurement-tools-highlighted-on-the-cebc/) and the National Child Traumatic Stress Network (http://www.nctsnet.org/resources/online-research/measures-review) both maintain lists of free and paid assessment tools relevant to adopted adolescents and families.

Therapeutic Interventions

In a review of outcomes for services for adopted children and families, Barth and Miller (2000) conclude that empirical evidence for post-adoption psychotherapeutic interventions is weak. However, existing research suggests that interventions such as psychoeducation (Bammens, Adkins, & Badger, 2015; Murray & Sullivan, 2017; O'Dell, McCall, & Groark, 2015; Riley & Meeks, 2005) and family-based (Barth & Miller, 2000) models may be efficacious for adopted adolescents. Given the limited research in this area, the following are interventions with promising research support or expert recommendations.

Psychoeducation

Psychoeducation involves giving clients information about adoption that can help them understand their situation or know what to expect in the future.

For adopted adolescents and their families, psychoeducational interventions can include basic information on child development, attachment, the impact of separating children from birth parents, the impact of trauma, effective parenting practices, and psychological experiences commonly faced by adopted adolescents and adoptive parents. We have not found evidence-based psychoeducational curricula for adopted adolescents, but clinicians can use other resources to develop psychoeducational materials for their clients. For example, factsheets on adoption and adolescent topics are available through the Child Information Gateway (https://childwelfare.gov). These factsheets include topics such as "Parenting Your Adopted Teenager" (https://www.childwelfare.gov/pubPDFs/parent_teenager.pdf) and "The Impact of Adoption on Adoptive Parents" (https://www.childwelfare.gov/pubpdfs/impactparent.pdf). The Child Welfare Information Gateway (https://www.childwelfare.gov/) is a public resource funded by the Children's Bureau, an Office of the Administration for Children and Families, U.S. Department of Health and Human Services. Their website provides resources on a variety of child welfare topics, including adoption (https://www.childwelfare.gov/topics/adoption/), developmental stages, ethical issues in adoption, and adoption laws.

The California Evidence-Based Clearinghouse (http://www.cebc4cw.org/) is an excellent resource for effective programs and practices. The focus of this database is on effective interventions for children and families who come into contact with public child welfare systems. Researchers at the California Evidence-Based Clearinghouse gather data on treatment programs and provide an easy-to-read research summary. Current topics on the website include attachment interventions, behavioral management programs, family stabilization programs, kinship caregiver support, placement stabilization programs, and post-permanency services.

The Center for Adoption Support and Education (http://adoptionsupport.org/), has resources and trainings for both adoptive parents and therapists. For parents, this website lists information and fact sheets on adoption, as well as webinars on how to talk to children about adoption, grief and loss, and related topics. For professionals, this website lists books and trainings to help therapists understand the impact of adoption and learn effective strategies for communicating about adoption.

The website of the National Child Traumatic Stress Network (NCTSN; www.nctsn.org) lists resources for children who have experienced traumatic events. This website is useful for clinicians working with any adolescents who have experienced trauma. NCTSN offers information on the types of trauma children may experience, as well as interventions for clients with trauma. The website offers the Resource Parent Curriculum, a free training for foster and adoptive parents (https://learn.nctsn.org/enrol/index.php?id=67). This training helps parents understand the impact of trauma on children. All of the resources listed here can be useful sources for your psychoeducational interventions with adoptive parents and adolescents.

Family Interventions

Family therapy with adopted adolescents and their families may include psychoeducation, skill building, parent training, and/or relational approaches. Because research on therapeutic interventions for adoptive adolescents and their families is sparse (Barth & Miller, 2000), clinicians should consider interventions which show efficacy across adolescent populations. For example, multidimensional family therapy (MDFT; http://www.mdft.org) is a therapeutic intervention used in community mental health, child welfare, and juvenile justice settings. MDFT is a family-based intervention that shows efficacy in improving family relationships and some adolescent concerns (Liddle, 2016a, 2016b; van der Pol et al., 2017). See Chapter 8 for a lengthy discussion on MDFT, how to administer it, and how to get trained in the model.

Case Examples

Since adopted adolescents vary widely in their histories, presenting problems, and needs, we present two case examples below to illuminate what treatment looks like with different adopted adolescents and their families.

Case Example: Parenting Supports

Derek, 34, and Aniyah, 33, were an African-American couple who presented to outpatient treatment regarding their recently adopted foster child Anthony, a 14-year-old African-African boy. Derek and Aniyah lived in a major metropolitan area, in a different area than Anthony's biological family, and had no other children. Aniyah was an attorney and served as the primary breadwinner for the family. Derek worked part-time with at-risk youth in an inner-city after-school program. Derek and Aniyah presented to therapy alone, without Anthony, as he told them he did not want to participate in therapy. Anthony explained to his adoptive parents that he associated therapists with his removal from his home and the ripping apart of his family. He was not interested in sharing details of his life with someone he didn't know.

Anthony was placed with Derek and Aniyah as a foster child with the intention that they would adopt him. Anthony lived in different foster homes for several years as his biological mother worked to completed treatment for substance abuse. His three biological siblings were placed in two other foster homes. After several years in foster care, the state decided it was in Anthony's best interest to be placed with a family that was interested in adoption. Anthony moved in with Derek and Aniyah approximately 6 months ago and they adopted him 1 month ago.

Anthony's life with his biological family had been challenging. Anthony's mother struggled with substance use for Anthony's entire life, maintaining sobriety only for brief periods and holding jobs only occasionally. Anthony's role as the oldest child in his biological family's home meant he took care of his siblings while their mother was at work, high, or away from their apartment. Anthony and his siblings had often been left alone, with Anthony as the caregiver. Anthony's biological father had never been a part of his life; a constellation of neighbors and extended family often stepped in to assist Anthony and his siblings.

Derek and Aniyah described Anthony as "sweet," "gentle," "shy," and "sad." He loved to draw and play games on the computer. He often spent hours in his room reading or playing computer games. Without his siblings or mother to care for, Anthony seemed sad and a little lost. He denied suicidality to his adoptive parents, but often seemed down.

Derek and Aniyah reported Anthony had adjusted adequately to their home in the previous 6 months. But they were worried that he was depressed because he spent so much time alone in his room. They reported that, although he was clearly sad, he had begun bonding with Derek over a mutual love of computer games they could play together. Derek and Aniyah sought counseling now because they were unsure how to help Anthony adjust to their home and wanted to ensure they were making the best parenting choices for Anthony. Derek and Aniyah indicated they were nervous that they didn't have the skills to parent Anthony in the ways that he needed.

On a screening form completed by Aniyah, she noted that Anthony cried when asked about his mother and siblings and that he showed low mood and seemed depressed daily. She described her relationship with Anthony as "mostly positive." She denied any other behavioral problems for Anthony. The therapist administered a parenting stress assessment, finding that most domains were within normal limits, though adolescent moodiness/emotional lability and parent incompetence/guilt were in the borderline range.

The therapist felt that psychoeducation about adolescent development, adoption, depression, and attachment would be the most effective interventions for the family. The therapist gave Derek and Aniyah the handout "Parenting Your Adopted Teenager" (https://www.childwelfare. gov/pubPDFs/parent_teenager.pdf). The therapist also explained that adoption in adolescents can be particularly difficult, given the stage of brain development and hormonal changes that take place during puberty. These developmental issues can make it difficult to parent an adolescent, even though adolescents are in need of supervision, guidance, and support. The therapist reviewed ways Derek and Aniyah could provide support to Anthony, such as being open in talking to him about his birth family and adoption, helping him to create a memory book where he could record his life history, helping him reach out to his biological siblings, and helping him connect to other adopted adolescents through support groups. The therapist also provided psychoeducation on adolescent depression, teaching the parents what symptoms to watch out for and when referring Anthony to individual therapy might be necessary.

The therapist explored with Derek and Aniyah how to foster Anthony's healthy adaptation to his new environment, including building strong attachment relationships with both Derek and Aniyah. The therapist explained that Anthony might blame himself for the breakup of his family because he saw himself as the caretaker for his siblings. Perhaps he thought he failed somehow by not keeping his family together. The therapist encouraged Derek and Aniyah to engage Anthony in conversations about his biological family members, what he missed about them, and what was hard for him about his new life. Anthony was adjusting to life without his family members, as well as a new school and an entirely new community.

We can conceptualize that, from an attachment perspective, Anthony hadn't yet constituted strong attachment relationships in his adoptive family, relationships which served to soothe him when he was distressed and which he sought out for closeness and warmth. In order for Anthony to use his adoptive parents as attachment figures, he would need to bond with them both over time and through warm, authentic communication. From an attachment perspective, Anthony's internal working model likely contained introjects (internalized versions of important relationships) which expected that important adults would be unavailable, high, or at work.

Anthony likely didn't expect to share his feelings with Derek or Aniyah. He probably didn't think that they would be emotionally available to connect. He needed to experience that his adoptive parents could be a safe haven for him, offering emotionally safe relationships to which he could return when in distress. He also needed to experience his adoptive parents as a secure base, a safe environment from which he could feel free to explore and then return. He needed comfort and protection, as well as support for exploration. He needed parents who could help reflect and organize his difficult feelings. These kinds of parenting functions typically begin in children's infancy and toddlerhood, but Anthony may never have had a parent who could help him to regulate his emotions, reflect them, and help manage them.

The therapist summarized some of this conceptualization, encouraging Derek and Aniyah to reflect on their own attachment relationships, their own internal working models. She encouraged the parents to express their hopes for their individual relationships with Anthony. Aniyah became tearful, explaining that she wanted a close and warm relationship with Anthony and was confused and upset by his emotional distance and depression. Derek and Aniyah both shared feelings of inadequacy as parents and their doubts about their parenting abilities. The therapist provided ego-supportive interventions, reflecting how most parents experience their inadequacies and reinforcing Derek and Aniyah's strengths as parents. She emphasized their strength in seeking therapeutic support when they felt overwhelmed as adoptive parents.

The therapist explored with Derek and Aniyah ways they might build bonds with Anthony. She helped them to identify activities they enjoyed together and recommended doing several of these weekly, identifying positive traits in one another and speaking those aloud to each other, and engaging in ongoing, open, and respectful dialogue. The therapist suggested that they prepare themselves to expect enjoyable and tough times, but explained that even if Anthony rejected them or began to be defiant, what he needed most was stable, consistent, warm and empathic parenting.

The therapist provided some psychoeducation to Derek and Aniyah regarding Anthony's attachment needs. She explained how they could watch for his attachment signals: looking for how he used (or didn't use) his adoptive parents when he was distressed, how he managed separations, reunions, and transitions between activities or settings. She encouraged them to present themselves as available to Anthony to help him, but not force him to share feelings with them. In session, the therapist coached Derek and Aniyah in role plays that practiced how to support Anthony when he seemed particularly low or was triggered by overt reminders of his mother or siblings.

By the fourth session with the parents only, the therapist felt Derek and Aniyah had made progress, gaining information and skills on parenting, adoption, and attachment. The therapist checked the couples' level of comfort with parenting and their feelings about Anthony's current needs. Derek and Aniyah reported that Anthony still seemed down, but they were optimistic about their increased skills and taking time to build relationship with him. Derek reported that, although Anthony was sad about not being reunified with his mother, he had opened up to Derek on a few occasions when playing computer games, discussing how upset and angry he was with his mother. Derek and Aniyah reported they had done their best to validate his feelings of loss and anger. They also indicated that Anthony said he still did not want to see a therapist.

Based on the parents' self-reported feelings of increased competence with parenting and their description of Anthony, the therapist felt that treatment was, for now, complete. The therapist felt Derek and Aniyah had described effective use of new parenting skills. Though she had some concerns about Anthony's adjustment, she felt that he was coping well and would likely begin to build attachment relationships with Derek and Aniyah. She recommended they respect his choice not to participate in therapy at this time. However, she recommended that they return to treatment if Anthony's feeling of sadness worsened or impaired his functioning. The therapist terminated the treatment after the fourth session.

Case Example: Transracial Adoption

Shaylee was a 16-year-old-Latina female adopted at birth by a Caucasian couple, Jennifer and James. Jennifer and James were business owners, married and in their early fifties. They reported that Shaylee's teenaged biological parents did not feel they could adequately care for a baby. Shaylee's adoptive younger sibling, Isabelle, aged 10, was also Latina and adopted at birth from a different biological family. The family lived in a suburb where most in the community were Caucasian.

James reported that he and Jennifer wanted Shaylee to get counseling because she seemed withdrawn. He reported she did not have any behavioral problems and did well in school. On the initial screening tool, James noted, "She is withdrawn from her mother and me, stays in her room most of the time, and has little interest in activities she used to enjoy, such as singing and music club." He described his relationship with Shaylee as "mostly positive."

In the initial session with Shaylee alone, Shaylee shared with the Caucasian therapist that she felt she didn't fit in anywhere. She said that she loved her adoptive family, but felt as though she was betraying her biological heritage by living in an affluent White area. Shaylee indicated that she had friends at school, but struggled to find her place in school environment with little racial or ethnic diversity. She said she tried to talk to her parents about these issues, but that they just didn't understand. The therapist administered the APA Depression—Child Age 11–17 measure (https://www.psychiatry.org/psychiatrists/practice/dsm/educational-resources/assessment: American Psychiatric Association, 2013) to rule out depression; scores were elevated, but within normal limits. The therapist noted Shaylee's strengths in her engagement in the treatment process, warmth in relationships with family members, and academic talents. The therapist identified concerns in terms of Shaylee's racial and cultural isolation, creating stress as she developed her identity in adolescence. The therapist engaged Shaylee in treatment planning at this point: they decided together to begin a combination of family and individual therapy with the goal of providing Shaylee with individual and familial support, thus reducing her isolation.

The therapist began individual therapy with Shaylee by providing psychoeducation that many adopted adolescents have similar experiences, struggling with feeling stuck between two different worlds. Shaylee expressed relief that these feelings were normal because she felt like she was betraying everyone and, at times, was hostile to her adoptive family. The therapist also shared that it was common to feel curious about birth parents and the reasons her biological parents chose adoption and to feel upset about not knowing everything about her birth family.

The therapist explored with Shaylee what she thought about her adoption, how that influenced her current identity, and how she felt about herself today.

Shaylee expressed that the difference in race between her and her parents was always in her face because everyone asked how she was related to her parents—and that her parents did not understand what it was like to experience the bias that she experienced as she moved through their mostly-White affluent community. The therapist and Shaylee explored Shaylee's ethnic identity and identified ways she could celebrate her biological family's racial and cultural identity in her home and community, both individually and in shared experiences with her adoptive family. They also discussed strategies for conveying her experiences of racism and bias with her parents to help them understand her experiences.

In family sessions, the therapist encouraged Shaylee to share things she had shared in individual therapy with her parents. The goal here was to help Shaylee to feel more connected to her parents and to have an authentic dialogue about how difficult it was for her to be a person of color and a transracially adopted adolescent in a mostly-White community. Shaylee's parents became tearful when Shaylee shared how difficult aspects of her life had been. They expressed concern and interest in serving as greater supports for Shaylee. They blamed themselves for not recognizing what Shaylee needed and how alone she felt. They made a commitment as a family to spend time celebrating Shaylee's biological and ethnic heritage by attending events in their community together. Therapy terminated once Shaylee and her family agreed that treatment goals regarding increasing familial support for Shaylee and reducing her isolation had been met.

Conclusion

The body of literature in this chapter suggests that adopted children face particular challenges during adolescence. These challenges may relate to adolescents' search for identity, push for autonomy, and/or shift in attachment relationships. Adopted adolescents face challenges at home and in school, in mental health and physical health. Adopted adolescents who have incomplete information about their birth family or adoption, who feel different than their nonadopted peers, who feel insecure that they may lose their adoptive family, who want to connect with their birth family, or who want to reconcile their biological ethnic and cultural identity with that of their adoptive family—all may seek therapy. These adolescents will have varied needs, so clinicians will need to customize treatment to each adolescent client, using knowledge of evidence-based practices and each adolescent's particular relational and attachment needs. Adopted children and their families will need the support of skilled and attuned clinicians to navigate the challenging waters of adolescence.

References

Achenbach, T. M., Humphreys, K. L., Katz, S. J., Lee, S. S., Hammen, C., Brennan, P. A., & Najman, J. M. (2013). Child behavior checklist and profile for ages 6–18. *The association of ADHD and depression: Mediation by peer problems and parent-child difficulties in two complementary samples, 122*, 854–867.

American Psychiatric Association. (2013). *Depression—Child age 11–17*. Retrieved from https://www.psychiatry.org/File%20Library/Psychiatrists/Practice/DSM/APA_DSM5_Level-2-Depression-Child-Age-11-to-17.pdf

Bammens, A.-S., Adkins, T., & Badger, J. (2015). Psycho-educational intervention increases reflective functioning in foster and adoptive parents. *Adoption & Fostering, 39*, 38–50. doi:10.1177/0308575914565069

Barroso, R., Barbosa-Ducharne, M., Coelho, V., Costa, I.-S., & Silva, A. (2017). Psychological adjustment in intercountry and domestic adopted adolescents: A systematic review. *Child & Adolescent Social Work Journal, 34*, 399–418. doi:10.1007/s10560-016-0485-x

Barth, R. P., & Miller, J. M. (2000). Building effective post-adoption services: What is the empirical foundation? *Family Relations, 49*, 447–455.

Beckett, C., Maughan, B., Rutter, M., Castle, J., Colvert, E., Groothues, C., . . . Sonuga-Barke, E. J. S. (2006). Do the effects of early severe deprivation on cognition persist into early adolescence? Findings from the English and Romanian adoptees study. *Child Development, 77*, 696–711.

Beijersbergen, M. D., Juffer, F., Bakermans-Kranenburg, M. J., & van Ijzendoorn, M. H. (2012). Remaining or becoming secure: Parental sensitive support predicts attachment continuity from infancy to adolescence in a longitudinal adoption study. *Developmental Psychology, 48*, 1277–1282. doi:10.1037/a0027442

Bettmann, J. E., Demong, E., & Jasperson, R. A. (2008). Treating adolescents with adoption and attachment issues in wilderness therapy settings. *Journal of Therapeutic Schools and Programs, 3*, 117–138.

Bettmann, J. E., Freeman, P. C., & Parry, K. J. (2015). Differences between adopted and nonadopted adolescents in wilderness and residential treatment. *Journal of Experiential Education, 38*, 245–261. doi:10.1177/1053825915569056

Borders, L. D., Penny, J. M., & Portnoy, F. (2000). Adult adoptees and their friends: Current functioning and psychosocial well-being. *Family Relations, 49*, 407–418. doi:10.1111/j.1741-3729.2000.00407.x

Brown, A., Courtney, M. E., & Curtis McMillen, J. (2015). Behavioral health needs and service use among those who've aged-out of foster care. *Children & Youth Services Review, 58*, 163–169. doi:10.1016/j.childyouth.2015.09.020

Burrow, A. L., Tubman, J. G., & Finley, G. E. (2004). Adolescent adjustment in a nationally collected sample: Identifying group differences by adoption status, adoption subtype, developmental stage and gender. *Journal of Adolescence, 27,* 267–282. doi:10.1016/j.adolescence.2004.03.004

Carnes-Holt, K., & Bratton, S. C. (2014). The efficacy of child parent relationship therapy for adopted children with attachment disruptions. *Journal of Counseling & Development, 92,* 328–337. doi:10.1002/j.1556-6676.2014.00160.x

Cassidy, J., & Shaver, P. R. (Eds.). (1999). *Handbook of attachment: Theory, research, and clinical applications.* New York, NY: Guilford Press.

Courtney, M. E., Dworsky, A. L., Cusick, G. R., Havlicek, J., Perez, A., & Keller, T. E. (2007). *Midwest evaluation of the adult functioning of former foster youth: Outcomes at age 21.* Retrieved from https://www.chapinhall.org/wp-content/uploads/Midwest-Eval-Outcomes-at-Age-21.pdf

Courtney, M. E., Needell, B., & Wulczyn, F. (2004). Unintended consequences of the push for accountability: The case of national child welfare performance standards. *Children and Youth Services Review, 26,* 1141–1154. doi:10.1016/j.childyouth.2004.05.005

Dunbar, N. (2003). *Typologies of adolescent adoptive identity: The influence of family context and relationships.* (Unpublished doctoral dissertation), University of Minnesota.

Dunbar, N., & Grotevant, H. D. (2004). Adoption narratives: The construction of adoptive identity during adolescence. In M. W. Pratt, B. H. Fiese, M. W. Pratt, & B. H. Fiese (Eds.), *Family stories and the life course: Across time and generation.* (pp. 135–161). Mahwah, NJ: Lawrence Erlbaum.

Dykas, M. J., Woodhouse, S. S., Cassidy, J., & Waters, H. S. (2006). Narrative assessment of attachment representations: Links between secure base scripts and adolescent attachment. *Attachment & Human Development, 8,* 221–240.

Erikson, E. H. (1968). *Identity: Youth and crisis.* New York, NY: Norton.

Evan B. Donaldson Adoption Institute. (2008). *Finding families for African American children: The role of race and law in adoption from foster care.* Retrieved from https://www.adoptioninstitute.org/wp-content/uploads/2013/12/MEPApaper20080527.pdf

Feigelman, W. (2001). Comparing adolescents in diverging family structures: Investigating whether adoptees are more prone to problems than their nonadopted peers. *Adoption Quarterly, 5,* 5–37.

Feigelman, W., & Silverman, A. R. (1984). The long-term effects of transracial adoption. *Social Service Review, 58,* 588–602.

Foli, K. J., Hebdon, M., Lim, E., & South, S. C. (2017). Transitions of adoptive parents: A longitudinal mixed methods analysis. *Archives of Psychiatric Nursing, 31,* 483–492. doi:10.1016/j.apnu.2017.06.007

Grotevant, H. D. (1997). Coming to terms with adoption: The construction of identity from adolescence into adulthood. *Adoption Quarterly, 1,* 3–27.

Grotevant, H. D., Lo, A., Fiorenzo, L., & Dunbar, N. (2017). Adoptive identity and adjustment from adolescence to emerging adulthood: A person-centered approach. *Developmental Psychology, 53,* 2195–2204. doi:10.1037/dev0000352

Harwood, R., Xin, F., & Yu, S. (2013). Preadoption adversities and postadoption mediators of mental health and school outcomes among international, foster, and private adoptees in the United States. *Journal of Family Psychology, 27,* 409–420. doi:10.1037/a0032908

Hussey, D. L., Falletta, L., & Eng, A. (2012). Risk factors for mental health diagnoses among children adopted from the public child welfare system. *Children & Youth Services Review, 34,* 2072–2080. doi:10.1016/j.childyouth.2012.06.015

Johnson, F. L., Mickelson, S., & Davila, M. L. (2013). Transracial foster care and adoption: Issues and realities. *New England Journal of Public Policy, 25,* 1–14.

Juffer, F., & van Ijzendoorn, M. H. (2005). Behavior problems and mental health referrals of international adoptees: A meta-analysis. *JAMA: Journal of the American Medical Association, 293*, 2501–2515.

Juffer, F., & van Ijzendoorn, M. H. (2007). Adoptees do not lack self-esteem: A meta-analysis of studies on self-esteem of transracial, international, and domestic adoptees. *Psychological Bulletin, 133*, 1067–1083. doi:10.1037/0033-2909.133.6.1067

Keyes, M. A., Sharma, A., Elkins, I. J., Iacono, W. G., & McGue, M. (2008). The mental health of us adolescents adopted in infancy. *Archives of Pediatrics & Adolescent Medicine, 162*, 419–425. doi:10.1001/archpedi.162.5.419

Kreider, R. M., & Lofquist, D. A. (2014). *Adopted children and stepchildren: 2010.* Washington, DC: U.S. Census Bureau.

Laible, D. (2007). Attachment with parents and peers in late adolescence: Links with emotional competence and social behavior. *Personality and Individual Differences, 43*, 1185–1197. doi:10.1016/j.paid.2007.03.010

Landsverk, J., Burns, B., Stambugh, L., & Rolls Reutz, J. (2006). *Mental health care for children and adolescents in foster care: Review of research literature.* Retrieved from http://lacdcfs.org/katieA/practices/docs/Foster%20Care%20MH%20Review%20(Casey_2006).pdf

Liddle, H. A. (2016a). Multidimensional family therapy. In T. L. Sexton, J. Lebow, T. L. Sexton, & J. Lebow (Eds.), *Handbook of family therapy* (pp. 231–249). New York, NY: Routledge/Taylor & Francis.

Liddle, H. A. (2016b). Multidimensional family therapy: Evidence base for transdiagnostic treatment outcomes, change mechanisms, and implementation in community settings. *Family Process, 55*, 558–576. doi:10.1111/famp.12243

McCauley, C., Pecora, P. J., & Rose, W. (2006). *Enhancing the well-being of children and families through effective interventions: International evidence for practice.* London/Philadelphia: Jessica Kingsley.

Miller, B. C., Fan, X., Grotevant, H. D., Christensen, M., Coyl, D., & van Dulmen, M. (2000). Adopted adolescents' overrepresentation in mental health counseling: Adoptees' problems or parents' lower threshold for referral? *Journal of the American Academy of Child & Adolescent Psychiatry, 39*, 1504–1511. doi:10.1097/00004583-200012000-00011

Miller, I. W., Epstein, N. B., Bishop, D. S., & Keitner, G. I. (1985). The McMaster family assessment device: Reliability and validity. *Journal of Marital and Family Therapy, 11*, 345–356. doi:10.1111/j.1752-0606.1985.tb00028.x

Murray, K. J., & Sullivan, K. M. (2017). Using clinical assessment to enhance adoption success. *Families in Society, 98*, 217–224. doi:10.1606/1044-3894.2017.98.29

Naccarato, T., Brophy, M., & Courtney, M. E. (2010). Employment outcomes of foster youth: The results from the Midwest evaluation of the adult functioning of foster youth. *Children & Youth Services Review, 32*, 551–559. doi:10.1016/j.childyouth.2009.11.009

Nickman, S. L., Rosenfeld, A. A., Fine, P., Macintyre, J. C., Pilowsky, D. J., Howe, R.-A., ... Sveda, S. A. (2005). Children in adoptive families: Overview and update. *Journal of the American Academy of Child and Adolescent Psychiatry, 44*, 987–995.

O'Dell, K. E., McCall, R. B., & Groark, C. J. (2015). Supporting families throughout the international special needs adoption process. *Children & Youth Services Review, 59*, 161–170. doi:10.1016/j.childyouth.2015.11.008

Pecora, P. J., Kessler, R. C., O'Brien, K., White, C. R., Williams, J., Hiripi, E., ... Herrick, M. A. (2006). Educational and employment outcomes of adults formerly placed in foster care: Results from the Northwest Foster Care Alumni Study. *Children & Youth Services Review, 28,* 1459–1481. doi:10.1016/j.childyouth.2006.04.003

Pecora, P. J., Kessler, R. C., Williams, J., Downs, A. C., English, D. J., White, J., & O'Brien, K. (2009). *What works in foster care? Key components of success from the Northwest Foster Care Alumni Study.* New York, NY and Oxford, England: Oxford University Press.

Pecora, P. J., Whittaker, J. K., Maluccio, A. N., Barth, R. P., DePanfilis, D., & Plotnick, R. D. (2009). *The child welfare challenge: Policy, practice, and research* (3rd ed.). New York, NY: Routledge.

Reilly, T. (2003). Transition from care: Status and outcomes of youth who age out of foster care. *Child Welfare, 82,* 727–746.

Riley, D., & Meeks, J. (2005). *Beneath the mast: Understanding adopted teens.* Silver Springs, MD: C.A.S.E. Publications.

Seiffge-Krenke, I. (2006). Coping with relationship stressors: The impact of different working models of attachment and links to adaptation. *Journal of Youth & Adolescence, 35,* 24–38. doi:10.1007/s10964-005-9015-4

Sheras, P. L., Abidin, R. R., & Konold, T. R. (2001). *Stress index for parents of adolescents.* Lincoln, NE: University of Nebraska Press.

Shoshani, A., Nakash, O., Zubida, H., & Harper, R. A. (2014). Mental health and engagement in risk behaviors among migrant adolescents in Israel: The protective functions of secure attachment, self-esteem, and perceived peer support. *Journal of Immigrant & Refugee Studies, 12,* 233–249. doi:10.1080/15562948.2013.827769

Simmel, C. (2007). Risk and protective factors contributing to the longitudinal psychosocial well-being of adopted foster children. *Journal of Emotional & Behavioral Disorders, 15,* 237–249.

Sroufe, L. A. (2005). Attachment and development: A prospective, longitudinal study from birth to adulthood. *Attachment & Human Development, 7,* 349–367.

Thompson, R. A. (2008). Early attachment and later development: Familiar questions, new answers. In J. C. Cassidy & P. R Shaver (Eds.), *Handbook of attachment* (2nd ed., pp. 348–365). New York, NY: Guilford Press.

Tan, T. X., Marfo, K., & Dedrick, R. F. (2010). Early developmental and psychosocial risks and longitudinal behavioral adjustment outcomes for preschool-age girls adopted from China. *Journal of Applied Developmental Psychology, 31,* 306–314.

U.S. Department of Health & Human Services. (2017). *The ACFARS report #24.* Retrieved from https://www.acf.hhs.gov/sites/default/files/cb/afcarsreport24.pdf

van den Dries, L., Juffer, F., van Ijzendoorn, M. H., & Bakermans-Kranenburg, & M. J. (2009). Fostering security? A meta-analysis of attachment in adopted children. *Children and Youth Services Review, 31,* 410–421. doi:10.1016/j.childyouth.2008.09.008

van der Pol, T. M., Hoeve, M., Noom, M. J., Stams, G. J. J. M., Doreleijers, T. A. H., van Domburgh, L., & Vermeiren, R. R. J. M. (2017). Research review: The effectiveness of multidimensional family therapy in treating adolescents with multiple behavior problems—a meta-analysis. *Journal of Child Psychology and Psychiatry, 58,* 532–545. doi:10.1111/jcpp.12685

van Ijzendoorn, M. H., & Juffer, F. (2006). The Emanuel Miller Memorial Lecture 2006: Adoption as intervention. Meta-analytic evidence for massive catch-up and plasticity in physical, socio-emotional, and cognitive development. *Journal of Child Psychology and Psychiatry, 47,* 1228–1245.

van Ijzendoorn, M. H., Juffer, F., & Poelhuis, C. W. K. (2005). Adoption and cognitive development: A meta-analytic comparison of adopted and nonadopted children's

IQ and school performance. *Psychological Bulletin, 131,* 301–316. doi:10.1037/0033-2909.131.2.301

Vandivere, S., Malm, K., & Radel, L. (2009). *Adoption USA: A chartbook based on the 2007 national survey of adoptive parents.* Retrieved from https://aspe.hhs.gov/report/adoption-usa-chartbook-based-2007-national-survey-adoptive-parents

Wherry, J. N., Huffhines, L. P., & Walisky, D. N. (2016). A short form of the trauma symptom checklist for children. *Child Maltreatment, 21,* 37–46. doi:10.1177/1077559515619487

Yoon, D. P. (2001). Causal modeling predicting psychological adjustment of Korean-born adolescent adoptees. *Journal of Human Behavior in the Social Environment, 3,* 65–82. doi:10.1300/J137v03n03_06

Yoon, D. P. (2004). Intercountry adoption: The importance of ethnic socialization and subjective well-being for Korean-born adopted children. *Journal of Ethnic & Cultural Diversity in Social Work: Innovation in Theory, Research & Practice, 13,* 71–89. doi:10.1300/J051v13n02_04

13

Family Therapy With Adolescents

Joanna E. Bettmann, Michael Riquino, and Jake L. Checketts

Doing therapy with adolescents usually involves working with their families. Since adolescents' caregivers typically have custody and the legal responsibility to make medical decisions for their children, working with adolescents involves coordinating with their families, making sure that treatment is cohesive with family values, and working with adolescents to ensure the home is a place where they feel valued and respected. Conflicts resulting from adolescents' wishes and those of their families are common and complex.

This chapter provides tools for new clinicians to navigate these difficult waters, addressing how to work with clients who are legally minors, how to navigate complex countertransference, and how to promote parental insight. The chapter also presents family systems theory as a useful model for this work. Finally, the chapter presents two evidence-based models for working with families, provides a case study illuminating each of these approaches, and concludes with a lengthy multimodal case study.

Adolescents as Legal Minors

Doing psychotherapy with adolescents necessarily involves their parents to some extent, since adolescents are minors under U.S. law. Laws vary state by state, but typically parents of adolescent clients have the right to access their child's mental health records, including psychotherapy records. Parents also have the legal right to receive a written summary of psychotherapeutic treatment. Most expect to receive regular treatment updates and speak to the clinician about what their child is saying and what is covered in treatment. How then can a psychotherapist navigate these tricky waters between adolescents who often feel extremely protective of their privacy and unwilling to disclose some issues to parents, and their parents who have a legal right to know what treatment is provided to their children?

I (JEB) worked for some months in weekly outpatient therapy with an 18-year-old client who was regularly abusing drugs on the weekends, resulting in what I believed were unsafe conditions for her. My client's mother was paying for this course of individual therapy and knew nothing of her daughter's drug abuse. I counseled the daughter on her troubling drug abuse and encouraged her to be more careful for her own safety, but I did not legally have the right to share this information with her mother given the laws in my state. The mother asked to know what the daughter had been disclosing to me. When I stated that I couldn't legally tell her, but could encourage the daughter to share this information with her mother, the mother immediately terminated the treatment. I never saw the daughter again. This case illustrates how challenging it can be to navigate these difficult dynamics between what adolescent clients share with us after we earn their trust and what they are willing to share with their parents, as well as parents' reasonable right to know critical information about their children and the role of state laws in such disclosures.

It is best to set clear ground rules when beginning treatment with an adolescent client. See the section "Confidentiality Concerns" in Chapter 4 regarding how I (JEB) set these ground rules in an initial session with a client. Your adolescent clients need to know what you will keep confidential and what you will have to tell their parents. I always explain to my adolescent clients that, in the state where I practice, parents have the legal right to view their child's medical record, which includes mental health records. However, I also encourage adolescents to confide in me, explaining that I can't help them if I don't know what is going on. If I have earned trust with my adolescent clients by being consistent, open, and honest, my clients usually do want to share with me what is paining them, even if they don't want their parents to know. I sometimes explain to my adolescent clients, "the details of what you share can stay between us, but what we're working on, your parents need to know about since they are ultimately responsible for you. I only see you once a week and they are with you the rest of the time, so they need to know so that they can support you." These kinds of statements help adolescents to see how sharing information with their parents and even engaging them in treatment can be helpful.

Countertransference When Working with Families

You might have strong countertransference when working with families. For example, if you are a parent yourself, you might have strong feelings of connection and alliance with the parents of your adolescent client. Or you might have strong judgments about the problematic parenting you witness in a family session, comparing their parenting behaviors to your own. If you are not a parent, you might side particularly strongly with your adolescent client, identifying with the child perspective since that is an identity you share with your client. Or you might feel none of these things. In any case, be sure to monitor your own internal processes carefully when you are working with families. Think about how your childhood family structure influences what you think of as a "normal" or "regular" family. What feels like "normal" family communication to you? The norms of your own childhood family are likely to influence how you evaluate families as clients. In order to make good clinical decisions, you will need to be aware of this countertransference. Monitor yourself carefully so that you can bring to conscious awareness your opinions about families and their norms. Then you can explore in supervision or consultation how these opinions or your own history might influence the family treatment you provide.

Promoting Parental Insight

One of the most important things that a clinician working with adolescents can do is to help parents better understand their children. In working with adolescent clients, I (JEB) have often found that I spend time talking to their parents and interpreting the adolescent's behavior. "Yes, he said he hated you and stomped out, but what I think he meant was 'I need some space and I'm feeling trapped right now.'" "Yes, I know she is refusing to speak with you about her feelings, but I think that she is feeling rejected by your . . . ."

Parental insight into their children's behavior is critically important to strong familial attachment relationships (Koren-Karie, Oppenheim, Dolev, Sher, & Etzion-Carasso, 2002; Marcu, Oppenheim, & Koren-Karie, 2016). We define parental insightfulness here as "parents' capacity to consider the motives underlying their children's behaviors and emotional experiences in a complete, positive, and child-focused manner while taking into consideration their children's perspectives" (Koren-Karie et al., 2002, p. 534). Simply, parental insightfulness is the ability of parents to step into their children's shoes, to see things from the child's perspective.

In thinking about a recent conflict with their adolescent child, parents should be asking themselves: What do I think was going through my child's head when this happened? What do I think my child was needing or wanting in this situation? Parents' ability to be insightful about their adolescent's behavior engenders stronger relationships between the parent and adolescent. Sometimes parents are too close to the situation or the relationship or too overwhelmed by their own emotional response in a heated exchange to see clearly what an adolescent is seeking or needing. This is where an adolescent clinician can be powerful: helping the parent to interpret the adolescent's behavior. Clinicians should coach parents to see things through their children's eyes: What do you think he was wanting just then? When he spoke those angry words, what do you think he was feeling or wanting from you?

Clinician in the Middle

Being a psychotherapist for an adolescent client can put you in the middle between parents/guardians who are typically paying for treatment and adolescent clients who want their privacy protected. You will need to show both the parents/guardians and the adolescent that you are on their side, that you understand their perspective. Alienating parents, as the case study earlier in this chapter illustrated, can result in early termination of treatment. You must communicate to both your adolescent clients and their parents that you understand their perspectives and support them. This is a balancing act, but alienating one side or the other can result in poor treatment or early termination.

It is particularly important that the adolescent's parents/guardians experience your respect for their values. Many adolescents are experimenting with identities or behaviors that are uncomfortable for or alien to their parents/guardians. You must communicate both to your adolescent clients and their families that you are supportive and respectful of both parties. Given these challenging dynamics, all clinicians who work with adolescents need strong skills in family therapy. A solid understanding of family systems theory can help ground us in an understanding of family structure and dynamics. This understanding may enable more effective intervention with our adolescent clients and their families.

Family Systems Theory

Psychiatrist Murray Bowen (1972) defined each family as *a system* in which "a change in the functioning of one family member is automatically followed

by a compensatory change in another family member" (p. 260). His conceptualization of family systems has significant implications for adolescent treatment: it suggests that any assessment of adolescents requires an assessment of
their family structure and relational dynamics. In an essay focused on alcoholism, Bowen posited that alcoholism is a response to high familial anxiety
and that "the process of drinking to relieve anxiety, and increased family anxiety in response to drinking, can spiral into a functional collapse or the process can become a chronic pattern" (1974, p. 259). Bowen's substance abuse
example highlights how individual symptomology is not an isolated event. The
behavior of one family member links to the dynamics and relationships with
all other members. In contrast to the medical model which locates pathologies
within an individual, Bowen (1975) conceptualized a model in which a family's
dynamics create and maintain illness within individual family members.

A case example may help illustrate Bowen's model. As a staff in a wilderness therapy program, I (JEB) worked for 7 weeks with an adolescent whose
anger at the beginning of the program was extreme. On the day that I met her,
she built graves for me and all the staff on our treatment team. She labeled the
graves with our names and wrote an elaborate poem which was our eulogies.
Her anger took my breath away. How could she hate me that much? I didn't
even know her! When I learned more about her history, I developed enormous
empathy for her and eventually a strong therapeutic relationship. This girl and
her siblings were survivors of years of incest perpetuated by her live-in uncle.
For years, she never told her mother or stepfather of the abuse. Her anger was
an effective defensive wall, built to protect her from dangerous adults. Since the
adults in her family were unable to protect her from years of sexual abuse and
one that abused her, she developed the idea that adults were generally not to be
trusted. Her anger, resistance to authority, running from home, and truancy
from school were not isolated behaviors, but behaviors which occurred in the
context of a particular family system. She was running from danger, running
away from those who hurt her and who failed to protect her. Her relationships
with each of her family members played a role in the development and manifestation of her symptomology. Her individual symptoms were best viewed in
light of the history and dynamics of her family system.

Bowen also defined an individual's ability to differentiate as essential to individual health and familial needs (Bowen, 1972, 1974; Haefner, 2014). Bowen
(1972) defined differentiation of self as the ability to distinguish oneself psychologically from one's family of origin. Differentiation of self implies that
an individual is able to function autonomously while maintaining important

emotional connections with family (Haefner, 2014). The opposite of differentiation of self is emotional fusion (Bowen, 1972). Emotionally fused individuals are both vulnerable and highly reactive to behaviors and emotions of other family members (Bowen, 1972; Haefner, 2014). Such individuals struggle to define their own needs, reacting emotionally out of fear and anxiety of possible rejection (Bowen, 1972; Haefner, 2014). As we work with adolescents, we often see this tension between differentiation and emotional fusion. We often see adolescents' push for independence and autonomy, their attempts at differentiation appropriate to developmental stage and culture. However, they are often emotionally fused in unhealthy ways with family members, manifesting high reactivity and unable to distinguish their own emotional needs from others.

Bowen's family systems theory offers a particularly useful lens for clinicians. Adolescents belong to a family system in which all members influence each other. The Bowenian model suggests that when a family member is referred for mental health services, that action is likely to influence family functioning and every family member (Withers, Cooper, Rayburn, & McWey, 2016). Bowen's model helps us to see that family-based interventions are likely to be useful for adolescents and their family systems, especially when parent-adolescent relationships are poor (Withers et al., 2016). Due to their age, adolescents are generally dependent upon the family system to provide for their basic needs such as relational support, housing and food, and access to education. As clinicians, we cannot view their symptoms in isolation, but should regard them as occurring within a particular family context and reacting to particular family dynamics.

Evidence-Based Models for Family Therapy With Adolescents

Research suggests the efficacy of two models for adolescent-family intervention: attachment-based family therapy and functional family therapy. We will explain both of these models here and present a case example to illuminate each.

Attachment-Based Family Therapy

Attachment-based family therapy (ABFT) is an attachment-focused family therapy model developed for work with depressed adolescents (Diamond,

Siqueland, & Diamond, 2003). Recent research also shows its efficacy in treating adolescents with unresolved anger (Steinmann, Gat, Nir-Gottlieb, Shahar, & Diamond, 2017), suicidal ideation (Diamond, Creed, Gillham, Gallop, & Hamilton, 2012; Diamond et al., 2010; Feder & Diamond, 2016), and self-injury (Kissil, 2011). ABFT focuses on reparative processes between the parent and child in order to engender greater attachment security between adolescents and their caregivers. The objective of ABFT is to foster a healthy parent-child relationship and reattach the child to the parent, while empowering the adolescent with stronger ability to communicate and regulate emotions (Kissil, 2011).

Significant literature suggests ABFT's effectiveness with adolescents who have mental health challenges. One study showed ABFT's efficacy in treating adolescent depression, showing statistically significantly lower depression scores in 62% of adolescents participating in 12-week ABFT compared to only 19% in the control group, who received 15-minute phone calls weekly for the first 6 weeks and then ABFT during the final 6 weeks (Diamond, Reis, Diamond, Siqueland, & Isaacs, 2002). In another study, adolescents with unresolved anger reported greater ability to express their feelings openly to the person of offense after receiving ABFT, which strengthened their relationships (Steinmann, Gat, Nir-Gottlieb, Shahar, & Diamond, 2017). ABFT also appears to decrease attachment avoidance and attachment anxiety, improve anger resolution, and reduce psychological symptoms in young adults with unresolved anger (Diamond, Shahar, Sabo, & Tsvieli, 2016). After receiving ABFT, suicidal LGBTQ adolescents showed reduced suicidal ideation and decreased depressive symptomology (Diamond, Diamond, et al., 2012).

A manualized treatment, ABFT guides families through a reparative process between parents and adolescents. ABFT consists of five therapeutic tasks which take place over approximately sixteen therapy sessions. Each of these tasks is explained below.

Relational reframe. The first major task of ABFT is to shift families' perspectives from thinking of the adolescents and their symptoms as the source of problems. The *relational reframe* task focuses on enhancing family relationships as a key component of relieving familial stress (Ewing, Diamond, & Levy, 2015). The clinician learns about the adolescent and family at this stage and supports the adolescent in expressing feelings. Clinicians may see a clear connection between the adolescent's depression and familial dynamics; for example, constant familial arguing might contribute to an adolescent's low mood. Or family relationships may not be linked to the adolescent's depressive symptoms, but these relationships could serve as a source of stress rather than comfort. Clinicians should question adolescents at this point in treatment: "When you are feeling hopeless, suicidal, or wanting to self-harm, what gets in the way of going to your caregivers for help?" By not focusing on the rift between the parents and adolescent but the consequences of it, the clinician centers the therapy on strengthening family relationships. ABFT here focuses on the familial relationships, rather than the adolescent's symptoms. This first task is typically completed within one 60–90 minute therapy session (Ewing et al., 2015).

Adolescence alliance. This second task typically takes two to four sessions and involves the clinician meeting individually with the adolescent (Ewing et al., 2015). The intent here is to explore adolescents' awareness of the relational barriers between themselves and their parents and how it relates to their depression. The clinician aims to increase the adolescent's expectations that her thoughts and feelings will be heard and to prepare the adolescent to speak respectfully and assertively to parents. The clinician gains the adolescent's trust by asking about her life, using emotion-focused techniques to explore feelings of isolation and depression. The clinician explores links between the adolescent's feelings and relationships with caregivers. The clinician helps the adolescent to explore relational ruptures between her and her parents, increasing the adolescent's tolerance for difficult emotions and her understanding of what influences her depressive symptoms. If clinicians encounter hesitation and resistance from adolescent clients, they may need to explain that therapy is likely to improve their parental relationships.

Parent alliance. This third task is often completed concurrently with the adolescent alliance task and requires the same number of sessions (Ewing et al., 2015). The clinician may choose to hold one weekly session with the adolescent alone and another weekly session with parents alone. The goal of this task is to engage the parents' motivation to rebuild relationally with their child and to reshape their interactions with that child. The clinician begins by exploring the parents' backgrounds. Then the clinician asks parents to explore how stressors with their child have affected family life and explore their own parental relationships. These conversations are often emotional for parents and may spark statements like, "I want to be the kind of parent I wished I had," and "I want to be there for my child the way my mother was for me." The clinician at this stage also teaches parents skills to strengthen the parent-child relationship, skills such as reflecting and validating their child's emotions.

Repairing attachment. Taking place over one to three sessions, this task asks the family to practice interpersonal skills in sessions (Ewing et al., 2015). The clinician encourages the adolescent to share experiences, thoughts, and feelings that reduced or changed the trust the adolescent had in parents. The clinician then encourages the parents to respond to their child's statements in a calm, compassionate, and empathetic manner, apologizing when appropriate. This task reworks relational schemas between the parents and adolescent, buffering the adolescent's feelings of worthlessness and depression with parental warmth. From an attachment standpoint, this task aims to rebuild the adolescent's trust in parents as attuned and available for support, with the goal of enhancing attachment security.

Autonomy promotion. With the foundation for a secure attachment in place, parents and adolescent work on improving their communication so they can maintain a supportive and meaningful bond (Ewing et al., 2015). The clinician focuses sessions at this point on communication and negotiation. This task typically occurs over four to eight sessions, with the goal of promoting adolescent autonomy and competence with guidance and support from parents. During this task, families might explore household rules or activities. Encouraging collaborative problem solving between adolescents and their parents is important here. This collaborative dialogue should increase adolescents' sense of competency and serve as a gateway into further discussions between the adolescent and parents regarding other coming-of-age topics such as sexuality, spirituality, and future goals. The clinician here aims to assist adolescents in taking responsibility for themselves and to challenge parents to find an appropriate balance between encouragement and support (Diamond, Russon, & Levy, 2016).

To deliver the ABFT model, you must be trained in it. The first level of training is a 3-day workshop which includes role-plays, case studies, and review of tape to build competencies in delivering the model. Level two training is an advanced 3-day workshop as well as follow-up work, and level three training focuses on certification in ABFT (Attachment-Based Family Therapy Training Program, 2017). More information on ABFT certification and training is available here: http://drexel.edu/familyintervention/abft-training-program/overview/

Case Study Using ABFT

The following case study illustrates what ABFT might look like with an adolescent client and her family. Maria, a Latina 16-year-old female, presented for individual outpatient treatment with symptoms of depression and suicidal ideation. Maria also described significant symptoms of anxiety. She reported that she lived with her married parents, her biological mother and father. Maria's mother, Nicole, worked as an administrative manager at a community college and her father, Tomas, was a teacher. Maria had three older siblings, all of whom lived independently outside of the family home. Maria reported having little to no relationship with her siblings, describing that she felt like an only child growing up because of the large gap in age between her and her siblings.

Maria reported that she had attempted suicide three times. The first attempt came after she was bullied in school at age 12. She explained that the bullying started when the family moved to a new home and she began attending a new school. She stated that the majority of the bullying comments were because she was "different" from her peers. Maria was too embarrassed to tell her parents, so the bullying went undetected until Maria tried to commit suicide by taking a bottle of Advil. She became scared and informed her parents, who promptly took her to the hospital where she got her stomach pumped.

Maria reported a significant trauma which occurred when she was 14. During a trip with family friends, Maria met a teenaged boy in the friends' neighborhood. Maria reported sneaking out to spend time with him when everyone else was sleeping. She explained that she went into a park with this boy and was raped. She reported that she never saw the boy again and that she told no one about the rape. But she began to feel extremely anxious. Maria worried that no one would love or accept her if they knew what had happened. She detailed an increasing distance in her previously warm relationship with her father and mother. She explained that she didn't want to tell her parents about the rape because she thought it was her fault. Two months after the rape, Maria attempted to commit suicide by swallowing phenobarbital, Ibuprofen, and Adderall. Her parents found her unconscious and called emergency services. The hospital pumped her stomach; the hospital social work encouraged the family to bring her to treatment.

During the intake session, Maria sat close to her mother on a loveseat. Her father sat on a couch across the room from them. When Maria was asked about her relationship with her father, she reported that she struggled to communicate with him because he seemed disconnected and unwilling to share in response to the things she had to say. When her father was asked about that response, he stated that he struggled communicating because he thought that Maria seemed very private about her life, more so recently. Immediately, Maria's mother jumped into the conversation, scolding her husband by saying, "he never listens and is being judgmental" while putting her arms around Maria. At this point, Maria's father rose from his seat and walked out of the room. He did not return. The clinician later reached out via phone and Tomas agreed to attend subsequent sessions. During the initial few sessions, the clinician works through the first task of ABFT by identifying factors that impaired trust within the familial relationships. The clinician did this here by exploring how family members felt about each other, what recent conflicts had emerged, and what alliances existed between family members. The alliance between Maria and her mother seemed clear, as did the disconnection of Tomas from his wife and Maria. The clinician explored with Maria what kept her from using her parents as supports and resources, information she struggled to share.

The next few sessions were individual sessions with Maria, working on the ABFT task of building a therapeutic alliance with the adolescent. The clinician did this by amplifying Maria's strengths and goals, as well as exploring family dynamics within the home. Maria reported that she had a great relationship with her mother. But she explained that when her mother sided with her during family conflicts, it typically caused a fight between her parents. Maria felt bad because her dad was always the "bad guy" and the one saying "no." She described him as "the odd man out." Maria said that she wanted a better relationship with her father. The clinician worked on the first task of ABFT, the relational reframe, by pointing out to Maria how much she cared about her father because she was able to see him as the "outsider" and the one having to push back against her and her mother. The clinician also pointed out how much she valued her mother. The clinician focused little on Maria's symptoms, instead on relational reframing, therapeutic alliance, and family assessment.

The next two sessions involved individual sessions with first Tomas and then Nicole. The ABFT task here was to build therapeutic alliance with parents. The clinician explored Tomas's perspective of his relationship with his daughter and his desired therapeutic outcomes. Tomas explained that his wife sided with Maria regardless of what the subject was. Tomas reported that this made it very difficult for him to communicate with Maria because Nicole would immediately side with Maria and the conversation would be over. Tomas said that he felt like a single parent always battling a set of twin girls under the tenet "majority rules." The clinician taught Tomas some skills to incorporate into his parenting including supporting and reflecting his daughter's feelings. Sessions also explored Tomas's early attachment relationships, his own parents, and how his upbringing influenced his parenting.

An individual session with Nicole identified her perspective on treatment goals and family needs, as well as her own early attachment relationships and parenting skills. Nicole shared the distance she experienced in her relationship with Tomas, her anger at him, and her emotional reliance on Maria. The clinician practiced communication skills in session with Nicole to prepare her for future sessions with Maria. The subsequent session with Nicole and Tomas together focused on establishing family goals for treatment. These sessions collectively provided the clinician with opportunities to build a therapeutic alliance with the parents, explore their perceptions of family dynamics, and prepare them for joint sessions where the focus would be on empathetic communication with each other and Maria.

In the next session with all three family members together, the clinician invited Tomas to share his feelings. Tomas shared that he wanted Maria to come to him when she experienced difficulties, needed to vent, or feel heard. After Tomas was finished sharing, they shared a warm embrace. Through tears, Maria whispered, "I love you dad, and I am sorry I have been so distant lately." She disclosed the rape to her parents, and both parents expressed warmth, support, and grief. The three hugged together for several minutes during the session and cried.

In subsequent sessions, the warmth between Tomas, Nicole, and Maria was clear. They sat more closely together in session, talked warmly, and often laughed. They began to take risks in session, sharing emotions openly and having honest dialogue about difficult topics like Maria's sexuality. This work constituted key pieces of the fourth ABFT task: the repairing, rebuilding, and/or creating of attachment bonds between parent and child. During later sessions, family members practiced communication skills and risk taking they learned in earlier sessions.

The clinician encouraged Tomas and Nicole to begin marital therapy with another clinician to address the issues in their marriage. The family therapy with Tomas, Nicole, and Maria terminated some weeks later, the clinician feeling confident in family members' reconnection with each other and their new skills for relational connection and healthy boundaries. The case of Maria and her family illuminates the structure and tasks of ABFT. Specifically, you can see how the clinician carefully worked through the five therapeutic tasks of ABFT, helping family members to improve relational skills and connect more strongly to each other.

Functional Family Therapy

Another evidence-based family therapy approach is functional family therapy (FFT). Developed by psychologists James Alexander and Tom Sexton, FFT focuses on reducing adolescents' negative feelings by reframing them and enhancing family problem solving by pointing out strengths that already exist (Alexander, Waldron, Robbins, & Neeb, 2013; Sexton, 2010). The clinician reframes statements that clients make and alters them slightly, shifting to a relational (rather than behavioral) focus. FFT evidences efficacy with adolescents who have disruptive behavior disorders, conduct disorder, delinquency, and substance use disorders (Hartnett, Carr, Hamilton, & O'Reilly, 2016; Hartnett, Carr, & Sexton, 2016; Sexton & Turner, 2011). FFT appears effective in working with adolescents who possess callous-unemotional traits (who lack guilt or empathy and show little to no emotion) and antisocial aggressive behaviors (White, Frick, Lawing, & Bauer, 2013). Research indicates parental engagement in FFT reduces behavioral and family problems both during and after treatment (Hartnett, Carr, & Sexton, 2016).

The FFT approach involves five components typically covered in 12 to 14 therapy sessions (Functional Family Therapy, 2017). The five components are *engagement, motivation, relational assessment, behavioral change,* and *generalization.* The engagement component involves the clinician building relationship with adolescent clients and their families in culturally sensitive ways that engender clinician credibility. The clinician focuses on "matching" during this stage. "Matching" refers to responding similarly to family members' communication styles in order to engender family members' comfort with the clinician.

During the second stage, motivation, the clinician aims to reduce familial hostility, blame, and conflict by helping family members to ally with each other. The clinician uses a strength-based relational focus, reframing family members' observations and disrupting negative interaction patterns. In order to do this, the clinician identifies strengths already existing within the family that they might not recognize. When the clinician points out family strengths, she is disrupting typical interaction patterns, shifting family members' views of their family to more positive ones. The clinician notes positive familial themes and patterns to help family members reframe.

The third phase of FFT, relational assessment, focuses on familial relational patterns between dyads, taking the spotlight off individual family members. The clinician focuses on the connections between family members and the hierarchal patterns within the family. The clinician identifies antecedents and consequences of dysfunctional familial behaviors, exploring these in session.

The fourth component of FFT, behavioral change, targets individual skill development and family functioning. At this point, the clinician provides family members with training on communication techniques and conflict resolution skills. The goal here is to reduce or eliminate problem behaviors and negative interactions, help to prevent relapse into maladaptive behavior patterns, and build positive self-sustaining relationships. The clinician matches intervention goals and tasks with each family member's needs.

The fifth stage of FFT, generalization, aims to extend positive family functioning into a variety of different systems and situations. The clinician connects the family with community agencies and supports, such as the adolescent's school, the juvenile justice system, or other local resources. The clinician then assists the family to strengthen their relationships with these systems. During this stage, clinicians teach family members how to communicate effectively with these systems without the clinician, encouraging self-reliance in preparation for independence from the clinician (Alexander, Waldron, Robbins, & Neeb, 2013; Sexton, 2010). Therapy termination occurs after family members work through the tasks in all five FFT stages.

Certification in FFT occurs at the agency level, rather than through individual clinician certification. FFT certification is a three-phase process that consists of clinical training in phase one, supervisor training in phase two, and maintenance in phase three. FFT certification requires that agencies complete all three phases of training to become certified facilities. The overall expense of FFT training is quite high (Functional Family Therapy, 2017). More information about the training and certification process is available here: http://www.fftllc.com/about-fft-training/implementing-fft.html

Case Study Using FFT

The following case example illuminates tasks and process from the engagement and motivation phases of FFT. Nick was a 15-year old Asian-American male who presented with a history of delinquent behaviors such as vandalism, bullying, and school truancy. He was referred to therapy by his juvenile probation officer. Nick had been in and out of treatment and juvenile detention centers for the last 3 years. During his time in treatment and detention, he engaged in consensual sexual behaviors with female peers that were against the rules of the facility and bullied his male peers, behaviors that resulted in him being expelled from one facility. Nick lived with his single mother and younger brother in a low-income community. Nick's mother Sue was the primary caretaker and financial provider for Nick and his brother, because Nick's father left the family when Nick was 3 years old. His father had not been a part of his life since then. Sue explained that Nick's father had been both verbally and physically abusive with her and the boys. She reported that Nick's father, a veteran, also abused opiates daily when he lived with the family. Sue reported that she worked two jobs to be able to pay the family's rent and other bills.

Upon receiving the referral from Nick's probation officer, the clinician made a direct call to Nick rather than calling his mother to set up the appointment. The clinician aimed to help Nick feel that he had some control in the situation and to begin to build therapeutic alliance. Nick was cold during the initial call. He provided brief responses to the clinician's questions, with little to no change in voice tone. Nick stated that therapy "was a place where he had to go and talk about feelings" and that it was "super boring." He said that he did not understand why he needed to attend. The clinician asked him what he might get out of therapy. Nick explained that the biggest thing that he wanted from therapy was "to get my mom and the school off of my back. Sometimes my mom just yells at me so I need to leave the room because it's too much." The clinician responded that he could help with that. They established a meeting time and place for the initial meeting. Nick then put his mother on the phone and the clinician confirmed the time and place with her.

When the clinician arrived for the first meeting with Nick and his family at the family home, Nick was in the basement playing video games. He yelled upstairs that he did not want to participate in any therapy. Sue then yelled into the basement that Nick needed to come upstairs since he said he would be at therapy. When Nick got upstairs, he slumped onto a couch, crossing his arms and keeping his head down. The clinician greeted Nick and Sue, thanking them for meeting. Nick commented, "this is such a waste of time" and "everything is fine the way it is." Then Sue listed her concerns about Nick, detailing the impact that it had on her. She said,

> You definitely need this, you skip too much school. You bully other kids to the point that the school kicks you out. You are super disrespectful to me and all of your teachers and your brother. I know you intentionally break rules lots of times, you know this will get you into trouble. I know you are a good boy, but sometimes it just doesn't seem that way. I'm ready to rip my hair out, you stress me out so much.

After listening to some of Sue's concerns, the clinician intervened by making relationally focused statements: "Sue, it's amazing to me that you're able to juggle all of your different jobs. Even though it has been difficult, you are still concerned with trying to help Nick with everything going on in his life. It seems like you have big hopes for him." The clinician then spoke to Nick: "You seem really connected to your mom and her feelings. Leaving conversations before they get too heated is your way of preserving the relationship with your mom." The clinician's statements here focused on relational reframing rather than the problematic behaviors. The clinician was working through some of tasks of the motivational phase of FFT, emphasizing strengths that already existed in their relationship. The clinician showed a strength-based relational focus, reframing family members' observations and disrupting negative interaction patterns. The clinician also worked in the session to "match" Nick and Sue's voice tone and communication style, establishing connection by modeling similar communication patterns. By the end of the initial therapy session, Nick and Sue were less defensive, communicating more calmly, and less reactive to statements made by the other.

The case example illuminates one component of a longer treatment process. FFT typically occurs over 12 to 14 sessions. Future sessions with Nick and his mother would involve Nick's younger brother and would focus on goals for treatment, familial communication patterns, familial strengths, links between Nick's behaviors and familial dynamics, and connecting the family to community supports. Nick's case highlights how an FFT-trained clinician begins the treatment process by matching family communication styles, reframing familial conflicts, and highlighting familial strengths.

The Critical Importance of Family Therapy:
A Case Study

We will present here one final case study which does not utilize ABFT or FFT. This case used a multimodal approach with an adolescent struggling with non-suicidal self-injury (NSSI) and suicidal ideation (Jacobson & Batejan, 2014; Klonsky, 2007). Using components of CBT and psychoeducation, the case highlights how family interventions can be key in adolescent treatment.

Aaron (a pseudonym) was a 14-year-old White male with a history of depression and anxiety symptoms. When the second author (MR) was initially contacted by Aaron's biological parents, they requested to meet in person to consult about their concerns regarding their son's NSSI. Specifically, they reported discovering bloody razors and tissues in his bathroom and confronting him about what they found. He revealed to them that he had been cutting on his upper arms, stomach, and thighs, but assured them he was not trying to kill himself. Given that Aaron had previously worked with a clinician to manage his depression and anxiety symptoms, his parents recognized that the pattern of isolation, failing grades, and anhedonia he exhibited during the previous several months was indicative of a recurrent depressive episode. However, Aaron's parents reported feeling unprepared and overwhelmed by his NSSI. They expressed confusion about the behavior itself and wondered if it was an unhealthy way of gaining attention.

Aaron came from a middle-income family, born to heterosexual married Caucasian parents. His parents described themselves as competent, accomplished, and capable people, who expected their children to perform as capable and responsible adolescents. Both parents had completed bachelor's degrees; Aaron's father served as a supervisor in an engineering firm and his mother worked as an administrative staff person in an agency. Aaron was the oldest of two children and the only boy. Aaron described himself as being much like his mother, experiencing deep emotions including depression and sadness. Aaron described his sister as more like their father: easy-going and taking difficult situations in stride.

During the initial consultation session, Aaron's parents were critical of how they reacted to his disclosure of NSSI. Although they expressed genuine concern and fear for their son's well-being while meeting with me, they remarked that they were unable to express this while talking with Aaron. Instead, Aaron's parent stated that they expressed feelings of anger and disappointment at him initially and made remarks such as, "Why would you do this to yourself?" His mother explained that she engaged in NSSI several times when she was a teenager, but she was "struggling to know how to support my son through this." Aaron's father expressed feelings of guilt and remorse about "the damage I've done to our relationship" because of his initial angry reaction to discovering his son's NSSI. I validated the difficult emotions parents experience when they learn their children are hurting themselves and noted that psychoeducation would be an important part of treatment to provide them with the tools necessary to better support their son. They requested that their son meet with me for an initial assessment to determine what treatment options would be appropriate for him and whether I (MR) would be the right therapeutic fit.

When Aaron arrived for his initial assessment, I met with him and his parents to review the presenting problems and their hopes for treatment. His mother reiterated her concerns about Aaron's NSSI and the recurrence of his depressive symptoms. His father expressed worry about Aaron's recent lack of interest in pleasant activities: "He doesn't want to play video games or even spend time with his friends. He's always enjoyed doing those things." Although Aaron agreed with his parents' observations of his behaviors, he appeared withdrawn when I asked about his perspective on what they reported. His affect remained flat during the entire time his parents were in the room. With Aaron's permission, I asked Aaron's parents to return to the waiting room in order to independently gather more information and begin building rapport.

Given that the primary behavioral concern was NSSI, I was especially interested in gathering information about the functions of Aaron's self-injurious behaviors. However, I wanted to attend to Aaron's mood and affect at the beginning of the assessment. So I inquired about Aaron's strengths and interests: "What do you like to do for fun in your free time?" Aaron agreed with his father's assertion that he historically enjoyed playing video games and spending time with his friends, but that he recently had spent his time watching television, listening to music, and reading books. When asked if the shift in activities had anything to do with social withdrawal, avoidance, or isolation, Aaron explained that spending time with friends had become anxiety provoking in recent months due to "the drama" his peers engaged in. He described that he preferred staying in his room alone where he could avoid interacting with anyone that might cause him distress.

I noted that Aaron's isolative behaviors of watching television, listening to music, and reading books served as adaptive coping mechanisms for the depressive symptoms he was experiencing. So I asked, "If the reason you do those things is to help you cope with your depression, what is the reason that you hurt yourself?" Aaron replied that it was easier to deal with physical pain than to deal with emotional pain—an explanation often given by adolescents who use NSSI as an emotion-regulation strategy. When pressed further to explain what he meant by "emotional pain," Aaron commented that he often felt lonely, unwanted, and worthless. Aaron remarked that spending time with others resulted in feelings of anxiety, spending time alone resulted in feelings of loneliness, and cutting himself relieved all of these distressing emotions. In order to convey acceptance and validation of Aaron's feelings without reinforcing his maladaptive behavior, I maintained an attitude of emotional neutrality and genuine curiosity about Aaron's experiences when discussing his NSSI.

Based on Aaron's description, his NSSI seemed to serve an emotion regulation function. To further elucidate the functions of Aaron's NSSI and elicit responses from him, I employed a combination of psychoeducation and open-ended statements: "It sounds like cutting yourself helps relieve all of those painful things you're feeling—this is a common reason teenagers give for hurting themselves. When they feel sad, anxious, angry, or overwhelmed, hurting themselves helps them manage those emotions. Other teenagers sometimes report hurting themselves when they feel numb, hollow, or empty inside. They sometimes say they would rather feel something, even if it's physical pain, than feel nothing at all. I'm wondering if you've ever hurt yourself for that reason." Aaron agreed with my description and reported that he often felt numb after being flooded by anxious and depressive thoughts. He explained that "feeling so much for so long is exhausting," noting that he eventually "turns off" his feelings to cope. He also stated that if he hadn't cut himself because of the overwhelming feelings, he would cut himself in response to the numbness in order to "bring me back to me"

When I observed that Aaron's NSSI seemed to be motivated by the belief that he deserved to hurt himself because he believed he was bad and worthless, Aaron explained that he had such thoughts and feelings daily. Feelings of worthlessness, recurrent depressive symptoms, and overlap between NSSI and suicidal behaviors prompted me to inquire about past and present suicidal ideation. Aaron reported that he had thoughts of suicide, both in the remote past and in recent months, but asserted, "I would never do it." He said that he had never attempted suicide. When asked to elaborate, Aaron explained that his thoughts revolved around not wanting to live anymore because life was so painful and wishing he was dead so that he didn't have to suffer anymore. However, he denied having any plan to kill himself and easily was able to describe what kept him rooted in life.

Because Aaron described engaging in NSSI and experiencing suicidal ideation, I used that moment as an opportunity to provide psychoeducation regarding the differentiation and overlap between the two constructs, as well as the counterintuitive function of NSSI known as anti-suicide (i.e., managing suicidal ideation and avoiding suicidal behaviors by engaging in NSSI instead). Aaron remarked that he never engaged in NSSI with an anti-suicide purpose. At this point in the assessment, Aaron and I discussed a broad functional conceptualization of his NSSI: (a) Aaron would cut himself in response to emotional dysregulation and subsequently experience relief; (b) after a period of relief, Aaron would experience feelings of guilt, shame, and worthlessness, which sometimes resulted in suicidal ideation; (c) his enduring feelings of guilt and shame sometimes resulted in emotional numbness and subsequent NSSI in order to feel again; and (d) his pattern of self-injurious behavior would repeat itself in iterative cycles depending on his emotional state, thought processes, and perception of self in any given situation.

After reviewing the functions of Aaron's NSSI, I returned the conversation to Aaron's report regarding watching television, listening to music, and reading books. I explained how each of those activities could be thought of as an adaptive coping mechanism—a potentially healthy way to manage distressing emotions. By helping Aaron think of NSSI as a maladaptive coping mechanism that served specific functions, I was able to help him see his healthy coping behaviors from a functional perspective. Additionally, I wanted to raise Aaron's level of consciousness regarding the self-denigrating thoughts that seemed to contribute to his feelings of worthlessness. I instructed Aaron to become more aware of his own internal monologue and the kind of language he used when thinking about himself. Although our therapeutic focus would be on changing those destructive thought patterns, the initial goal was helping Aaron be more mindful of his own thought processes, recognizing how they influenced his emotional well-being, and increasing his capacity to be aware of his own internal states.

Before inviting Aaron's parents back into the room, I asked Aaron, "What was it like meeting with me today?" Aaron hesitated at first, but then observed that he was initially uncomfortable with the idea of returning to therapy and meeting with a new clinician, but that he was surprised at how comfortable he felt. He stated that even though we were discussing personal and difficult subjects, it felt like "just having a conversation" where it was acceptable to talk about whatever he needed. I followed up by asking, "How are feeling about returning to therapy? What do you think you might get out of it?" He described feeling validated and understood, expressing the belief that therapy could help him manage his recurring depressive symptoms and learn how to stop hurting himself.

When I invited Aaron's parents back into the room to discuss the next steps in the therapeutic process, I reviewed the psychoeducation I provided Aaron in our individual session. I explained the interpersonal functions of NSSI, explored why Aaron might be engaged in NSSI, and assisted his parents in addressing their misconceptions about NSSI. Although Aaron hid his NSSI for several months, his parents still wondered if his NSSI was motivated by attention seeking. They explained initially, "Every time he's really stressed, he does this. When he does this, he keeps it a secret. It must *not* be for attention." I was able to address these misconceptions, explaining how Aaron's NSSI did serve important interpersonal functions for him and communicated messages to his parents, but that his NSSI didn't appear driven by his need for attention. I often explain to parents that everyone needs attention—children, adolescents, and adults. Sometimes children and adolescents evidence behaviors which appear to be attention seeking blatantly. I encourage parents to reframe their understanding of such behaviors as simply adolescents' requests to get their needs met. Aaron was trying to meet his own emotional needs through his NSSI—not trying specifically to influence his parents.

Aaron had reported during the course of the assessment that he disclosed his NSSI to several close friends, but felt intense guilt and shame about their expressions of fear that he might try to kill himself. The four of us discussed how NSSI can serve the function of interpersonal influence when teenagers lack the skills necessary to communicate their internal suffering or are attempting to emotionally influence others around them. Aaron's parents had already started experiencing the interpersonal effects of his NSSI based on their reports of uncertainty on how to respond to him or implement boundaries without instigating an episode of NSSI. In reviewing the intrapersonal and interpersonal functions of NSSI with Aaron and his parents, I laid the foundation for a treatment structure that would include the teaching of emotion regulation skills and tools for effective communication.

Treatment with Aaron progressed well, with weekly meetings for approximately 1 year. Sessions in the first few months followed this structure: at the beginning of each session, I would meet with Aaron, his mother, and his father together for a few minutes to discuss recent concerns. Then I would meet individually with Aaron for the bulk of the hour to discuss his concerns and his distress and then teach new skills for managing emotion dysregulation. For the last 5 minutes of each hour, I would meet again with Aaron, his mother, and his father to talk about skills we worked on during the therapy session, any current safety issues, any current NSSI that Aaron hadn't already disclosed to his parents, and Aaron's goals for the week ahead.

I explained to Aaron that the details of each session would stay confidential, but that his parents needed to know what was worked on in therapy so that they could support him during the week. Aaron was present for all of these parent check-ins, so that no dialogue with me would occur without his involvement.

After a few months of this kind of treatment and family check-ins, Aaron's NSSI and SI slowed to a stop. Individual weekly treatment continued, but family check-ins were no longer needed. I asked the parents to join a session when NSSI, SI, or family conflict re-emerged in subsequent months. Treatment ended when Aaron and his parents concluded he now had strong enough coping skills to manage his emotions, his NSSI and SI having been absent for 6 months.

Case Study Analysis

The case of Aaron illuminates how family members can be engaged in adolescent treatment as equal partners in the treatment process. The clinician engaged Aaron's parents in the assessment process to gauge their perspective on his issues, involved them in the goal-setting process, and finally utilized them as resources by framing each individual session with parent check-ins at the beginning and end. Aaron's case is an example of how family interventions can serve critical roles in adolescent treatment.

Part of the clinician's responsibility in providing psychoeducation to Aaron's parents was framing his presenting problems in its developmental and relational contexts. For example, while reviewing the links between Aaron's emotional experiences and subsequent NSSI, the clinician explained how Aaron's self-perception and feelings of worthlessness informed that process. The clinician shared with the parents how identity development is a key part of adolescence and that Aaron's sense of self was rooted in his previous childhood and early adolescent experiences.

Aaron's NSSI had a relational context to it, as his withdrawal from family and friends was compounded by their responses to his disclosure of engaging in NSSI. The clinician's psychoeducational interventions with Aaron's parents helped them to understand better his NSSI and depressive symptoms, as well as how to respond to his disclosures more supportively. NSSI often serves an interpersonal function, helping an individual to set boundaries with others (Jacobson & Batejan, 2014; Klonsky, 2007). This is particularly salient for adolescents, many of whom have so little control within their families that NSSI serves a function of establishing a sense of control. With NSSI, the adolescent can establish an arena in which they have control, since they often experience little sense of control within the larger family dynamic. For adolescents who struggle to identify and explain their internal experience, NSSI serves as a form of communication, a way of expressing the depth of their emotional distress. Aaron's NSSI occurred within the relational context of his family; thus, engaging his parents in the treatment process was critical in helping him to manage and reduce depressive symptomology.

Aaron's NSSI served to help him manage his emotional dysregulation and feeling of numbness. However, his NSSI was typically followed by a feeling of shame and guilt, feelings which further reinforced his belief of being worthless and bad. This cycle perpetuated his use of NSSI. When depressed, Aaron thought, "I'm never going to be good enough for my parents, they are never going to love me." Aaron's parents needed coaching in session to express their love and support for him openly. As adolescent clinicians, we often tell parents, "You may not have been part of the problem that got your child here, but you need to be part of solution." Aaron's parents did not create his NSSI and depression, but he needed their help to recover. An adolescent's chances of successful treatment improve when his family participates actively in therapy.

Conclusion

Working with adolescents' caregivers in tandem with adolescent individual therapy may improve the therapy's efficacy, but the clinician should be attuned to when caregivers' involvement is appropriate (Whitefield & Midgley, 2015). Some adolescents may want to feel that individual therapy is their space alone, without the intrusions of family members. Other adolescents may become nervous that the clinician will share adolescents' private information with their families. So, familial involvement in treatment needs to engage the adolescent client first in making decisions regarding this component.

When families are involved, clinicians need strong skills sets: the ability to perceive the relational contexts of adolescents' behaviors, an understanding of adolescents' attachment relationships and the security of those relationships, and the ability to coach adolescents' parents on how to increase insight into their child's behaviors. Helping both adolescents and their caregivers experience that you are on their side and want to help them achieve their goals gives you the strongest chances for success in adolescent treatment. While challenging, engaging families in every step of the treatment process is critical when working with adolescents.

References

Alexander, J. F., Waldron, H. B., Robbins, M. S., & Neeb, A. A. (2013). *Functional family therapy for adolescent behavior problems.* Washington, DC: American Psychological Association. doi.org/10.1037/14139-000

Attachment-Based Family Therapy Training Program (ABFT Training Program). (2017). Retrieved from https://www.goodtherapy.org/training-courses/attachment-based-family-therapy-training.html

Bowen, M. (1972). *Family therapy in clinical practice.* New York, NY: Jason Aronson.

Bowen, M. (1974). Alcoholism as viewed through family systems theory and family psychotherapy. *Annals of the New York Academy of Sciences, 233,* 115–122.

Bowen, M. (1975). Family therapy after twenty years. In Bowen, M., *Family therapy in clinical practice,* (pp. 285–320). New York, NY: Jason Aronson.

Diamond, G., Creed, T., Gillham, J., Gallop, R., & Hamilton, J. L. (2012). Sexual trauma history does not moderate treatment outcome in attachment-based family therapy (ABFT) for adolescents with suicide ideation. *Journal of Family Psychology, 26,* 595–605. doi:10.1037/a0028414

Diamond, G. M., Diamond, G. S., Levy, S., Closs, C., Ladipo, T., & Siqueland, L. (2012). Attachment-based family therapy for suicidal lesbian, gay, and bisexual adolescents: A treatment development study and open trial with preliminary findings. *Psychotherapy, 49,* 62–71. doi:10.1037/a0026247

Diamond, G. S., Reis, B. F., Diamond, G. M., Siqueland, L, & Isaacs, L. (2002). Attachment-based family therapy for depressed adolescents: A treatment development study. *Journal of The American Academy of Child & Adolescent Psychiatry,* 41, 1190–1196. doi:10.1097/00004583-200210000-00008

Diamond, G. S., Russon, J., & Levy, S. (2016). Attachment-based family therapy: A review of the empirical support. *Family Process, 55,* 595–610. doi:10.1111/famp.12241

Diamond, G. M., Shahar, B., Sabo, D., & Tsvieli, N. (2016). Attachment-based family therapy and emotion-focused therapy for unresolved anger: The role of productive emotional processing. *Psychotherapy, 53,* 34–44. doi:10.1037/pst0000025

Diamond, G. S., Siqueland, L., & Diamond, G. M. (2003). Attachment-based family therapy for depressed adolescents: programmatic treatment development. *Clinical Child & Family Psychology Review, 6*, 107–127.

Diamond, G. S., Wintersteen, M. B., Brown, G. K., Diamond, G. M., Gallop, R., Shelef, K., & Levy, S. (2010). Attachment-based family therapy for adolescents with suicidal ideation: A randomized controlled trial. *Journal of the American Academy of Child & Adolescent Psychiatry, 49*, 122–131.

Ewing, E. S. K., Diamond, G., & Levy, S. (2015). Attachment-based family therapy for depressed and suicidal adolescents: Theory, clinical model and empirical support. *Attachment & Human Development, 17*, 136–156.

Feder, M. M., & Diamond, G. M. (2016). Parent-clinician alliance and parent attachment-promoting behaviour in attachment-based family therapy for suicidal and depressed adolescents. *Journal of Family Therapy, 38*, 82–101.

Functional Family Therapy. (2017). Clinical model. *About FFT Training*. Retrieved from http://fftllc.com/about-fft-training/clinical-model.html

Functional Family Therapy. (2017). FFT training. *About FFT Training*. Retrieved from http://fftllc.com/about-fft-training/implementing-fft.html

Haefner, J. (2014). An application of Bowen family systems theory. *Issues in Mental Health Nursing, 35*, 835–841. doi:10.3109/01612840.2014.921257

Hartnett, D., Carr, A., Hamilton, E., & O'Reilly, G. (2016). The effectiveness of functional family therapy for adolescent behavioral and substance misuse problems: A meta-analysis. *Family Process, 56*, 607–619. doi:10.1111/famp.12256

Hartnett, D., Carr, A., & Sexton, T. (2016). The effectiveness of functional family therapy in reducing adolescent mental health risk and family adjustment difficulties in an Irish context. *Family Process, 55*, 287–304.

Jacobson, C. M., & Batejan, K. (2014). Comprehensive theoretical models of non-suicidal self-injury. In M.K. Nock (Ed.), *The Oxford handbook of suicide and self-injury* (pp. 409–418). New York, NY: Oxford University Press.

Kissil, K. (2011). Attachment-based family therapy for adolescent self-injury. *Journal of Family Psychotherapy, 22*, 313–327. doi:10.1080/08975353.2011.627801

Klonsky, E. D. (2007). The functions of deliberate self-injury: A review of the evidence. *Clinical Psychology Review, 27*, 226–239.

Koren-Karie, N., Oppenheim, D., Dolev, S., Sher, E., & Etzion-Carasso, A., (2002). Mothers' insightfulness regarding their infants' internal experience: Relations with material sensitivity and infant attachment. *Developmental Psychology, 38*, 534–542.

Marcu, I., Oppenheim, D., & Koren-Karie, N. (2016). Parental insightfulness is associated with cooperative interactions in families with toddlers. *Journal of Family Psychology, 30*, 927–934.

Sexton, T. L. (2010). *Functional family therapy in clinical practice*. New York, NY: Routledge.

Sexton, T., & Turner, C. W. (2011). The effectiveness of functional family therapy for youth with behavioral problems in a community practice setting. *Couple and Family Psychology: Research and Practice, 1*, 3–15. doi:10.1037/2160-4096.1.S.3

Steinmann, R., Gat, I., Nir-Gottlieb, O., Shahar, B., & Diamond, G. M. (2017). Attachment-based family therapy and individual emotion-focused therapy for un-resolved anger: Qualitative analysis of treatment outcomes and change processes. *Psychotherapy, 54*, 281–291. doi:10.1037/pst0000116

White, S. F., Frick, P. J., Lawing, K., & Bauer, D. (2013). Callous-unemotional traits and response to functional family therapy in adolescent offenders. *Behavioral Sciences & the Law, 31,* 271–285.

Whitefield, C. & Midgley, N. (2015). 'And when you were a child?': How clinicians working with parents alongside individual child psychotherapy bring the past into their work. *Journal of Child Psychotherapy, 41,* 272–292. doi:http://dx.doi.org/10.1080/0075417X.2015.1092678

Withers, M., Cooper, A., Rayburn, A., & McWey, L. (2016). Parent- adolescent relationship quality as a link in adolescent and maternal depression. *Children and Youth Services Review, 70,* 309–314. doi:10.1016/j.childyouth.2016.09.035

Index

Figures are indicated by *f* following the page number

For the benefit of digital users, indexed terms that span two pages (e.g., 52–53) may, on occasion, appear on only one of those pages.

9 780190 880064